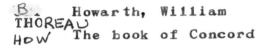

The
Book of
Concord

ALSO BY WILLIAM HOWARTH

Thoreau in the Mountains

Walden and Other Writings (editor)

The John McPhee Reader (editor)

The Literary Manuscripts of Henry David Thoreau

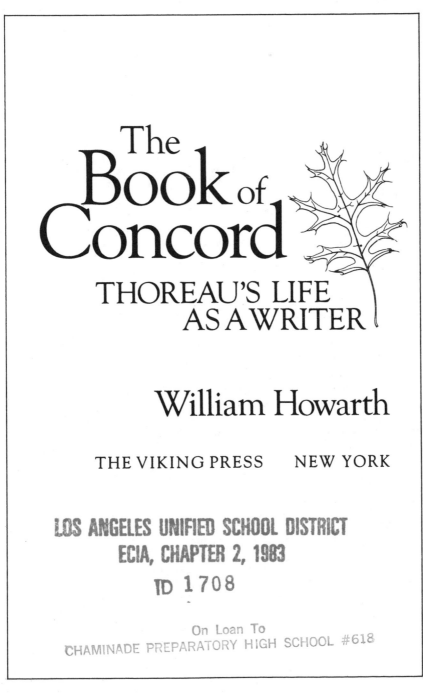

The
Book of
Concord

THOREAU'S LIFE
AS A WRITER

William Howarth

THE VIKING PRESS   NEW YORK

First published in 1982 by The Viking Press
625 Madison Avenue, New York, N.Y. 10022
Published simultaneously in Canada by
Penguin Books Canada Limited

LIBRARY OF CONGRESS CATALOGING IN PUBLICATION DATA
Howarth, William L., 1940–
    The book of Concord.
    Bibliography: p.
    Includes index.
    1. Thoreau, Henry David, 1817–1862.   2. Authors,
American—19th century—Biography.   I. Title.
PS3053.H63   818'.309   [B]   81-7487
ISBN 0-670-23706-X   AACR2

Work on this book was supported by research grants from Princeton University
and the National Endowment for the Humanities.

Maps in this volume were compiled by the author and drawn by Tom Funk of
Westport, Connecticut. The drawing from Thoreau's Journal on page 128 is
reproduced with the permission of The Pierpont Morgan Library, New York. All
other drawings are reproduced from *The Journal of Henry David Thoreau* (Boston,
Houghton Mifflin Co., 1906).

Printed in the United States of America
Set in CRT Goudy Old Style

For Bonnie

For a long time I was reporter to a journal, of no very wide circulation, whose editor has never yet seen fit to print the bulk of my contributions, and, as is too common with writers, I got only my labor for my pains. However, in this case my pains were their own reward.

—*Walden*

His journals should not be permitted to be read by any, as I think they were not meant to be read. I alone might read them intelligently. To most others they would only give false impressions. I have never been able to understand what he meant by his life. Why did he care so much about being a writer? Why did he pay so much attention to his own thoughts? Why was he so dissatisfied with everybody else, etc.? Why was he so much interested in the river and the woods and the sky, etc.? Something peculiar, I judge.

—ELLERY CHANNING, ON HENRY THOREAU

CONTENTS

CONTENTS

LIST OF MAPS

FOREWORD

Lately I have been thinking of how this book began. I first read Thoreau in my teens, while living in central Illinois. A job one summer put me outdoors for long hours of solitude, and in that unsupervised freedom I read. Late in August, when cicadas sing high in the trees, I came to *Walden*. The voice I heard there struck deep, though not for the deepest reasons: to me Thoreau seemed angry yet clear, a man living exactly the way he thought.

In college I again read *Walden*, where it stood out in the shuffle of survey courses, and I heard a professor describe the Journal that Thoreau never published: "Perhaps someone will explain his unfinished work one day." At graduate school I read his books and Journal, learned to pronounce his name (stress the *first* syllable), then wrote some early thoughts about him.

After coming to teach at Princeton, I went to see the manuscripts of Thoreau's Journal at the Morgan Library in New York. I expected to learn from these bound, handwritten volumes something about how Thoreau composed, but soon I found that many of the early Journal pages were elsewhere—some just a few blocks away, others in New England or out on the West Coast. I would not know how Thoreau wrote until I had seen all of his working papers, both the Journal and the publications it spawned.

So I began to compile a census of his manuscripts, a task that eventually took me to research libraries in over twenty states, from Maine to California. For several years I worked on this project, traveling summers in a camper bus with my family. In the bus we kept one suit; I put it on to meet librarians.

My book on the manuscripts described how and when Thoreau composed. He always began with Journal entries, then moved slowly through separate, multiple drafts, endlessly tinkering with his words and thoughts. I learned more about this process while directing a new Thoreau edition at Princeton, one based on his manuscripts rather than on the texts of previous editors. In the manuscripts are several of Thoreau's unpublished writings (now being prepared for publication), which I have described here for the first time.

During these years my family and I also went to Concord, where we lived for several months on Nawshawtuct Hill. With the help of friends I began to follow Thoreau's canoe and foot trails about the town. I came to see how he "travelled a good deal in Concord," for those twenty-six square miles often correspond to the world he found in books. Concord even resembles our larger continent: the town has northern forests, river savannahs in the south, a sandy eastern plateau, and out west some grazing land, part of it known as "Texas." In Concord I began to learn natural history, the facts about plants and animals that Thoreau converted into higher ideas.

After Concord I began to write this book, working in various retreats and against the distractions that can—and probably should—interrupt a long project. I wrote on other subjects, worked with students who clarified my ideas. Then the National Geographic Society invited me to study Thoreau in the field, where his books began.[*] With family and friends I retraced his journeys. We hiked the length of Cape Cod, climbed in the White Mountains, canoed the lakes and rivers of northern Maine. Not far from Webster Stream, where Thoreau also had trouble, my party destroyed its two canoes in a stretch of heavy rapids. I remember standing in icy water, on lacerated feet, trying to calculate the miles to safety—and silently asking why I was not on the trail of Henry James.

Since then my adventures have been on paper, as I sought to give this book its final form. I have chosen to describe the part of Thoreau's life that mattered most to him (but is still largely unknown), his life as a writer. At the center of that life is his Journal, the private

[*]See "Following the Tracks of a Different Man: Thoreau," *National Geographic* 159, 3 (March 1981), 349–86.

history of his imagination. At the heart of his Journal is Concord, the place that he came to see as a microcosm, a whole earth living in organic harmony.

Previous accounts of Thoreau have made little use of his Journal, probably because it is so massive (over two million words) and—in the later years—so apparently "scientific." My purpose is to suggest a different reading of Thoreau's life and art. I have written not a biography but a natural history of his career. The prevailing view of his career has been that *Walden* is the climax, preceded and followed by work of lesser importance. I see his career as a continuous ascent, sustained by the Journal, and rising from youthful confusion into a triumphant maturity.

In telling this story I have contended that popular images of Thoreau—the radical, the mystic, the naturalist—come from *a writer* who projected those roles. I have focused on how he wrote, what he thought about writing, and how the two affected each other. That sequence reveals the principles that shaped his works. The Thoreau I depict is a conscious literary artist, one who uses the devices of his art—style, images, structure—to make facts flower into truth. The subjects are literal, his vision metaphorical. Concord is not unlike Joyce's Dublin or Faulkner's Mississippi, a ground of reality that inspired high levels of art. But Thoreau's genius was for nonfiction, the sort of creative journalism that has flourished in America, producing writers as different as Agee, Didion, McPhee, and Mailer. Thoreau launched this tradition; his career stands as a reminder to readers that no fact is trivial, if seen in the proper light—and with an observant eye.

A word about the drawings in this book. After 1850 Thoreau filled his Journal with crude line sketches: the shape of a leaf, a feather, a tree, or a river bank. I see these markings as efforts to read the world without words, to record—as he said in *Walden*—"the language which all things and events speak without metaphor." The drawings are silent and skeletal; they go beneath the skin of apparent reality to show its essential form. No drawing better expresses this motive than the one he used in "Autumnal Tints," the simple outline of a Scarlet Oak leaf. The leaf is a cipher, a hieroglyph "not found on the Rosetta Stone," an object defined by its lines *and* by the emptiness around

"There they dance, arm in arm with the light. . . . you can hardly tell at last what in the dance is leaf and what is light."

them. Here in one natural form lie all of the world's conditions, as he saw them: fact and idea, flesh and spirit, land and water, life and death. The leaf seems rough, ragged, and irregular at first, but in the end it proves to be symmetrical and coherent. Thoreau had the same life as a writer; out of inchoate experience he built The Book of Concord.

Reading *Walden* in that long-ago August, I could hardly see how far Thoreau would take me—or how many friends I would be thanking today for their aid and encouragement. They are:

My editors at Viking Press: Alan Williams, Elisabeth Sifton, Virginia Avery, and Nanette Kritzalis. And Beth Tondreau, the designer.

Computer experts who introduced me to the IBM 3033, on which I wrote, edited, indexed, and typeset this book: Hannah Kaufmann, Velga Stokes, Lee Varian, and Melinda Varian.

Colleagues who read—and advised: Carlos Baker, John Broderick, Edward Davidson, Emory Elliott, Walter Harding, Laurence Holland, John McPhee, Joseph Moldenhauer, James Olney, Thomas Roche, Robert Sattelmeyer, Robert Sayre, Walter Teller, and Willard Thorp.

Friends of the Thoreau Edition: Herbert Bailey, Thomas Blanding, Herbert Cahoon, Wendell Glick, Carl Hovde, Linck Johnson, Carolyn Kappes, Arthur Link, Walton Litz, Carol Orr, Leonard Neufeldt, Lyndon Shanley, Kevin Van Anglen, Paul Williams, and Elizabeth Witherell.

Fellow students: Mo Bragdon, Mimi Danly, Mary Ann Franke, Royce Flippin, Beth Friskey, Jane Hamilton, Paul Judge, Bill Kelly,

Liz Muñoz, Caroline Moseley, Mike Northrop, Gabriel Seymour, Nancy Simmons, Meg Tuttle, Charles Whitin, Wistar Williams, and John Williamson.

Fellow travelers on Thoreau's trails: Victor Boswell, Warren Elmer, Mary Fenn, Mary Gail Fenn, Farrell Grehan, Steve Harbison, Roland Robbins, Anne McGrath, Marcia Moss, Robert Peck, Eugene Walker, Mary Walker, and Ruth Wheeler.

Former mentors, east and west: Lester Beaurline, Russell Hart, and Floyd Stovall; Edward Davidson, William Rueckert, and Jack Stillinger; Lois Body and Nina Chesebro.

My extended family: Will and Agnes, Nelson and Mary, Ruth and Don, Susan and Dana, David and Marian, Bob and Nancy, Lydia, Dana, Jo, Jenny, and Jeff. They join me in saluting my life's companion, to whom these years—and this book—are dedicated.

—WILLIAM HOWARTH
Princeton, New Jersey

Prologue

1
HIS BROKEN TASK

It seems an injury that he should leave in the midst his
broken task which none else can finish, a kind of indignity
to so noble a soul that he should depart out of Nature
before yet he has been really shown to his peers for what he
is. But he, at least, is content.
                    —R. W. EMERSON, "THOREAU"

Concord, Massachusetts, May 6, 1862. At the town hall a clerk enters
the latest death: "Henry D. Thoreau. 44 years, 9 months, 24 days.
Natural Historian."*

Word passes quickly to his friends Ellery Channing, Bronson Alcott, Waldo Emerson. Thoreau has been dying of tuberculosis for
months, but they grieve nonetheless. Emerson alone has lost a father,
two brothers, and a young wife to this disease. His obituary tribute
appears in the Boston *Daily Advertiser* on May 8: "The premature
death of Mr. Thoreau is a bitter disappointment to many friends."

Exactly how bitter, Emerson will soon reveal. A former Unitarian minister, he insists on holding the funeral services at the First Parish meeting house. Twenty years ago Thoreau resigned from this
church, saying: "I do not wish to be considered a member of the First
Parish in this town." A service outdoors would be more appropriate,

*See page 221 for Sources.

but on May 9 the church is filled to hear Emerson read "an address of considerable length." Nathaniel Hawthorne is there, also the publisher James T. Fields, and Concord's rising young author, Louisa May Alcott. She thinks Emerson's address is too critical, "good in itself, but not appropriate to the place and time."

Fields at once offers Emerson a second occasion: why not expand the address into an essay for the *Atlantic Monthly?* Emerson agrees; in an essay he can draw upon his own journal volumes, where entries about Thoreau have piled up for twenty-five years. Also useful is one of Ellery Channing's notebooks, in which he had copied extracts from Thoreau's Journal ten years ago. Emerson finds some suggestive phrases, then decides to go to their source. After putting off his deadline an extra month, he asks Sophia Thoreau for permission to see the Journal volumes.

The only survivor of four Thoreau children, Sophia is a spinster of forty-two, endowed with the family's plain looks and agile mind. She worships Henry's memory, having become in recent months his nurse, secretary, copyist, and editor. Often she climbed to his third-floor study to find books and papers, then brought them to his sickbed in the front parlor. Together they prepared several texts for Mr. Fields, who now wants to publish all of Henry's work, even the Journal. She is reluctant. Those papers are sacred to her, and so is the room where they are kept.

This large attic domain has slanting walls, with windows at either end and a stairwell in the center. The stairs form a Y, rising straight from the second floor, then turning left and right. Henry divided his time there: at one gable end stands his cane bed, a bureau, and a washstand; at the other is a study. His things are in order, but dusty—he said this dust was like the bloom on plants, not to be swept away.

Everything here speaks of his life and work. Two writing desks, supplied with paper, ink, pens, and sand for blotting. A pile of old business letters, the clean backs ready for notes or rough outlines. His many collections, housed in drawers or cases: Indian relics—arrowheads, axes, mortars, and pestles; bird relics—eggs, nests, stuffed skins; unusual rocks and lichens; albums of dried flowers with botanical labels. His flute, his music book (also used to press flowers), his surveyor's tools, his walking stick, notched in feet and inches; his library. He built the bookcases of salvaged driftwood, then lined them with hundreds of volumes, mostly of literature, philosophy, travel, and natural history.

Only two books bear his name: *A Week on the Concord and Merrimack Rivers* (1849) and *Walden* (1854). His essays and travel stories are uncollected; a group of recent papers—on fruits, seeds, trees —seems largely unfinished. On a separate shelf are nearly seventy handwritten volumes, the ones Sophia holds most dear. These are "blank books" from the local stationers: about twenty Henry used for notes and quotations from his reading; the rest are his Journal, over two million words of original, unpublished text.

Like the man who wrote them, the Journal volumes are not uniform. Some are octavos of less than sixty pages, barely the length of Sophia's hand; others are five-hundred-page ledgers, wider than sheet music. The volumes from 1837 to 1850 are in tattered condition, for he clipped many of their pages to use in his drafts. In the 1840s he nearly devoured some volumes this way, leaving behind only unbound fragments. But after 1850 few pages are missing; the entries grow longer; the paper and bindings have an expensive, handmade quality. In some volumes he left minor souvenirs: bits of dried plants, rough sketches and maps, newspaper stories attached with sealing wax. And an odd little page marker made of brass—one side a pointing hand, the other a boot. He bought lined paper, in a vain effort to control his rapid, careless scrawl, but he refused books that were ruled in columns for dollars and cents. The only reckonings here are his indexes, usually at the end of each volume. The indexes help Sophia to locate favorite passages.

Even in these private pages Henry was too reticent to be confessional. He left out many episodes from his life: a long-ago romance, the time he nearly died of grief, the night he spent in jail. Most of his days at Walden Pond are missing; so are the early trips to Cape Cod and Canada. But the Journal also tells more about him than readers ever knew. Here he wrote of long moonlight walks lasting until dawn, of days spent in the swamps and mountains, of encounters with new books and old neighbors. This work tells of his love for Concord's scenery, his good humor about its people. Many called him a hermit, a loafer who never amounted to much. The Journal tells a deeper truth: he worked hard all his life, and not for selfish reasons. Should others now read these pages? Sophia has no orders to destroy them, no reason to think he wanted them kept secret any longer. With a reluctant sense of duty, she turns them over to Mr. Emerson.

For the rest of June Emerson reads in the volumes with great pleasure. In his own journal he sets down ideas and phrases that fill out a portrait of Thoreau: "I read him not only truely in his Journal, but he is not long out of mind when I walk." He detects "a little strut" in Thoreau's style, which may someday go on parade: "If we should ever print Henry's journals, you may look for a plentiful crop of naturalists."

Yet Emerson's own opinion is firmly fixed. Thoreau was an early disciple, a trusted colleague in the 1840s, when they shared the high ambition of reforming American ideals. But after 1850 Thoreau withdrew his allegiance and took a solitary path. Their friendship declined throughout the decade, even as the Union collapsed into secession and war. In this summer of 1862 America's future looks bleak: Confederate armies are winning battles; Union volunteers are on the wane; Wall Street is in a panic. Emerson's youthful optimism has faded; at fifty-nine he sees the past as so many lost opportunities. When his essay "Thoreau" appears in August, its mood of injury and regret is evident.

Emerson portrays Thoreau as a hermit and stoic, military in his bearing and rarely tender. He had a sturdy frame, acute senses, and a photographic memory, but with these gifts he renounced "the natural expectations of family and friends" (Ex, 8).* The Journal reveals Thoreau's intimate knowledge of Concord, but Emerson decides this work is "without apparent method," that Thoreau was wrong to think of one town as "the most favored centre for natural observation" (Ex, 19). He was industrious, yet lacked ambition. He scorned wealth, fame, even influence. His death was premature, a bitter disappoint-

*See page 222 for a listing of Source abbreviations.

ment to friends; it left them with unfulfilled expectations and unpublished papers, "his broken task, which none else can finish" (Ex, 33).

———

Thus began the legend of Thoreau as a writer who fell into early decline. He carved many youthful works from the Journal, but after *Walden* only scraps reached print: some chapters on Cape Cod, one on Maine, a few lectures on antislavery and nature. Yet the Journal for his last eight years is prodigious: sixteen large volumes with more than four thousand pages of writing—easily a million words—but to what end?

Friends like Alcott, Emerson, and Channing tried to guess. During the 1860s they helped Sophia edit five volumes of Thoreau's writings. They also read through the Journal, Emerson "with ever mounting estimation," and tried to decide how its contents might be published. Emerson favored creating topical anthologies, what Alcott called *Field and Table Talk* in February 1865, and "Natural History . . . Morals . . . Religion" in October 1869. Alcott's own preference was an arrangement like that of his diary, in which he wrote a page or more for each day of his life, a volume for each year. When he published excerpts in *Concord Days* (1872), he proposed that a similar book could be drawn from Thoreau's Journal "by selecting what he wrote at a certain date annually, thus giving a Calendar of his thoughts on that day from year to year."

Ellery Channing thought this plan agreed with Thoreau's intentions, which he described in *Thoreau, the Poet-Naturalist* (1873): "The idea he conceived was that he might, upon a small territory—such a space as that filled by the town of Concord—construct a chart or calendar which should chronicle the phenomena of the seasons in their order, and give their general average for the year."

Channing was notoriously imprecise; in his own journal at this time he admitted: "I have always been surprised at the pertinacity with which Henry kept to the writing of his Journal. This was something truly heroic. I should have thought his thoughts would have run out—that the stream would have become dry. But there are the thirty

[sic] volumes, all done in ten [sic] years, besides all the other writing (and no little, truly) that he must have done in the same period."

Out of loyalty to Thoreau, Alcott and Channing had sought an answer to Emerson's lament. Thoreau had not worked in vain: he must have planned to write a book about Concord, shaped as a calendar year; his friends would take up this broken task and publish the Journal accordingly. By 1876 Emerson was fading into senility, unable to challenge their view. Now he only regretted that Thoreau's unpublished papers "had remained so long so near, & I never found time to read them."

Sophia found an editor for the Journal in Harrison Blake, Henry's old friend and correspondent from Worcester. Blake followed Alcott's suggestion for arranging calendar excerpts, first as a trial run in the *Atlantic Monthly* for April–June 1878; then as a full set of "seasons": *Early Spring in Massachusetts* (1881), *Summer* (1884), *Winter* (1888), and *Autumn* (1892).

The "calendar" was now a fact in literary history, canonized in the ten-volume edition of Thoreau's writings in 1893 and promulgated by an apparently complete twenty-volume edition in 1906. (The fourteen volumes of Journal have many omissions and errors in their text.) This fuller version, with its frequent cross-references to Thoreau's other published writings, provoked controversy: was the Journal, as Mark Van Doren charged in 1916, a "vacuous and expansive effort," or better than the books Thoreau "extorted" from it, as Norman Foerster wrote in 1921?

From then until the present, readers have speculated about the Journal's ultimate purpose. Leon Balzagette saw it as "fragments of a great poem"; Henry S. Canby invented titles for Thoreau's "hypothetical book": *The Concord Year, Kalendar, Concord*. A hypothetical book can embrace many corollaries: Sherman Paul saw the Kalendar as "a Walden writ large"; Laurence Stapleton said this "Concord mythology" resembled the *Georgics*; Edwin Fussell envisioned its stature as an "epic of the New World." Thoreau's failure to edit the Journal spawned many anthologies and articles about its contents, ranging from politics to diet. Other readers took an opposite view, that Thoreau made it into "a deliberately constructed work of art," in Perry Miller's words.

The truth seems to lie somewhere between these poles. Thoreau himself never promised to write a "calendar"—that idea came from friends who wanted to justify his peculiar career. (They also spread rumors about an intended book on Indians.) On the other hand, his Journal is not entirely a conscious work of art. It did not arise from premeditated design; often its story is clogged by repetition and undigested trivia. The Journal is never more or less than the antipodes of its author.

This homely fellow—dark and hairy, with short legs and long arms, a great hooked nose and wide gray eyes—was a natural introvert, most at ease when alone. In solitude he could live freely, without accommodating others. Yet he was eloquent, and he burned to announce this gift to the world. Like Emily Dickinson he poured his energy into a private forum, a Journal that was ever responsive and tolerant, always leading him on to higher levels of effort. Outside the Journal he was insecure, beset by friends, readers, and editors who criticized—and often twisted—his words.

Unlike most writers, he could not accept the proprietary will of readers. He feared their literalism, their indolence, their casual disregard for fact and form. His publications did not help, for often they expressed ideas he had already abandoned in private. Within the Journal he was free to grow and change, writing for himself and for an idealized reader.

This dual compulsion of Thoreau's, to write and to conceal, has suggested to some readers that he never found his true "vocation" or "identity." But the Journal seems to verify E. B. White's belief that Thoreau was born to be a writer. He spent a lifetime learning to master that art, and the Journal effectively tells the story of his development. At the same time the Journal describes his long search for a trustworthy vision of Order, some principle that unifies the disparities of experience.

At first he directly imitated Emerson's journal, creating a workshop where materials were shaped for print. Hence he clipped those many pages in the 1840s or scribbled indiscriminately in several volumes at once. His first writings were transcendentalist "mosaics" assembled from the Journal, and they reflected the motley nature of their source. When he and Emerson parted, this method of writing changed: Thoreau left the volumes intact, preserving their chronology, and he imitated that continuity in his better published works.

In the early 1850s his Journal allowed Thoreau to grow through self-expression; it became a mirror reflecting himself and Concord, in which he transformed the particulars of nineteenth-century New England into universal symbols. His pleasure in writing the Journal increased, but his publications often lagged behind its current level of ideas and style. A book like *Walden* could emulate those principles, but not embody them with the same vitality or apparent ease.

In the years after *Walden* his Journal became a massive compilation of natural history data, a self-justifying book that taught him to live patiently, growing in confidence as his knowledge of nature expanded. Writing became more important to him than publishing, yet his lectures of this period—"Cape Cod," "Walking," "Allegash" —went beyond his private concerns to present a new vision of America's destiny: the country was not immortal, moving always onward and upward, but was caught in cycles of birth and death, the law of natural succession.

The Civil War seemed to confirm this prophecy, yet in his last years the Journal became a celebration of Concord, one town that represented the unity of all space and time. Before dying Thoreau attempted to extract writings from the Journal that emulate its calendar form, using the organic cycle of leaf, fruit, and seed as a metaphor for America's evolution. In those unfinished projects he expressed what the Journal had taught him: left to its own course of development, free of blundering ambition, life moves to its natural climax, a whole and perfect concord. Had he lived, new books might have announced this conviction; but in any case his Journal made the statement for him. This Book of Concord was his main achievement, a place where art and life merged at the highest level.

Although he died too soon, Thoreau apparently had no regrets or unfulfilled ambitions. The Journal would survive him, and it proclaimed his central discovery: that true exploration lies within, in the country of the mind. In June of 1863 Waldo Emerson first began to sense this possibility: "In reading Henry Thoreau's Journal . . . I find the same thought, the same spirit that is in me, but he takes a step beyond, and illustrates by excellent images that which I should have conveyed in a sleepy generality." Those volumes resting in Thoreau's study told an eloquent story. His task was not broken but alive and growing. Each year he took a step beyond his previous thoughts; each year he wrote more pages and clipped fewer.

Workshop of the World Maker

"A Scotch lass ushers you into the second story front chamber, which is the spacious workshop of the world maker." Here he sits a long time together, with many books and papers about him; many new books, we have been told, on the upper shelves, uncut, with the "author's respects" in them. . . .

—"THOMAS CARLYLE AND HIS WORKS"
MARCH 1847

2
GLEANINGS FROM THE FIELD

> My Journal is that of me which would else spill over and
> run to waste, gleanings from the field which in action I
> reap. I must not live for it, but in it for the gods.
> —FEBRUARY 8, 1841

The first volume of Thoreau's Journal contains a title page, inscribed "Gleanings—Or What Time Has Not Reaped Of My Journal," and these opening words:

> OCTOBER 22, 1837. "What are you doing now?" he asked. "Do you
> keep a journal?" So I make my first entry to-day.

This mentor was probably Emerson, whom the shy, reticent Thoreau had typically left unidentified. In the fall of 1837 Thoreau was twenty years old, a recent graduate of Harvard, and he had just lost his first job: he taught briefly at the Center School in Concord, until his overseers insisted that he flog the students. Prospects for employment were dim that year, for the country was in a financial depression. Thoreau's true ambitions were literary, and any conversation with Emerson would have turned to books and writing. After Emerson moved to Concord in 1834 he wrote *Nature* (1836), a bold, rhapsodic treatise that propelled him into leadership of the movement known as transcendentalism. *Nature* was Emerson's hymn to radical individuality, to the sublime powers inherent in language and letters. At Harvard Thoreau had read and concurred: some of his senior essays were virtual paraphrases of *Nature* (EE, 102–103).

Emerson would have recommended a journal because he had kept one since boyhood, using it to store thoughts, quotations, and bits of nascent composition. As he matured these volumes became an essential part of his literary method. Some contained original jottings, written in sequence but not always dated; others compiled facts and quotations, often under topical headings. He indexed most volumes, gave them coded titles, then sifted the pages for his lectures and essays. He called the journal his "Savings Bank," which implies just how valuable it was to him. Although untidy in appearance, with scrambled page numbers and entries written sideways, these volumes served a prudent end. They were the workshop of a professional writer, his place to store tools and scrap materials for future projects.

The earliest volumes of Thoreau's Journal look nothing like Emerson's, but they had a similar function. These five small ledgers, with the main title "Gleanings," are filled with pages of careful script, with entries that bear neat titles and dates. The entries date from 1837 to 1841, but in fact Thoreau copied them all in late 1841 from two earlier volumes. That proto-Journal contained almost one thousand pages; these Gleanings are about half as long. Probably Thoreau gleaned the new text as well, for he had the leisure in 1841 to smooth and improve his prose as he copied. He was living at Emerson's home then, much under the influence of his host. Yet his harvest metaphor was more somber than Emerson's Savings Bank: Thoreau thought of his early Journal as living material that he and Time had reaped together.

When he began the Journal in October 1837, Thoreau had two ambitions: to be a writer and to live in Concord. He was born in that small market town, which lies eighteen miles west of Boston, and he had grown up there. He knew its twenty-six square miles intimately, from its forests and swamps to the modest hills and three small rivers. Concord held all of Thoreau's childhood memories. His parents were hard-working and affectionate, and they had built a close-knit family.

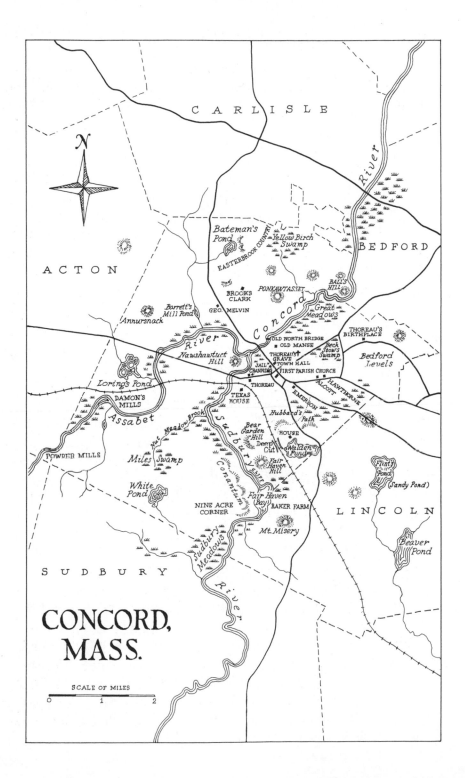

CARLISLE

N

ACTON

BEDFORD

Bateman's
Pond

EASTERBROOK COUNTRY

Yellow Birch
Swamp

BALL'S
HILL

BROOKS
CLARK

PONKAWTASSET

GEO. MELVIN

Great
Meadows

Barrett's
Mill Pond

Annursnack

River

THOREAU'S
BIRTHPLACE

OLD NORTH BRIDGE

OLD MANSE

THOREAU'S
GRAVE

Beck
Stow's
Swamp

Nawshawtuct
Hill

JAIL
CHANNING

TOWN HALL

FIRST PARISH CHURCH

Bedford
Levels

Loring's Pond

THOREAU

EMERSON

HAWTHORNE

ALCOTT

TEXAS
HOUSE

DAMON'S
MILLS

Wet Meadow Brook

Hubbard's
Path

Assabet

Bear
Garden
Hill

HOUSE

POWDER MILLS

Miles Swamp

Deep
Cut

Walden
Pond

Flint's
Pond

Conantum

Fair
Haven
Hill

(Sandy Pond)

White
Pond

Fair Haven
(Bay)

BAKER FARM

NINE ACRE
CORNER

LINCOLN

Mt. Misery

Sudbury

Beaver
Pond

SUDBURY

Sudbury
Meadows

River

CONCORD,
MASS.

SCALE OF MILES

0   1   2

John Thoreau was a pencil-maker by trade; Cynthia Dunbar Thoreau provided room and board to paying guests. She was a great talker, quick and firm in her opinions; he was quiet, but fond of books and music. Together they raised four children: Helen, John, Henry, and Sophia. The family lived on a modest scale, taking walks and picnics together, tending a garden and some livestock. Yet their ideals were lofty: the children went to Unitarian services, to antislavery lectures at the Lyceum, and to local schools. They all became teachers, but only Henry went on to college.

At Harvard Thoreau had sorely missed Concord, yet once he was home he made some gestures of independence. During the winter of 1837–38 he looked for a teaching post elsewhere, sent applications and made journeys to other small towns, to no avail. He had more success in altering his name from its christened form, David Henry, to Henry David. Named for an uncle David, Thoreau was known to his family as Henry, and apparently he did not fancy "D. Henry" as a signature. He made the change informally at this time, but correspondents soon accepted it without comment. Certain neighbors in Concord were less tolerant, and in later years they perpetuated stories that David Henry was an affected crank.

In mid-March of 1838 he wrote to his brother John, then teaching in Taunton, and suggested that they go west, either to set up a school jointly or to find separate jobs. John would make a new location tolerable, for he had been a close friend since childhood. They were only two years apart, a balanced pair of temperaments. John was an open, sunny character, quick and playful rather than deep. His jokes and stories had a tonic effect on Henry, and for quiet moments they had the outdoors to share. At parties and dances John made up for Henry's reserve; in conversations Henry steered John toward new ideas.

By September Henry had established his own school in the Concord Academy building, and early in 1839 John returned to join the enterprise. This school was far more progressive than any they had ever attended, for Henry had strong ideas about education. Harvard gave him many negative examples, since its curriculum offered little science and almost no practical courses. Classes were dull, taught by recitation rather than lectures. The college maintained an elaborate marking system of "points" for deportment and learning, with demerits given for infractions of the many rules. The cumulation of points determined class ranking—and discouraged independent study or good student-faculty relations. In Thoreau's freshman year a massive rebellion against this system disrupted college life for several days.

Life at the Concord Academy was entirely different. The school was coeducational, and it accepted both day and boarding students. Needy pupils received free tuition, flogging was banned—an honor code maintained discipline. John taught English and mathematics; Henry offered languages and science. They gave informal talks, encouraged discussion, and—a striking innovation—arranged frequent field trips. Outdoors the students collected flowers, dug for Indian relics, practiced making surveys and maps. Their school was all of Concord, from the woods and rivers to the shops of local printers or blacksmiths. These were exciting days for the young schoolmasters, yet teaching drained their energies. Within two years John's health began to decline. Henry spent many hours on student compositions and only rare moments of solitude with his Journal.

In the pages of his Gleanings not much of an intimate nature survives, but the original Journal was probably not confessional, either. John and Henry made a boat and hiking journey to the White Mountains in 1839; only a few sketchy notes survive in the Gleanings. Elsewhere, Thoreau writes of a deceased friend without identifying the person; he turns stories about finding arrowheads or losing a tooth into solemn little allegories. Some of this writing is as stiff as his early college essays, in which the traditional ideas and styles of Augustan authors—of Gray and Burke, Adam Smith and Samuel Johnson— dominate his prose. His entry titles (probably afterthoughts) are didactic, exemplary: "Still Dreams Run Deepest," "Every Man is a Roman Forum."

Many entries are simply calisthenic drills for the young writer. As a Harvard sophomore Thoreau wrote an essay on the importance of keeping a journal; he concluded that a writer must reckon his "daily gains" and detect his "false coins" on a regular basis (EE, 8). This utilitarian attitude also influences the Gleanings, in which Thoreau works hard to balance his accounts. In *Nature* Emerson had announced a romantic credo, "this radical correspondence between visible things and human thoughts," and many of Thoreau's entries try to build those analogies: a morning fog beclouds his soul, a cricket's song marks the "still eventide" of his life. These similes resemble the conceits of his favorite metaphysical poets, but Thoreau's contention is romantic, that the mind shapes reality. In later years he would reverse this belief, saying that the mind must absorb facts and adjust to their complexity. But for now a Platonic bias colored his work as writer and schoolmaster. He asked students to write frequently, probably along the lines suggested to his sister in October 1838: "Set one up to a window to note what passes in the street, and make her comment thereon; or let her gaze in the fire, or into a corner where there is a spider's web, and philosophize—moralize—theorize, or what not."

In the Journal he pursued his own muse by writing down comments on other writers. The habit of commentary had developed at Harvard, where he wrote critical essays for English courses and delivered book reviews to a literary club. In a series of early notebooks he copied favorite quotations, indexed by topics and authors—a reference aid that became his lifetime habit. The Journal entries on authors functioned as a form of self-analysis. In February of 1839 Zeno becomes an alter-ego, one devoted to a similar "system of bookkeeping"; then in November Thoreau writes (in his attic study) of Aeschylus, who led "his own healthy Attic life." A writer had to be a skilled reader; Thoreau studied Homer and Goethe because he expected to emulate their success.

The author who most obviously inspired young Thoreau was Ralph Waldo Emerson (whose journal contains similar calisthenics). His career had bloomed in recent years, when friends like Bronson Alcott began to call Emerson "the high literary name of this age." Thoreau was strongly drawn to Emerson, his senior by fourteen years, while Emerson behaved toward Thoreau as a benevolent but distant mentor. The two men walked together, exchanged books and ideas; to some critics, they seemed to become unconscious duplicates. James Russell Lowell met Thoreau in Concord during the summer of 1838; to a friend he wrote: "it is exquisitely amusing to see how he imitates

Emerson's tone & manner. With my eyes shut I shouldn't kn[ow] them apart." (Mrs. Thoreau had her own version of this matter: "How much Mr. Emerson does talk like my Henry.") Actually, they were quite dissimilar: both had prominent noses and hesitant, solemn speech, but Thoreau was short and dark-complexioned, Emerson tall and fair.

Even sharper differences characterized their ideas about a literary career. Although cool and reserved, Emerson burned with ambition for himself and his friends. On their behalf he organized meetings and lecture series, then lobbied for them with Lyceum committees and publishers. He encouraged novices to bring him manuscripts, which he read as a severe critic. His comments on some of Bronson Alcott's diary entries in 1838 made their author conclude that silence "was a fairer style of publication," and he published little from his diary for the next twenty years.

Emerson had too much energy and talent to remain silent; always he urged his fellow idealists not to ignore the logistics of their careers. Young Henry Thoreau, an expert carpenter and gardener, seemed far less enterprising as a man of letters. In February 1838 Emerson urged him to write a history of college life; in November he said poetry would kill "this maggot of Freedom & Humanity" in Thoreau's brain. Thoreau saw his thoughts in more flattering terms; to him an un-formed moment of intuition was vastly superior to any attempt at ex-pressing it. A Journal entry written in early March 1838 seemed "stale, flat, and unprofitable" to him only hours later; in December he conceived of a perfect book in impossible terms, as "a foil whereon the waves of silence might break."

Emerson was patient with this would-be Hamlet; in April he said Thoreau should follow his impulses but still write for a public; in No-vember he listened quietly when Thoreau argued against revision, say-ing that a writer who "took too many pains with the expression . . . was not any longer the idea himself." Emerson would see to the revi-sions himself. In 1839 he helped to launch a new transcendentalist quarterly, The Dial, and as one of its editors he solicited Thoreau to submit his works. Thoreau came up with a short paper on Aulus Per-sius Flaccus, the Latin satirist, in March 1840; after seeing Emerson's "rewritten" text in April Thoreau took it back for "recorrection." The version published in July expressed his earliest reservations about editors: "The word that is written may be postponed, but not that on the lip . . . The artist and his work are not to be separated" (EE, 126–27).

That same month John and Henry Thoreau nearly separated, over the surprising issue of romance. One of their pupils, Edmund Sewall from Scituate, had an attractive older sister named Ellen. On her visits to Concord the Thoreaus both sought her affections, a rivalry that was no less intense for their long friendship. John made a proposal of marriage in July; Ellen accepted—and then swiftly declined. She may have actually preferred Henry, but her parents objected to both of the Thoreaus, who had a reputation for espousing radical ideas. John's reactions are unknown; Henry put his energy into an essay on the radical as hero.

In this work he tried to reconcile his conflicting estimates of thought and expression. His inspiration was an actual incident, watching the local militia gather for Concord's Fourth of July muster. The troops met at dusk on July 3, pitched tents, and slept through a tranquil night, then awoke to a bugle's morning call. These were men of action, tempered by rest and thought, and thus prepared to lead heroic lives. "The whole course of our lives should be analogous to one day of the soldier's," Thoreau wrote on July 4. He knew this one day could be an appropriate framework for an essay, but in preparing a text he had to ransack many previous days of Journal entries, plucking out useful passages and drafting fresh thoughts in later entries. This piecemeal method (so exactly like Emerson's) belied the very congruity of theme and form Thoreau had sought.

Eventually his original concept eroded away, leaving a finished essay—"The Service"—that uses military images but has no clear pattern of thought or action. Repeatedly Thoreau describes "the brave man" in odd paradoxes, shifting to new images before he has explored the old ones, invoking his favorite notion that silence is not passive but active: "A man's life should be a stately march to an unheard music . . . which only his nicer ear can detect" (RP, 11). (In Walden Thoreau discarded this apology for inertia, using the same figure to create his vigorous—and most famous—phrase: "If a man does not keep pace with his companions, perhaps it is because he hears a different drummer" [Wa, 326]).

One editor of The Dial was a brilliant and vigorous critic herself, and Margaret Fuller saw little in "The Service" to merit publication. On December 1 she returned it, pointing instinctively to Thoreau's lack of form and method: "I never once felt myself in a stream of thought, but seem to hear the grating tools on the mosaic." This rejection did not sting as much as another that winter. Henry also proposed to Ellen Sewall, but she—embarrassed by the earlier fiasco with John —followed her father's wishes and sent an immediate refusal. Margaret Fuller had been more generous: she invited Thoreau to resubmit the essay if he thought her strictures too harsh. He declined, writing in the Journal for January 1841 that any experience was useful: "So is all misfortune only a stepping-stone to fortune."

Outside the Journal he had little control over events, but Thoreau seized the initiative when possible. Rather than allow the town treasurer to charge him both taxes and a church assessment (then a common practice in Massachusetts), on January 6 Thoreau formally "signed off" from the First Parish, where his family and the Emersons continued to attend. His loyalty to John was constant, even more so after their loss of Ellen: in late January they upheld the affirmative side in a Lyceum debate on the question "Is it ever proper to offer forcible resistance?"

His life was often inconsistent and fluctuating, but the Journal encouraged him to see this condition as useful. The entries were never wholly predictable, he wrote on January 29. At the time of writing "my counter seems cluttered with the meanest home-made stuffs; but after months or years I may discover the wealth of India." This image suggests how much Thoreau saw his early Journal as a workshop where raw materials might in time become salable goods; but that idea also contradicted his belief that writing should be immaculately conceived, without reference to future publications.

Sometimes he wrote entries that had no apparent purpose, except to address the pleasures and problems of composition. At Walden Pond on January 30 he saw some fox tracks curving across the snow; they represented to him "the fluctuations of some mind . . . The pond was his journal, and last night's snow made a *tabula rasa* for him." But his own Journal was not a blank slate, to be filled and cleaned as though by magic; when he tried to join its separate parts, the resulting whole seemed pallid and artificial. Nature would not transplant a primrose from the river's edge to a mountain, he wrote in early February: "If sun, wind, and rain came *here* to cherish and expand it, shall not we come here to pluck it?"

He was beginning to argue that nature has one order and art another, a difference Emerson had resolved by declaring the supremacy of human consciousness. Thoreau was more certain that reality stands apart from the mind. He sensed what any farmer knows, that good ideas do not always yield a good harvest. The Journal, he wrote on February 8, represented the force of his own talent, for its entries were "gleanings from the field which in action I reap," yet that process converted these once living materials into a dry and withered artifact: "Like the sere leaves in yonder vase, these have been gathered far and wide."

Thoreau had thought of farming because he needed a new situation. The brothers had agreed to close their school in April; John's health had weakened, and Henry wanted to give more time to his writing. He inspected some properties for rent, caught a cold walking in the snow, and spent the rest of February convalescing. Writing Journal entries redeemed some of this time, he noted, for "Nothing goes by luck in composition . . . Every sentence is the result of a long probation." He then talked with Emerson about the future. Both men had been invited to join Brook Farm, the transcendentalist commune at West Roxbury, and neither wished to go. In his Journal for early March, Thoreau was blunt: "I would rather keep bachelor's hall in hell than go to board in heaven." Emerson sent a diplomatic letter to Brook Farm, saying he preferred to try some "domestic and social experiments" of his own.

In April Emerson unfolded a plan: Thoreau could have room, board, and access to Emerson's library, in exchange for a few hours of daily chores. They struck a classic Yankee bargain: one man sought liberty, the other a household appliance. On April 26 Thoreau moved into Emerson's large white manse on the Cambridge Turnpike. He

took a small room on the second floor, at the head of the stairs. Within days he registered a complaint in his Journal: "Life in gardens and
parlors is unpalatable to me. It wants rudeness and necessity to give it
relish."

———————

For nearly two years Thoreau lived with the Emersons, enjoying a productive but not always contented period of his literary apprenticeship.
This interval marks his apex as a poet, when he wrote most of his best
verses. Some are oddly contradictory, expressing with great skill his
distrust of authorship. "Sic Vita" (published in *The Dial* for July 1841)
is a shaped verse, the lines of each stanza printed to resemble a gift
bouquet—some violets, tied with a grass band—that is also an image
of its donor:

> I am a parcel of vain strivings tied
> By a chance bond together,
> Dangling this way and that, their links
> Were made so loose and wide,
> Methinks,
> For milder weather.

The poem goes on to describe how these rootless flowers, when placed
in water, will bloom "in mimicry of life" (CP, 81) and then pass away,
to be followed by new generations. This simple paradox, that art destroys life to create beauty, fed on his naïve ideas of organic processes
(greatly expanded in later years) and on large amounts of youthful self-
pity. A couplet in his entry for August 18 rationalizes this sense of
frustration:

> My life hath been the poem I would have writ,
> But I could not both live and live to utter it.

Some of this fatalism came from reading Hindu scriptures in Emerson's library, books that counseled patience and seemed "without

beginning or end, an eternal interlude without plot," all their parts equally important. Thoreau wanted to write a similar book, something close to his experience but also high-flown, poetic. In early September he fancied writing "a poem to be called 'Concord,' " an epic description of the town's woods and fields, days and seasons. Realizing that his two original Journal volumes were now too ragged for convenient use (he had torn out many pages), Thoreau decided to copy the surviving entries into five new blank books, the first one titled "Gleanings."

This work occupied most of October and November; he never wrote the "poem to be called 'Concord.' " Then he turned to a new idea, an anthology of English verse. He copied many pages from Chalmers' edition of *English Poets* and composed critical commentary in the Journal, but nothing came of this plan, either. His career was beginning to resemble a Hindu scripture, without plot or progress. Emerson grew uneasy about his young disciple: Thoreau had unerring perception, "yet he is impracticable, & does not flow through his pen or . . . tongue."

By December Thoreau wanted to leave, to live by Sandy Pond and "watch the progress of the seasons." He was fond of Mrs. Emerson and the children, enjoyed the role of seeing to their needs—building a drawer to hold dress gloves, cooking popcorn at the fire. Mr. Emerson was a bachelor in spirit; he kept to his study, published books on a regular schedule. Emerson knew that he was aloof, but only in his journal could he apologize: "Yet if I am born to write a few good sentences or verses, these shall endure & my disgraces utterly perish out of memory."

Then in January 1842 came tragedy, to both Thoreau and Emerson, which made them forget their differences for a while. After a shaving accident John Thoreau suddenly contracted lockjaw; he suffered fever and convulsions, and died in Henry's arms on January 11. In a grief-stricken reaction Henry also developed symptoms of the disease, but he recovered in a few weeks. Meanwhile, the Emersons' son, five-year-old Waldo, died of scarlatina on January 28. Thoreau consoled both families, then tried in vain to heal his own broken life. For the rest of his days he mourned this dead brother who had been his best of friends, virtually another self. John was Henry's ideal of youth and chastity; his memory became a substitute for love, marriage, and most other deep commitments.

When he resumed Journal entries on March 8, Thoreau was newly aware of the "long delay" that characterized his career. He now tried to accelerate his work by completing a verse translation of *Prometheus Bound* for *The Dial* (printed there in January 1843), which projects his own anguish into this story of an imprisoned hero: "In plain words, all gods I hate." Emerson then gave Thoreau a fresh assignment, to prepare for *The Dial* a review of several state reports on natural history.

In looking over his recent Journal entries, especially those in volume 6, Thoreau saw the possibility of writing more than a standard book review. His Journal entries were now more personal and anecdotal; they experimented with narrative effects by shifting tenses (from past to present) and person (from "I" to "you" or "we"). These new syntactical patterns were the elements of a maturing prose style —less didactic, more spontaneous and lyrical:

> May 27 [1841]. *Thursday* I sit in my boat on Walden, playing the flute this evening, and see the perch, which I seem to have charmed, hovering around me, and the moon travelling over the bottom, which is strewn with the wrecks of the forest, and feel that nothing but the wildest imagination can conceive of the manner of life we are living. Nature is a wizard. The Concord nights are stranger than the Arabian nights.

In the Journal he had begun to develop a new vision of nature, beyond the stable and orderly *design* of Locke and Newton that Harvard taught him, and toward the romantic vision of nature as a *process* of ceaseless, dynamic change, its patterns of life and death forming a single great poem. Recalling the tragedies of last winter, Thoreau saw this lesson in his own restored vigor: "If we see Nature as pausing, immediately all mortifies and decays; but seen as progressing, she is beautiful." Progress was also apparent in his Journal entries, which rose and fell with his daily fortunes, following the annual cycle of seasons. The

Journal was itself a natural history: it revealed the form of nature and the ideal shape his works could emulate.

By late March Thoreau was at work on his natural history essay, which he wanted to be as seamless as time, but still a record of his own imagination. He reviewed the Journal, selected entries from the past five years, then wrote a draft on the first ninety pages (now missing) of volume 7. These were the same working methods he had applied to "The Service," and they had an equally adverse effect on "Natural History of Massachusetts," printed in The Dial for July 1842.

After referring only briefly to the state reports, Thoreau moves to his own observations. He tries to portray a calendar of four seasons, but fails—because his Journal entries mostly described two seasons, the dramatic changes of spring and fall. He also tries to fit several classes of animals, from mammals to fish, into the seasonal progress —but his Journal evidence was ambiguous, so instead he arranges each class of animals in a separate calendar year. The essay constantly recycles, spring to fall, spring to fall; and it lists the animals in almost random order. Thoreau's style has improved and some of his descriptive passages—of a diving loon, or a fox tracked in snow—are impressive (Ex, 66–67). But the formal deficiencies remain; they illustrate the wide gap between his early theory and practice of writing.

This problem was common to other transcendentalists, for they could not find practical forms that clearly expressed their ideal convictions. Transcendentalism—which an advocate once defined as "a little beyond"—was an assault on materialism and conventional institutions. Any idea of Form, political or aesthetic, was contrary to the spirit of Reform. Emerson insisted that life is fluid and volatile, that the true work of art is "never fixed, but always flowing"; in his own lectures he used his preacher's gift, a deep, melodious voice, to cascade thoughts and images upon his audiences—who strained to keep pace. Most of The Dial authors preferred oral performance, the spontaneous Conversation or Orphic proverb that defied logical structure. After meeting Thomas Carlyle in June, Alcott noted in his diary the author's lack of conversation: "Another instance . . . of the suicide of the pen." Thoreau was surrounded by Talkers with soft, translucent visions and little in the way of tough practicality.

A different sort of writer arrived in Concord that July: Nathaniel Hawthorne, recently married and settling into the journeyman phase of his career. Behind him were years of hack writing and a brief taste of life at Brook Farm. He was quiet but witty, not overly reverent toward *The Dial* circle. After meeting Thoreau, Hawthorne read "Natural History of Massachusetts" and commented sharply in his notebook on September 1: Thoreau was wholesome but "imperfect in his own mode of action." Hawthorne saw a writer who had not yet found his native voice and subject matter. Yet Thoreau was amazingly skillful in handling his boat on the Concord River, as Hawthorne found during an excursion on September 2. Perhaps he suggested that Thoreau put this talent to use and write a travel narrative. Thoreau was already at work on a long version of his 1839 trip with John; a briefer story lay in some Journal entries (now missing) about his hike to Mount Wachusett in July. He quickly wrote a separate draft, in the back of John's old nature album, then made a fair copy and sent it to *The Boston Miscellany*, whose editors Hawthorne knew well.

"A Walk to Wachusett" (published in January 1843) was an entirely new piece of writing for Thoreau because he did not build it as a mosaic, by assembling Journal entries around a common theme. Instead, he took a well-defined sequence of entries, linked by his movement through space and time, and expanded their facts into metaphors. In the essay, landscape becomes a map of his mind; each step of his journey is an increment of thought. His central metaphor is Wachusett, a mountain on the western horizon "who like me / Standest alone without society" (Ex, 75); yet this emblem of isolation reunites him with humanity, for from the summit he sees the great Appalachian chain of mountains, running north to south, that shaped the history of America. The story's climax is both physical and intel-

"Wachusett from Fair Haven Hill looks like this:—the dotted line being the top of the surrounding forest."

lectual, as Thoreau finds in the mountains an embodiment of creative Form: "the hand which moulded their opposite slopes, making one to balance the other, worked round a deep centre, and was privy to the plan of the universe" (Ex, 91–92).

The shape of nature defined this story as well, and though poets have traditionally found revelation on mountaintops (he cites both Virgil and Wordsworth), for Thoreau this unity of form and theme was an original achievement. He, too, had molded opposites around a common center, discovering that "there is an elevation in each hour," and that his own "separate and solitary way" lies not on Wachusett but in returning to Concord. This rite of passage, going out into nature and then coming home, was Thoreau's greatest discovery; for that became the pattern of all his major narratives—the retreat into solitude that leads to reconciliation with society.

His success with this essay, about a mountain he addresses as "thy worthy brother," may have prompted Thoreau to impose a similar plan on the longer story of his 1839 journey. Since John's death that trip had assumed an elegiac significance; now Thoreau seemed ready to prepare a deliberate memorial. In the fall of 1842 he obtained a volume, called "long book" in later notes, and wrote this invocation on the first page:

> Where'er thou sail'st who sailed with me,
> Though now thou climbest loftier mounts
> And fairer rivers dost ascend
> Be thou my muse, my Brother.

He then leafed through the Gleanings and copied useful passages into "long book," a sequential procedure that gave him his narrative plan: descriptions of the journey—departure, the river, meals, camps—alternating with meditations on time, friendship, music, poetry. These were the opposite slopes of his story, action and thought, molded around the deep center of his unidentified companion, now fallen silent on the return voyage.

As this work proceeded Thoreau varied its rhythms, sometimes by writing new entries in "long book," dated September and October, then by dropping the 1839 dates for general titles, such as "Wednesday" or "Friday." He had decided to compress the two-week voyage into a span of seven days, but not to curtail the work of writing this story. More than four years were to pass before he had collected enough Journal passages to fill "long book," and by then its natural coherence had faded; the tribute to John had become instead a vast, unwieldy mosaic.

For the rest of 1842 Thoreau accomplished little, even though he was busy in many areas. He placed poems in the October *Dial* and helped Emerson with its proofreading; in November he was elected curator of the Concord Lyceum, a post that obliged him to set up a schedule of twenty-five programs, plus attend to a host of minor details. He had little time for leisure or solitude, and the first anniversary of John's death, in January 1843, left him profoundly depressed. To Emerson (then on a lecture tour) Thoreau sent an apology for his "meanness"; in the Journal he described himself as miserably dull and insipid, "a diseased bundle of nerves."

Yet by February he had regained his confidence, in part by completing a lecture on the heroic figure Sir Walter Raleigh. Thoreau delivered this lecture at the Lyceum on February 8, but he never published the full text, only a few passages (We, 104–105). As his sole effort in biography, "Sir Walter Raleigh" is not an impressive work; mostly it reflects the ideas of Emerson and Carlyle, who believed that historical heroes are symbolic versions of living men. Thoreau agreed; he tried to portray Raleigh as an ideal version of himself, the contemplative man of action.

Unfortunately, he had conflicting images of both men, because he did not see how to equate their separate realms of life and art. Although he depicts Raleigh as a man of "general information and universal accomplishment" (EE, 195), the lecture breaks into two stories, of deeds and of writings, their twin climaxes being Raleigh's imprisonment and his poems—which he actually wrote long before going to prison. This flawed plan reflects Thoreau's method of construction, as he tried to adapt Journal passages on widely varied subjects to suit the central figure of Raleigh. The mosaic had not worked satisfactorily on other themes, and it certainly would not admit Thoreau now "into the secret of a man's life" (EE, 208).

He was no longer making progress in Concord, as Emerson acknowledged in his journal that March: "Young men, like Henry Thoreau, owe us a new world, & they have not acquitted the fulfillment." Perhaps New York, where magazine and book publishers abounded, would offer him better incentives. Thoreau was willing to try a new domestic experiment; soon he agreed to work as a tutor and live in the home of Emerson's brother William, a county judge on Staten Island. Hawthorne liked the idea of New York; in April he wrote in his notebook that Thoreau would thus "take one step towards a circumstantial position in the world."

His friends expected the world of him, but Thoreau's six months in New York were largely a disaster. He hated the jostling crowds on Broadway, and he found that these Emersons gave him less privacy, and more idle chat, than their Concord kin. Much of his energy went into writing homesick letters, for city editors were not attracted to his wares. At the end of volume 8 of the Journal he drafted an essay about winter, then sent it to Emerson for inclusion in *The Dial*. Emerson disliked the piece, complaining to his journal that he felt "nervous & wretched to read it," and in a letter on September 8 he frankly scolded Thoreau for the "*mannerism*" of creating so many artificial paradoxes. He accepted the essay anyway, for publication in the October 1843 issue.

In "A Winter Walk" Thoreau tried to use the excursional pattern that had worked for "A Walk to Wachusett," but he was not writing now about one journey through a real landscape. Instead, he assembled many different Journal passages—some had nothing to do with winter—into an imaginary synthesis, and for some reason he decided to conceal all local references. The story moves from a village (Concord) to a pond (Walden) and returns along a river (Sudbury), but the anonymity of these landmarks blurs the essay's spatial design. His themes have no clear line of action, and his paradoxes—the woods are home, cold is fiery, solitude civilizes—seem largely unfounded. This journey has neither a climax nor a conclusion; at the end he ambles off into snowdrifts and never returns to the village. One of the closing lines best describes Thoreau's method and achievement: "In winter, nature is a cabinet of curiosities, full of dried specimens, in their natural order and position" (Ex, 129).

Thoreau felt equally out of place in New York, where he could make no progress with editors. To his mother he wrote on October 1: "My bait will not tempt the rats; they are too well fed." Yet editors were not entirely to blame, for in the gossipy, contentious atmosphere of New York journalism (where Edgar Allan Poe thrived) Thoreau was attempting to vend esoterica—like his recently completed translation of Aeschylus, *The Seven Against Thebes*, the story of another metropolis that would not fall to siege. In six months of solicitation he managed to place only two pieces, both in *The Democratic Review*: "The Landlord," a familiar essay, and "Paradise (To Be) Regained," a review of a Utopian tract by J. A. Etzler.

Neither work suggests that Thoreau had a bright future in journalism. "The Landlord" is nostalgic, recalling a village inn where the host charms his guests with lively stories, "what we would say provided we had an audience" (Ex, 106). "Paradise (To Be) Regained" is a critique of the then popular spirit of social reform, for Etzler envisions a city powered by the natural forces of wind, tides, and sun. Thoreau admires this scheme, but he doubts that current engineers can make it work. Better seek "the paradise within" mankind, he argues, than try to build a heartless social machine (RP, 47).

He distrusted apparatus, perhaps largely because he had not yet found appropriate forms for his own ideas. By December 17 he had left Staten Island for good and returned to his parents' house in Concord. He would not be a guest there, but instead worked in the pencil factory a few days each week to pay for his room and board. Emerson was gloomy about the new situation; in his journal he wrote: "H . . . will never be a writer; he is as active as a shoemaker." Yet *The Dial* for January 1844 carried Thoreau's latest effort, an essay called "Homer. Ossian. Chaucer.," which agreed with Emerson that thought supersedes poetic form. The essay demonstrates that principle by presenting yet another mosaic of Journal passages—one of them a redaction of the warning not to transplant primroses from their original site (EE, 171).

In the last two issues of *The Dial*, January and April 1844, Thoreau published translations of Pindaric odes and "Herald of Freedom," an essay on the antislavery writer N. P. Rogers. As in his later political essays, Thoreau saw public issues from a literary perspective: he praises both Rogers's ideas and his prose style, which resembles a rushing mountain stream (RP, 50–51). This analogy invokes an attractive series of Thoreau's own ideas and phrases, an indication that he had begun to shape a rhetoric that was more natural and logical. In the radicalism of one author, he glimpsed his own ambitions: "unfinished as his pieces were, yet their literary merit has been overlooked" (RP, 57).

On April 30 an event occurred that set his reputation in Concord back several distinct notches. With his friend Edward Hoar, then a senior at Harvard, Thoreau caught some fish along the Sudbury River and stopped to cook a chowder at Fairhaven Bay. The fire they kindled went out of control, and while Thoreau ran for help, nearly three hundred acres of forest were destroyed. For years he had to live with the epithet "woods-burner," since many neighbors thought the incident revealed how shiftless he had become, the college man with no career. His thoughts at the time are unknown. Although he may have written about the fire in volume 9 of his Journal, most of its contents are now missing. He did write an account in June 1850, and some later readers have attributed that six-year silence to Thoreau's repressed guilt. The 1850 version, however, appears among several passages that he had drafted for Walden and may have had a similar purpose. The story never reached his final text, in which he describes a woods fire set "by mischievous boys" rather than by himself (Wa, 259–60).

A one-year gap, March 1844 to March 1845, lies between volume 9 and his next datable entries, at the end of "long book." In those missing pages he probably wrote about a summer hike in the Berkshires and Catskills, since he later published a partial account (We, 180–86; 202–09). He may have written little in the fall, as he helped his father build a house out in "Texas," an area west of the new railroad tracks. With her characteristic energy, Mrs. Thoreau chose the house site and drew up plans; Henry later found she had forgotten to put stairs between the lower and upper floors.

His own designs were more careful. Early in 1845 he wrote "Wendell Phillips at Concord Lyceum," a flattering review of an anti-slavery lecture that W. L. Garrison printed at once in his militant weekly, *The Liberator*. On March 25 Thoreau delivered to the Lyceum his first installment of *A Week on the Concord and Merrimack Rivers*, a lecture called "Concord River." He was eager to work full-time on this book now, preferably under conditions that allowed maximum privacy and quiet. For years he had dreamed of living in the woods near a pond.

Emerson owned property on both sides of Walden, and he was agreeable to allowing Thoreau to build a house there. In March of 1845 he chose a site—on the north side, with easy access to town; on a slope above a deep cove, with a fine view and protection from winds. He dug his cellar in an old woodchuck burrow; the sand held without stones and guaranteed that his stores would not freeze. The house had a sensible design—windows and door facing the sun, space for a chimney on the cold north wall. His carpentry was economical—handcut framing and shingles recycled from an old shanty. The later refinements—plastered walls, a stone hearth, and a brick chimney—were made for practical comfort.

In all his days Henry Thoreau had not built a piece of writing as sound and tight as this small house. The whole process of construction—a place, a plan, a set of new uses for old materials—resembled his compositions, but here the form and function were consonant. Moving in on July 4, 1845, nearly eight years after he began the Journal, Thoreau must have believed that only good works lay ahead.

3
THE CUBES OF PYTHAGORAS

From all points of the compass, from the earth beneath and the heavens above, have come these inspirations and been entered duly in the order of their arrival in the journal. Thereafter, when the time arrived, they were winnowed into lectures, and again, in due time, from lectures into essays. And at last they stand, like the cubes of Pythagoras, firmly on either basis; like statues on their pedestals, but the statues rarely take hold of hands. There is only such connection and series as is attainable in the galleries. And this affects their immediate practical and popular influence.

—ca. AUGUST 1846

At Walden Pond Thoreau conducted a writer's sabbatical as much as an experiment in living, for he wanted time to concentrate on his poetry and prose. In this "wooden inkstand," as Channing later called it, the furniture expressed Thoreau's priorities: one bed, one table, one writing desk. Thoreau took fuel from the woods and food from his garden, but he was no hermit there. Readers of *Walden* often think he lived in utter isolation, yet (as the book reports) he frequently saw visitors or paid calls in town. Some villagers assumed he was "idling away his time," but idleness was an important part of his work.

As a writer, he was certainly busy. The "long book" now had

more than two hundred pages of transcribed entries, and he had a firm outline of A Week in mind: an introductory chapter on "Concord River," followed by seven others, "Saturday" to "Friday." In the margins of "long book" he numbered paragraphs 1 to 8, assigning them to chapters. During the summer of 1845 he began a first draft, much shorter than the final version, but remarkably similar in form and content.

He also knew that his life at Walden could be the subject of a future book. In addition to continuing the "long book," he began that summer two untitled notebooks (now called "Walden 1" and "Walden 2" by editors) for the new project. All three volumes were filled by late March 1846, whereupon he began a fourth, also untitled (called "Berg Journal," for its library location), which ran up to early 1847. With their overlapping chronology and contents these volumes still resemble Emerson's journal, a mix of dated entries and working drafts. Most pages of "Walden 1" describe Thoreau's immediate experiences at the pond, in present tense and with dates; those of "Walden 2" recast events and add later thoughts, usually undated. Often he gleaned the volumes for his drafts by copying or excising pages. More than ever, his Journal in these years served as a writer's workshop, flatly contradicting the principles of organic form and continuity Thoreau expressed in its pages.

In September, early in the "Walden 2" book, he confessed to strong reservations about these writing habits, so like Emerson's: thoughts came to the Journal from "all points of the compass"; he put them down "in their order of arrival"; then later he "winnowed" them into lectures or essays until they stood, "like the cubes of Pythagoras" or statues in a gallery, firmly independent and unconnected with each other. The images of this passage, themselves rather unconnected, reflect an important development in Thoreau's ideas about his work. In learning to make surveys he had used a compass and geometry, computing areas and right angles with the famous Pythagorean theorem. These tools produced accurate surveys, but only if his field notes and measurements were exact. Less accurate were the writings he "winnowed" from his Journal; they became mere "cubes" or statues, pale renditions of their original source.

His privacy at Walden encouraged Thoreau to blame readers for these lapses. If only they saw the work through *his* eyes, reading books "as deliberately and reservedly as they were written." Like a good friend, such an audience would provoke his best thoughts, make them actual by echoing the music he sounded: "an amended strain . . . corrected and repronounced for me." This listener was not an earthly companion; in a poem Thoreau described a "Great Friend" who merges with nature and becomes "the person in her mask" (CP, 141). The mystical notion of an Other—analogous to his departed brother —inspired a bold ideal for *A Week*: it would be the "perfect work of art" before which readers would "stand as mute though contented."

Life at Walden was quiet, and so are the pages of his three concurrent Journal volumes. Only one entry, in mid-July, comments on slavery, and none refer to the Mexican war, widely interpreted by other liberals as a plot to extend slavery farther west. Silence and withdrawal were Thoreau's forms of protest: he refused to pay his poll tax, and in the Journal he criticized an Irish laborer who would not drop his old customs "in this primitive new country." The writer's prerogative, he wrote in December, was to transform old modes of expression into new ones, creating a "fable which is truly and naturally composed" and thus has universal appeal. With this narrative ideal in mind, on December 23 he began to compose the earliest version of *Walden*, a lecture on "getting a living."

In the "long book" and "Walden 2" he also drafted a lecture on Thomas Carlyle, which he delivered in February 1846 and revised that spring for publication. Many passages he wrote first in the new "Berg Journal," begun in mid-April. This discourse on a famous author raised questions about his own mode of life. The days at Walden seemed rather too divided between physical labor and thought: "The poetic & philosophic have my constant vote—the practic hinders & unfits me for the former." Yet his mind and body were perhaps governed by "the law" he discovered in late April while surveying the pond. On his map the lines of greatest length and breadth intersected at the point of greatest depth, near the middle. A man's hidden, contemplative life should equal the visible and active one; that coherence made his work successful. "You only need to know how his shores trend . . . to know his depth and concealed bottom."

Emerson admired Thoreau's situation at the pond enough to consider building a "lodge" for himself on the opposite shore. In early May he asked Thoreau for a design, which Alcott embellished with a second story, but nothing came of these plans. In June Thoreau continued to fill many pages of the Journal with passages for A Week, from practical facts on natural history to long, contemplative extracts from the Hindu scriptures. In mid-July he read parts of the draft to Emerson, who at once concluded that the book was ready for publication. That plan was also fruitless, for an event suddenly interrupted Thoreau's work.

On a trip to town in late July he was arrested for failing to pay his poll taxes. Instead of seizing his property, the constable put Thoreau in jail; after a single night of confinement, someone (certainly not his parents; perhaps Aunt Maria) paid the arrears and Thoreau was released. This moment of resistance was brief, yet it was an action derived from principle, obeying the hidden "law" he had found at Walden. In the Journal he made some sharp comments on governments and taxes but gave no specifics about his night in jail.

Alcott wrote on July 25 that Emerson said Thoreau's act was "mean and skulking, and in bad taste," but Emerson's private estimate was less derogatory. In his journal he wrote that many abolitionists denounced war yet paid the taxes that supported it; that Thoreau's quarrel was not with Massachusetts but with "the State of Man." At the antislavery meeting held at Walden on August 1, Emerson spoke from Thoreau's doorstep. From there one could see the surface of the pond—if not its hidden bottom.

By this time Thoreau had sent the essay on Carlyle to Horace Greeley, founder and editor of the New York Tribune. Greeley was the best memory Thoreau retained of New York, for this important journalist had volunteered to serve as his unpaid literary agent. He was a hearty, energetic soul, always frank in his criticism (as Emerson was not), sympathetic to new ideas but practical about their popular appeal. Over the years he would encourage Thoreau to develop his own identity as a writer and reach a larger audience—which Greeley stimulated by printing excerpts and positive reviews. In his blunt fashion Greeley told Thoreau on August 16 that the essay on Carlyle was too long and intellectual for most journals, but eventually he placed it in *Graham's Magazine*, where—after many delays—it appeared as "Thomas Carlyle and His Works" in March and April of 1847.

In this essay Thoreau tries to avoid the problems of "Sir Walter Raleigh" by writing criticism, not biography. He does see Carlyle as a heroic figure, his study "the spacious workshop of the world maker" (EE, 220–21), but also as an outcast, whose books the world misreads as wild, formless, and overwritten. The fault lies with readers, not the author; to read him truly "you must almost have written these books yourself" (EE, 225).

As in the Journal, Thoreau was asking for a contract between reader and author that virtually eliminates objective criticism. His own identification with Carlyle is clear, especially in describing the author's style with Waldenic images: "cultivated spots, and belts of forests and blueberry-swamps round about it" (EE, 230). In an essay filled with praise, Thoreau's strongest objection is that "Carlyle indicates a depth . . . which he neglects to fathom" (EE, 257). That metaphor probably arose from the two books, of river and pond, which Thoreau was now drafting at Walden. The essay expressed bold hopes for writing, yet Greeley had implied that Thoreau's own workshop had produced only another irrelevance. The editors at *Graham's* were not reassuring; they delayed publication for six months and kept Thoreau waiting more than a year for his payment. Nor did Carlyle shower him with praise; on May 18, 1847, he wrote to Emerson only that the essay gave its subject "due entertainment and recognition."

By late August of 1846 Thoreau had drafted a brief account of hiking in the White Mountains for *A Week*; then he went to Maine for a journey to Mount Katahdin. Northern Maine exceeded his expectations, for this wilderness was not fully mapped or explored. Its roads gave way to footpaths, the rivers to lakes and rocky streams. His six-man party poled a heavy wooden bateau upstream, carrying it around the rapids and waterfalls. They hiked the last ten miles to Katahdin and camped on its southern slope. Twice Thoreau climbed alone to higher ground—first above treeline, later to a broad plateau just below the summit. Heavy clouds obscured his view and discouraged him from climbing to the highest peak. But he had gone far; in the annals of Katahdin only four recorded ascents precede his.

Three days after leaving Maine he was back at Walden and writing a swift summary of his trip in the Journal, laying out names, dates, and facts in their order of occurrence, from August 31 to September 10. From September to December he wrote an expanded version of the journey, eventually filling 168 pages of his Journal volume. Unlike A Week and Walden, this story described the face of "Demonic Nature," an untamed place that made previous seasons in his life seem "unsubstantial and . . . incredible." But the Journal account was elaborately substantial; more facts piled up than he could ever use in a publication. A noticeable change had come to his style and structure. Like his excursion to Wachusett, this mountain story was solid and orderly; no cube of Pythagoras, it came from only one point on the compass, and he wrote it in the Journal as a single, continuous account.

Other projects were developing along more familiar lines. Only scraps of a Journal volume, called in his indexes "n book" (for new or next) and later "I," survive between January 1847 and July 1848, when Thoreau was hard at work on both A Week and Walden. This new, roman-numbered series did not signify a change from his usual working methods; the missing pages probably went into his two book drafts. Emerson encouraged Thoreau's activity; on March 12 he urged Evert Duyckinck at Wiley & Putnam's to publish A Week, "a book of extraordinary merit," on terms favorable to its author. Thoreau was not eager to rush into print, perhaps because friends had expressed varying reactions to A Week. Channing rejected it altogether; Emerson told Duyckinck that the narrative was "a very slender thread for such big beads & ingots as are strung on it." The writings about Walden were more firmly organized. By early 1847 Thoreau had accumulated enough draft material to describe his "housekeeping" and the year-long cycle of seasons. Both elements he incorporated into a lecture, which he read to the Concord Lyceum on February 10.

Bronson Alcott often visited the Walden house that winter on Sunday evenings, walking two miles through the snow to sit before

Thoreau's fire and converse. In mid-March Thoreau read him parts of his two projects; Alcott responded in his diary as a transcendentalist. The new lecture seemed materialistic, with Thoreau "beating the bush and measuring his tread" too exactly. But the long, meditative book would be a popular companion to Emerson's *Poems*, "purely American . . . as picturesque and flowing as the streams [Thoreau] sails on." This admiration of "flowing" discourse betrayed Alcott's indifference to narrative form, one that Emerson did not share entirely. At a lecture on March 3 he had controlled his audience's attention by learning "to rein in [his] genius a little" whenever he heard the footsteps of late arrivals. He might have admired what Alcott disliked, a lecture that measured its tread with care.

In late May Thoreau completed a draft of *A Week*, but this story did not rein in his genius sufficiently: the seven-day account of his river voyage now had many leisurely digressions, with a lavish sampling of poems, translations, and quotations. The text was a virtual anthology of his early writings, twice (or thrice) revised and rearranged in mosaic order. Perhaps sensing these flaws, he continued to delay his search for a publisher. The manuscript left him in late May for an initial round of negotiations; then he recalled it on July 27 for further revision.

By the late summer of 1847 he was ready to leave Walden Pond. His work there seemed done, for he had finished *A Week*, together with early versions of *Walden* and his essay on Katahdin. Emerson proposed some work of a different nature: during his absence on a European tour, Thoreau could resume his post with the Emerson family. A related project there was the building of a "summer house" for Emerson from Alcott's designs. Thoreau had gone to Walden as a builder; he left in the same capacity. On September 6, 1847, he was back in the house on Cambridge Turnpike, living in the same tiny room he had occupied six years ago.

––––––––

Building a house with a philosopher proved a comical test of transcendentalist principles: Alcott refused to make exact plans or square off

"The whole house, methought, was well planted, rested solidly on the earth. . . ."

the timbers, preferring instead to accommodate the "fitness" of their original branches and curves. (Thoreau told Emerson that the work went slowly, "so many *knots* per hour.") This "Tumbledown Hall," as Emerson had called it in late August, was the antithesis of Thoreau's house at Walden, yet it emulated the very principles of spontaneous, meandering development he had praised in Thomas Carlyle's books and followed in *A Week*.

Before the house was finished Thoreau finally answered a letter he had received from his Harvard class secretary six months earlier. A decade had passed since commencement; Harvard wanted a summary of his achievements. On September 30 Thoreau replied, listing many trades—including the current venture as carpenter and mason—with this sarcastic request: "If you will act the part of Iolas and apply a hot iron to any of these heads, I shall be greatly obliged to you." In private, he was discouraged about his literary prospects. Emerson pressed him to keep up the hunt for a publisher, but Tumbledown Hall seemed a warning. When they talked of art this month, Thoreau blotted a paper with ink, folded it double, "and safely defied the artist to surpass his effect."

A month later Emerson was in Europe. Thoreau wrote him on November 14 that the summer house was done, "and the fame of the architect will endure as long as it shall stand." He also had rueful news of his own fame: a few polite conversations with an older woman, Sophia Foord, had somehow inspired her to send a marriage proposal, which he swiftly refused. His writings fared no better: because four publishers had declined *A Week*, he would yield to Emerson and take "the course you advised,—to let it lie." Emerson had actually advised the opposite course; his return letter on December 2 urged Thoreau to pay for the printing himself.

But Thoreau could not square his book's timbers. During the winter of 1847–48 he continued his new series of Journal volume numbers with "II," in which he drafted fresh materials for A *Week*. Possibly prompted by the misunderstanding with Miss Foord (she later threatened suicide), he began to assemble an essay on "Friendship," parts of which he read to an admiring Alcott in January. Throughout the spring of 1848 Thoreau drafted more passages in volume II, and eventually he inserted the essay into a second, longer draft of A *Week*. The book was "swelling again under my hands," he told Greeley on May 19.

At the same time he was diverted by two briefer works, both describing events from the summer of 1846: his night in jail and the trip to Maine. Alcott heard lecture versions that winter: at the Lyceum in December, "a very lively picture" of Maine; on January 26 and February 23, a two-part version of "The Rights and Duties of the Individual in relation to the Government." Throughout the early months of 1848 Thoreau worked on revising both lectures as well as A *Week*, apparently not in any fixed order but moving back and forth—rather like Iolas, applying hot irons as needed to the heads of Hydra. Work on one project probably affected the others, for better or worse.

The essay on Maine invoked a small but important change in his working habits. In his Journal was the long, continuous draft he had written in late 1846. Instead of excising the draft, he copied out a separate version and sent it to Greeley on April 3. Possibly Thoreau sent those pages now missing from volume II; in any case, his 1846 draft remained intact. Eventually he made a habit of separating the Journal and his drafts, thus preserving the integrity of each step in the creative process. He was beginning to find the form of *Walden*, a natural cycle of growth that replaced his early "cubes of Pythagoras." He was also developing the mode of his later Journal: after the spring of 1848 more of his entries in volume II are dated and left intact, in consecutive order.

Greeley placed the essay with the new *Union Magazine*, where it appeared as "Ktaadn, and the Maine Woods," in five installments, from July to November 1848. In the elegant pages of the *Union* "Ktaadn" was an anomaly, a frontier narrative set in the East instead of America's wild West. Before his death Thoreau corrected and revised this text for *The Maine Woods* (1864), but those changes did not substantially alter his earlier ideas and style.

Like two works he had recently read, Melville's *Typee* (1846) and Parkman's *The Oregon Trail* (1847), "Ktaadn" is an imaginative recasting of actual events. Although set in the pattern of rising and falling action Thoreau used for "A Walk to Wachusett," this excursion is not pastoral; its climax on Mount Katahdin (the usual spelling) is a sobering appraisal of civilized man's place in the wilderness. In this "bran new country" Thoreau finds that he can "no longer accuse institutions and society, but must front the true source of evil" (MW, 16).

That source is not nature but the "narrow, uninformed, and countrified mind" (MW, 22) he brings to the frontier. His journey is a story of struggle and submission, moving *against* the elements—paddling canoes upstream, hiking up the course of a mountain torrent —but never victorious over them. Each ascent leads only to a more arduous labor, until eventually he sees that the country is not "bran new" at all but older than his deepest dreams.

The import of this story unfolds in his mythological references to Katahdin, which he first sees in Olympian terms, "a dark isthmus . . . connecting the heavens with the earth" (MW, 33). But the difficulties of ascent challenge this illusion, as his journey becomes "scarcely less arduous than Satan's anciently through Chaos" (MW, 60). The summit, where he had expected heaven and earth to touch, is a "vast, Titanic" scene, reminding him of the place where Prometheus was bound (MW, 64). Here nature is "inhuman"; only "daring and insolent men" can travel in these "unfinished parts of the globe" (MW, 64–65).

The story's climax does not occur at the summit, for Thoreau's view there is obscured by dense, roiling clouds. Only after his descent to charred "Burnt Lands" (also recovering from disaster) can he see the meaning of what he failed to anticipate, "a region uninhabited by man" (MW, 70). The experience of utter isolation in this hard, brutally material realm makes his own bodily existence seem a fearful mystery: "rocks, trees, wind on our cheeks! the *solid* earth! the *actual* world! the *common sense*! *Contact*! *Contact*! Who are we? Where are we?" (MW, 71).

Those questions are unanswerable, yet by raising them he has retreated from his early dream-vision of Katahdin and prepared to return to the settled world. Moving downstream, his party gradually regains its confidence, running falls and rapids "which once had seemed terrible and not to be trifled with" (MW, 77). By journey's end he has set romantic illusions aside. Coming home he meets two Indians headed upstream. One of them, Louis Neptune by name, had promised to guide Thoreau at the outset. Now these once savage hunters seem to resemble "the lowest classes in a great city" (MW, 77). The wilderness is "more grim and wild" (MW, 80) than he had imagined, and therein lies its value to civilized men: "While the republic has already acquired a history world-wide, America is still unsettled and unexplored" (MW, 81).

In "Ktaadn" Thoreau began to evolve his distinctive prose style, spare and direct in describing physical forms—for example, this log shelter: "The interstices were filled with moss, and the roof was shingled with long and random splints of cedar, or spruce, or pine, rifted with a sledge or cleaver" (MW, 19). This realism complements his central theme and action; he works *with* scenes and events rather than *against* them by inventing conceits. As he wrote to Emerson in January 1848, "Ktaadn" had "many facts & some poetry." He was no longer writing much verse; now facts themselves were poetic, as when the actual map of Maine suggested his story's narrative line. If the movement of a river system later seemed "quite philosophical" to him, that was because the sequence of real place names—Lake, Deadwater, Stream, Falls—corresponded to his idea of a logical "order and identity" (MW, 46).

"Ktaadn" is the work in which Thoreau most obviously began to see and write with the confidence of his mature years. Every aspect of this experience conspired to turn him away from youthful, imitative standards: the wilderness itself, the pattern of his journey (and the story it created), the effort to *follow* his facts rather than lead them, the simple clarity of his words. This essay taught him how to write *Walden*. The excursion to Maine made him use the materials of his life—and Journal—in a new form of imaginative nonfiction.

The other lecture/essay from early 1848, on the individual and the state, was equally independent in ideas and form. Exactly why Thoreau decided to write about politics at this time is uncertain; he may have been stirred by the signing (on February 2) of the Treaty of Guadalupe, which ended the Mexican war on terms highly favorable to the United States. But Thoreau's reactions to public issues were always intensely personal. His friendship with Bronson Alcott was strained that winter, as Thoreau began to sense sharp differences between them. In 1843 Alcott had also gone to jail for nonpayment of taxes, an act that Thoreau had long admired. Yet the recent fiasco over Tumbledown Hall suggested that Alcott was not original, merely a faint imitation of others' ideas. As Thoreau wrote Emerson on December 29, 1847, "I think we must call him particularly *your* man."

Late in February of 1848 Thoreau was feeling even less companionable. Although Alcott had expressed "satisfaction" with the political lecture, Thoreau noted that in conversations his friend's thoughts roved like a band of disorderly soldiers, "firing behind—easily routed —not easily subdued—hovering on the skirts of society." Alcott apparently thought Thoreau had similar problems; in mid-March his diary described their mutual "inefficiency" in attracting disciples.

Thoreau could point to contrary evidence, for he was now rapidly becoming his own man. In mid-April "Ktaadn" was published, for a good fee—thanks to Greeley. Disciples were beginning to appear; on May 21 Thoreau wrote Emerson about receiving "earnest letters from H. G. O. Blake," an admirer from Worcester. Another frequent companion was Ellery Channing, who hiked with Thoreau in southern New Hampshire that summer—the trip surfaces briefly in A Week (We, 176). When Emerson returned to Concord in July, Thoreau promptly returned to his parents' house. His new essay defined the rights and duties of an individual, and so did his family circle.

Although essentially complete in 1848, the political essay was not published until a year later, in May 1849, under the title "Resistance to Civil Government." It appeared in the first (and only) volume of *Aesthetic Papers*, edited by Elizabeth Peabody, the vigorous reformer who ran a bookshop in Boston and had published *The Dial*. After Thoreau's death the essay appeared, somewhat revised, as "Civil Disobedience," a title that became widely known during the contentious twentieth century. The later title and revisions are possibly Thoreau's, but they do not significantly alter the text printed in his lifetime.

"Resistance to Civil Government" is more proof of Thoreau's growing maturity as a writer, for it has a sturdy narrative framework. The design governs his central statement: "Action from principle,—the perception and the performance of right . . . is essentially revolutionary . . . it divides the *individual*, separating the diabolical in him from the divine" (RP, 72). In part Thoreau is declaring his independence from old allegiances, but he has also defined the structure of his essay, a statement of principle followed by a story of action. He thus avoids the lapses of "The Service" and "Sir Walter Raleigh"; this time he unifies theory and practice by leaning them against each other.

In stating his principles Thoreau vigorously attacks democratic notions of government, citizenship, and majority rule, contrasting them with the Protestant ethic of individual conscience: "Let your life be a counter friction to stop the machine" (RP, 73–74). This opening barrage is radical stuff, but it stops short of advocating anarchy. Thoreau wants a few machines left running; he therefore urges acts of political dissent that are selective and symbolic.

The story of his incarceration becomes counter-frictional through paradox, as he uses the language and values of his antagonists to slow their machine. In an unjust State the just citizen belongs in prison; this captivity will liberate him by teaching him to separate falsity and truth, the diabolical from the divine. Going to jail is therefore "like travelling into a far country" (RP, 82), where he sees himself and society in a new light. After jail he leads a huckleberry party to one of Concord's highest hills, where the State does not rule and he can see politics "from a point of view a little higher" (RP, 86).

Like his previous stories of ascent, Thoreau's essay turns at the end back to its origin—in this case, to the opening theme of government, which his imagery transforms from a machine into a living organism: "A State which bore this kind of fruit, and suffered it to drop off as fast as it ripened, would prepare the way for a still more perfect and glorious State, which also I have imagined, but not yet anywhere seen" (RP, 90). The radical is not the enemy of society but a prophet of its redemption, symbolized by the village to which he may return.

By late 1848 Thoreau had written two of his best early essays,

"Ktaadn" and "Resistance to Civil Government," and his success in these works strongly affected the narrative plan of *Walden*. Both essays nicely modulate action and ideas, merging his paradoxical turns of language with the structural turns of an excursion; these elements he incorporated into the second and third drafts of *Walden*, written in 1848–49. During this time he continued to seek arrangements for the publication of both *A Week* and *Walden*. In February 1848 Ticknor & Company had offered to print both books, but only *Walden* at their expense. Thoreau declined. Occasionally he read portions of both manuscripts to audiences, and their reactions were not encouraging. After hearing some of *Walden* at Gloucester in December 1848, a reporter there wrote that missionary relief should be dispatched to Concord. Thoreau's sister Helen, gravely ill with tuberculosis (she died in June), declared that parts of *A Week* were blasphemous. One of his maiden aunts warned other relatives, "Henry is putting things into his book that never ought to be there."

Late in 1848 he contracted with James Munroe to publish *A Week*, at the author's cost, and soon Thoreau found that printers also had a way of putting in or taking out. When the proof sheets began arriving in March he discovered hundreds of errors, from simple misreadings of the manuscript to outright "corrections" of style and ideas. He was hard pressed for time in March and April, mailing both copy and proofs in batches, often barely keeping ahead of the printers. During this hectic rush he missed many errors, and the printers overlooked many of his corrections. When the book finally appeared in May 1849, he had to face a public whose ideas and tastes were as undefined as his own.

———

In *A Week on the Concord and Merrimack Rivers* Thoreau tried to combine the two modes of writing that had dominated his early career, the excursional narrative and the topical discourse. He told Hawthorne, "I have thought of you as a reader while writing it," probably remembering their early river trips together. The action of this story attempts to link a series of discussions, and both elements are meant to suggest

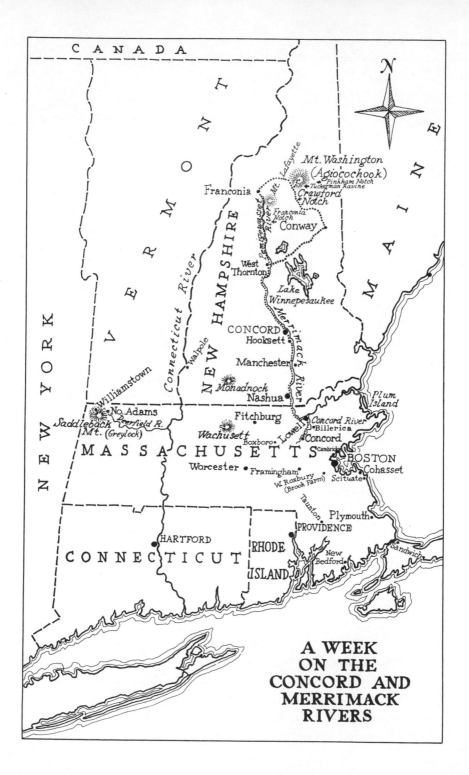

A WEEK
ON THE
CONCORD AND
MERRIMACK
RIVERS

the elegiac theme of grief transcended. In a letter Thoreau later defined the elegy as "some victorious melody in you escaping from the wreck." For him this journey memorialized a lost brother, whose death made the flowing river "an emblem of all progress," wherein all living things go downstream with the current (We, 111).

The rivers gave Thoreau a strong and logical pattern for his story, which moves down the "dead" or sluggish Concord and up the "living" Merrimack to the White Mountains, the high land where rivers are born. By seeking and finding this source of life, his travelers can accept their inevitable voyage downstream. The rivers also justify Thoreau's frequent digressions, which resemble the meanders and changes of current that vary the brothers' progress.

Yet the framework Thoreau chose for A Week emphasizes time rather than space: he condensed his original two-week trip into seven days and wrote a chapter for each. These divisions are merely arbitrary. Most units of time correspond to the solar cycle, but the week is a human convenience that provides a regular Sabbath for rest and worship. Although the English names of days have mythological origins, their sequence is meaningless. The "days" of Thoreau's journey therefore do not order his story, which has a spatial movement. In later books such as Walden, Cape Cod, and The Maine Woods, he learned to frame his narratives with geographic locales, set in the natural sequence of seasonal time.

Although flawed in design, A Week clearly expresses its elegiac theme (first established in the "long book" in September 1842). "Saturday" begins with a summery, youthful editorial on work, chaffing the fishers and farmers who plunder the earth before they are "cut down by the Great Mower" (We, 35). "Sunday" is a critique of Sabbath restrictions, set against the transcendentalist ideal of books that aspire—like the boaters—"to higher levels above and behind ourselves" (We, 103). "Monday" praises the Hindu seers, who counsel a vision beyond death: "Thus did one voyageur waking dream, while his companion slumbered on the bank" (We, 158). The chapter also describes an earlier hike to Wachusett, that "worthy brother" (We, 165) on the western horizon: this digression anticipates the later climax but violates the story's space and time. "Tuesday" has more digressions, this time to the Berkshires; back on the river some barges remind the travelers of youthful days and the prevailing "law of buoyancy" (We, 212).

"Wednesday" is the end of upstream boating; at this midpoint Thoreau inserts his longest digression, an essay on friendship that resolves the problem of grief: "He is my real brother. I see his nature groping yonder so like mine. We do not live apart" (We, 284). "Thursday" is the ascent "into the free air of Unappropriated Land" (We, 314), beyond the river's source until, "without its guidance," they reach the summit of Mount Washington. Their return journey moves with the river's flow, sailing downstream to autumn and the fruits of its harvest. "Friday" returns them to their village home, where Thoreau resolves to live on, becoming a man who writes of "the dreams of our childhood" (We, 380).

This narrative line is by no means clear in A Week; often the digressions—including many poems and quotations—obscure the trip entirely. The book is a fair approximation of Thoreau's early Gleanings, that motley mixture of bookish commentary and narrative modes. It favors the tools of his workshop yet praises the genius of nature: "Our art leaves its shavings and its dust about; her art exhibits itself even in the shavings and the dust which we make" (We, 319).

Ten years in the making, A Week reflects many of the contradictory ideas Thoreau developed—and discarded—during that period. Throughout the story he contrasts nature and society, the river and the shore. Ashore men wage war and clear the land; the river always moves in a gentle, undulating pace. The river is a superior creation, principled and harmonious, and the brothers who float on its surface share in that integrity. The works of men—boats, mills, canals—are not so handsome as trees, stones, and waterfalls; Thoreau insists that great works of art should imitate natural forms.

Only up to a point. He also praises gnomic, esoteric works that are puzzling—"Give me a sentence which no intelligence can understand" (We, 151)—and books with loose, open structures. Although the cursive, meandering form of a river seems to justify his loose miscellany, he alone built this imaginary story, which makes few concessions to its readers. In praising Goethe as a travel writer, Thoreau reveals his own ambitions: "He speaks as an unconcerned spectator, whose object is faithfully to describe what he sees, and that, for the most part, in the order in which he sees it" (We, 326).

That passage describes not A Week but Thoreau's early Journal, the workshop he ransacked to build his book. The final product was less coherent than his original materials; he had destroyed their natural order by fitting them into an artificial plan. In "Thursday" he comments on the difficulty of recording his 1839 voyage: "It is not easy to write in a journal what interests us at any time, because to write it is not what interests us" (We, 332). Extracting a book from that Journal had only compounded this problem.

When A Week was published in late May 1849, it met the fate of many first books: although widely reviewed, and for the most part favorably, it did not sell. Munroe gave away seventy-five copies and sold perhaps two hundred others. After four years the large stock of remainders was shipped to Thoreau, who wrote in his Journal: "I have now a library of nearly nine hundred volumes, over seven hundred of which I wrote myself."

In 1849 this failure was a bitter lesson, for it came as an anticlimax to his long apprenticeship in literature. He had mortgaged ten years to write this book, time when he served "the gods" in his Journal, striving to improve the flow of his style and stories. He had winnowed his best poems and essays for A Week, tried to build around them a strong narrative frame. And rivers were popular subjects for other writers; Washington Irving had reasonable success that year with his Book of the Hudson (1849).

A Week was a failure because Thoreau had conceived of it as a compilation of his early works. The book was retrospective; it looked back to earlier methods of writing and ignored his more recent successes in "Ktaadn" and "Resistance to Civil Government." His current sensibility was firm, empirical; in a letter the previous winter he had stressed the importance of learning mathematics, surveying, and technology: "I can build an engine myself when I am ready." In A Week he had built only his grandest mosaic, one gleaned from scattered sources and written at odd intervals over many years. The methods of Emerson were everywhere in these pages; yet Thoreau could blame only himself for the final product, a Pythagorean cube that had little continuity or popular appeal.

Even so, the failure of *A Week* soon effected a change in his long relationship with Emerson. A year earlier Thoreau had been publicly mocked in *A Fable for Critics* (1848) by Lowell, who accused him of picking up windfalls from neighbor Emerson's orchard. Now Thoreau blamed his neighbor for having grown any fruit at all. The Journal recorded this grievance in September 1849: "I had a friend, I wrote a book, I asked my friend's criticism, I never got but praise for what was good in it;—my friend became estranged from me and then I got blame for all that was bad, & so I got at last the criticism which I wanted."

Emerson said nothing; either he ignored these feelings or could not see how to ease them. In the space of four months he sent two recent windfalls to Thoreau, *Addresses and Lectures* and *Representative Men*; then in his journal for October he wrote that Thoreau was the Lilliputian equivalent of Napoleon, a man described in *Representative Men* as vigorous, realistic, and egotistical.

Whatever his faults, Thoreau was determined to remain a writer; he told the Harvard librarian on September 17, "I have chosen letters for my profession." But he could not afford to publish *Walden* now, as announced in the back pages of *A Week*. Other projects called him. He had begun his first "Indian book," a place to store facts and quotations from his reading on Indians. In October he went to Cape Cod with Channing, a trip that eventually gave him the narrative plan for *Cape Cod*.

His experiences on the Cape were a peculiar mix of the tragic and the comic. At Cohasset he saw a beach strewn with debris and corpses, the aftermath of a great shipwreck. In Wellfleet his host was a garrulous old oysterman, full of stories and tobacco juice, dispensed with incautious aim. The walking trip ended at Provincetown, where Thoreau and Channing caught a steamer to Boston. Shortly thereafter a bank in Provincetown was robbed, and for a while suspicion centered on the two hikers from Concord.

Thoreau certainly needed funds. He owed Munroe almost $300 for the cost of publishing *A Week*, an amount that exceeded his total income for several years. To pay the debt he tried selling cranberries and then pencils, but again lost money. Finally he bought surveying equipment and distributed handbills announcing his services as a surveyor. The choice was fortunate; gradually it helped to clear his debt and gave him at last a reliable source of personal income.

For the rest of his life he would run lot lines and compute acreage, writing the transactions in a surveyor's notebook—the most profitable of all his unpublished works. In December of 1849 he was looking to the future, with no regrets for the mistakes and losses of recent years. Failure had taught him a lasting principle: "No man's praise can cheat me into thinking that to be good which is really bad."

The Smooth Mirror

The poet must bring to Nature the smooth mirror in which she is to be reflected. He must be something superior to her, something more than natural.

—MAY 23, 1853

4
SAYS I TO MYSELF

"Says I to myself" should be the motto of my journal. It is
fatal to the writer to be too much possessed by his thought.
Things must lie a little remote to be described.
—NOVEMBER 11, 1851

Early in 1850 the Thoreaus prepared to move into a new house on
Main Street. With the deaths of John and Helen their family circle
had narrowed, but business had expanded and prospered, as they
shifted from making pencils to grinding plumbago, a fine graphite used
by printers for inking high-speed rotary presses. Invented in 1846, the
rotary press was rapidly transforming nineteenth-century tastes by producing cheap books and journals for mass audiences. Thoreau helped
his family's profits by improving the plumbago formula, but he could
not become a popular writer. Over the next four years he reported
mostly to his private Journal, for its audience of one.

    In January of 1850 Emerson saw this withdrawal coming, a time
when he and Thoreau would no longer "fuse all our repulsions & com-
patibilities." Thoreau also knew they were on diverging roads, but he
thought in February that distance would improve his perspective: "My
so-called friend comes near to being my greatest enemy!" He kept to
his own affairs, helping with work on the house, writing passages possibly intended for *Walden* in the Journal. One of these described a toy

waterwheel he found in April at Nut Meadow Brook; another—written in June, early in volume III—recalled his accidental burning of Fairhaven woods in 1844.

Despite their estrangement, Emerson continued to rely on Thoreau in practical matters: in July 1850 he dispatched his young friend to New York to help recover the remains of Margaret Fuller. She had been in Europe since 1846, writing for Greeley's *Tribune* and following the course of Roman politics. She married an Italian marquis, gave birth to a child, worked on a book about the revolution of 1848–49. On their return voyage to America, all were lost in a shipwreck off Fire Island. Thoreau's letter to Emerson on July 24 was grimly factual, sparing no detail about the demise of his former editor: "Margaret sat with her back to the foremast with her hands over her knees—her husband & child already drowned—a great wave came & washed her off." But a letter to Harrison Blake on August 9 was more artful, as Thoreau sifted his Journal passages into a meditation on the writer's indifference to death: "Our thoughts are epochs of our life: all else is but as a journal of the winds that blew while we were here."

The old mentors had passed, new ones were rising. Earlier that year Thoreau had completed an English translation of "The Transmigrations of the Seven Brahmans." This ancient Hindu parable tells a story of loss and restitution: seven brothers ignore their father's dying wishes and are therefore doomed to successive reincarnations as hunters, stags, geese, swans, and wild ducks. But their lives as humbler animals bring the promise of emancipation; they learn that "mysterious

"the undulating line of migrating geese against the sky"

words" will someday recall the past "concealed at the bottom of your souls." When the moment of divine illumination finally arrives, those words reveal "the borders of the sacred lake" where they had once lived in pure devotion.

This story, which Thoreau never published, foretold the evolution of both the Journal and *Walden* over the next few years, as they became joint narratives of his losses and gains, of his past recollected, of the mystery concealed at the bottom of Walden Pond. The transmigrations into animal forms may have suggested to him a metaphor for the losses all men must endure: "a hound, a bay horse, and a turtledove" (Wa, 17). The sacred lake was a mirror where seven brothers found their souls; for Thoreau, *Walden* and the Journal also came to reflect a true image of his art.

Settled in the new "Yellow House" by late August, he had an ideal situation: the entire upper floor became his quarters, and less than one hundred yards away (in Channing's backyard) was a landing place for a boat. From there Thoreau could sail on three different streams, each distinct in character: the Sudbury, which had a moderate current and open, meadowed banks; the Assabet, for adventures among the rocks and fast rapids; and the placid Concord, broad and stately in its sluggish flow. From the new house he could walk in any direction and soon reach glacial ponds or hills, the teeming riches of swamps and meadows.

Afternoon walks at once became part of his daily routine in August, providing material for the Journal and a new theme for *Walden*: "Concord is the oldest inland town in New England, perhaps in the States, and the walker is peculiarly favored here." Sometime late in 1850 he gathered a number of Journal passages into a draft, working from an index titled "Places to Walk to." The surviving pages of his draft describe places and old houses seen on walks to Lincoln and Sudbury, the towns lying south of Concord. He probably intended to put this material into the "Baker Farm" chapter of *Walden*, which begins with a general catalogue of local walks (Wa, 201–202). But the draft was too local and digressive; eventually he used only a few passages in *Walden* and his essay "Walking."

When not afield or with the family, Thoreau worked in his

study. The small slant-top desk from the Walden house was in place; he also had a large bureau for his papers, and along the wall stood shelves for a growing collection of books. At the age of thirty-three he had a more comfortable and settled life, and this stability gradually affected the Journal. The entries in volume IV become more narrative in late 1850, frequently including anecdotes about his neighbors and daily experiences. Surveying also had its effect, for the entries are detailed and carefully dated. Many of them are also longer—occasionally exceeding several thousand words.

Though the Journal was becoming more directly autobiographical, it continued to function as a storehouse for Thoreau's future publications. Sometimes he excised pages, like those describing his trip to Canada in September and October. Other entries were variants of the same story, written long after the fact (in August and October he twice described the same "drunken Dutchman"). Yet he no longer shared Emerson's notions of a literary career. When they talked in late October, Emerson praised England while Thoreau defended the obscurity and independence of American scholars. Emerson wanted writers to lead another sort of life, "bold, experimental, varied," but he also held the contradictory view that one's journal should be "a book of constants."

On November 16 Thoreau wondered if he were not writing a better work than Emerson had defined: "My Journal should be the record of my love. . . . I have no more distinctness or pointedness in my yearnings than an expanding bud. . . . I feel ripe for something, yet do nothing, can't discover what that thing is." The Hindu fable counseled patience and growth; his Yankee mentor wanted a harvest of fruits. What is a writer's proper course, secrecy or open confession? Hawthorne chose confession; in his preface to The Scarlet Letter (1850) he refers to Thoreau's "hermitage at Walden," then proceeds to dramatize the anguish of solitude.

As an antidote to Emerson, Thoreau had cultivated a friendship with Ellery Channing for several years. In that time they both passed through literary apprenticeships and came to share many interests. Channing was married, to a sister of Margaret Fuller, but he neglected his family and seemed to envy Thoreau's bachelor life. The two men frequently traveled together, from Cape Cod to Canada, and they spent many afternoons walking or sailing in Concord. They swapped stories and jests, tried to best each other with outrageous puns. Channing was the antithesis of Emerson: ribald, irreverent, eccentric, the poet *manqué*. He made Thoreau laugh, sometimes even at himself.

———

As he began volume V of the Journal in January 1851, Thoreau could sense that his life had assumed more predictable rhythms: two days a week in the shop, one or more for surveying; other days he spent the morning in his study, the afternoon outside. Yet the Journal was not so regulated; often he could not develop a proper interval between living and writing. He wanted the entries to record fleeting, evanescent moments: "I would fain keep a journal . . . which would have in one sense the greatest remoteness, in another, the greatest nearness to me."

According to Channing, Thoreau's solution was to make field notes, rough factual jottings on a sheaf of papers that he could later expand into entries. He had turned a surveyor's practice to literary advantage. Five minutes of notes might yield several pages of Journal; yet if he was ill and confined to bed (as in January and February), the entries might lapse altogether. Often he pretended to be writing entries directly in the field, but the excellent physical condition of his Journal volumes confirms that he left them at home, safe and dry.

The practice of writing notes and entries separately allowed Thoreau to shape the entries, either through reflective comments or by selecting and reshuffling episodes. His days were half-planned and half-accidental; the entries synthesized events into a single composition. He began each entry knowing how his day had ended, and often that hindsight allowed him to tell an effective story. February 12, 1851, is an example: the day provides a discovery, of "thin cakes of ice" on the Sudbury meadows, and this event becomes a fulcrum for

"Examined now the fleets of ice-flakes close at hand."

his entry, anticipated by "unexpected views and objects" and followed by other "surprises" that nature reveals to an attentive eye.

But he did not write with cold premeditation; many entries had no discernible form or purpose. Sometimes he wrote drafts of stories, like one about the capture of a fugitive slave (in March and April), which he did not revise and publish for several years. (Alcott had even less talent for purposeful reporting; on April 27 he complained in his diary: "A narrative is what I could never compass, and hanging were easier than testifying or telling a story.") Some days Thoreau might have welcomed a hanging to describe, instead of the ordinary events of his life—as on May 12: "If I have got false teeth, I trust that I have not got a false conscience."

This lack of design in the Journal—and his life—was less troubling as he grew older. In the botanical *Manual* of Asa Gray he read on May 20 that plants must grow before propagating, and this fact seemed "a perfect analogy" for his destiny. Emerson disagreed; in July he wrote that Thoreau would remain boyish and unambitious forever, since "instead of being the head of American Engineers, he is captain of a huckleberry party." Emerson did not know that Thoreau was engineering a new kind of journal. By early June it was no longer just a workshop to him but "a book of the seasons, each page . . . written in its own season and out-of-doors, or in its own locality wherever it may be."

During the summer of 1851 Thoreau began to use the Journal as a place to test his powers of seeing and hearing. The daily entries became a mirror for his senses, allowing him to raise the level of his experiences and move beyond the failures of his early writings. The observer at this glass was talking to himself, but his work also had a generous effect: by concentrating on one man's senses, he was learning to brag for humanity.

The climax of this development came in June and July, when Thoreau produced a magnificent series of entries about his moonlight walks. These nightly excursions, often lasting from sunset to dawn, offered him subtle variations of light and shadow, sound and silence; a chance to explore Concord and the growing concord of his mind and senses. The entries are highly charged, reminiscent of the great nocturnal poems of Coleridge and Keats, and they seem to have been written more for intrinsic pleasure than any projected publication. As Thoreau had learned from botany, now was a time for growth.

Some of the moonlight entries run to considerable length (up to 4,000 words on June 11), and most have descriptive passages far surpassing Thoreau's early prose. At Walden Pond on June 13 he observes the moon reflected on a shimmering surface:

> As I approached the pond down Hubbard's Path, after coming out of the woods into a warmer air, I saw the shimmering of the moon on its surface, and, in the near, now flooded cove, the waterbugs, darting, circling about, made streaks or curves of light. The moon's inverted pyramid of shimmering light commenced about twenty rods off, like so much micaceous sand. But I was startled to see midway in the dark water a bright flamelike, more than phosphorescent light crowning the crests of the wavelets, which at first I mistook for fireflies, and thought even of cucullos.* It had the appearance of a pure, smokeless flame a half-dozen inches long, issuing from the water and bending flickeringly along its surface. I thought of St. Elmo's lights and the like. But, coming near to the shore of the pond itself, these flames increased, and I saw that even this was so many broken reflections of the moon's disk, though one would have said they were of an intenser light than the moon herself; from contrast with the surrounding water they were. Standing up close to the shore and nearer the rippled surface, I saw the reflections of the moon sliding down the watery concave like so many lustrous burnished coins poured from a bag with inexhaustible lavishness, and the lambent flames on the surface were much multiplied, seeming to slide along a few inches with each wave before they were extinguished; and I saw how farther and farther off they gradually merged in the general sheen, which, in fact, was made up of a myriad little mirrors reflecting the disk of the moon with equal brightness to an eye rightly placed.

*Also spelled "cucuyo," a West Indian firefly.

This passage conveys an extraordinary energy, passionate in its sensuality but rational in developing the central image: the reflected moon is a flame, some burnished coins, a myriad of mirrors—all representing change, transformation, or enhancement. The description of reflections is itself "reflective," enlarging a vision of reality—as mirrors can —while pondering the thoughts it suggests.

He was pursuing a lonely occupation in July, considered the "least dignified man in the village," and at times he feared becoming too literal. At midmonth, as the end of volume V coincided with his thirty-fourth birthday, he had a spasm of regret: "In youth, before I lost any of my senses, I can remember that I was all alive. . . . " Mirrors give back reverse images, and so did the Journal at times. In the years to come Thoreau often sank into ritual laments, marking in July and January either his birthday or the anniversary of John's death. These intimations of mortality were as useful as they were brief. On July 18 he could write: "What is nature without this lofty tumbling? . . . Let me forever go in search of myself."

Walking and writing were related cycles in his daily life, one inspiring the other. Earlier in the year he wrote a lecture about walking called "The Wild," parts of which Alcott heard in mid-August and thought "too aboriginal." Thoreau had recently returned from a journey to Plymouth, which had not seemed aboriginal enough: "It takes a man of genius to travel in his own country, in his native village." His response to Alcott was that one township is a world, if reported faithfully to "a meteorological journal of the mind. You shall observe what occurs in your latitude, I in mine."

In imagination he ranged farther abroad by reading accounts of scientists, naturalists, and travelers from many lands. That August he began to keep a separate set of "Fact books," where he stored quotations or paraphrases from his reading. Ideas inspired by writers like Bartram, Kalm, or Linnaeus went directly into Journal entries.

The Journal had now become his major occupation, with entries growing so long that just two months, July and August of 1851, filled all of volume VI. The entries of late August frequently discussed his writing, which Thoreau saw as a concentrated version of life. His sentences were to be "not mere repetition but creation," depicting experiences as emblems of his spirit—fading flowers were "a symbol of my own change," while the river's surface "reflects heaven because my mind does." His figures had shifted from simile, in which a fact is *like* an idea, to metaphor, where the fact and idea are one. Emerson had taught him to impose thoughts upon the world; the Journal was a less aggressive means of seeking them out: "All perception of truth is the detection of an analogy; we reason from our hands to our head."

"The ripples on the river, seen in the moonlight . . ."

Living in Concord and working largely in isolation, Thoreau had conceived a form of metaphor that was strikingly similar to Melville's in works like *Mardi, White Jacket,* and *Moby-Dick* (1849–51). Melville had at first derived his symbols from sentimental works like *The Poetry of Flowers* (1846); not until he drew upon his knowledge of the sea did his writing become richly metaphorical. Thoreau was on a more direct course of development, as he wrote on September 8: "Shall I use any other man's word? A genuine thought or feeling can find expression for itself, if it have to invent hieroglyphics."

That month he found two major tropes in his Journal, the seasons and the telegraph harp. The seasons, put to dim use in early essays and poems, became an image for his own passing life, dull in the summer and revived by early autumn. The accuracy of previous entries kept this analogy under control; on September 12 he observed that seasons were as variable as his own character: "I can hardly believe that there is so great a difference between one year and another as my journal shows."

When touched by the wind Concord's new telegraph lines sang

like a great Aeolian harp, reminding Thoreau of his own artistic mission: "Thus I make my own use of the telegraph, without consulting the directors. . . . Shall I not go to this office to hear if there is any communication for me . . . ?" Throughout 1852 the harp became a recurrent analogy for both the seasons and his powers; singing a clear melody in late January, rusted by spring rains, slack in midsummer's heat, brought to life again by the winds of late October.

Like Narcissus gazing into a forest pool, Thoreau was using the Journal to mirror his love—not for himself, but for Concord. He knew that few other journals resembled this one. On September 7, near the end of volume VII, he tried to buy some new blank books, but most were ruled in columns for dollars and cents. The few published journals he had read, "—John Adams's not excepted—" were like opened tombs, he wrote on September 26; but the emblems he described for early October—milkweed, acorns, and blooming witch hazel—became signs of regeneration: "the life of Nature, by which she eternally flourishes, is untouched."

His friends did not read the Journal, but they could hear its themes when he talked. In their own accounts they reacted to his changing ways. On October 27 Emerson detected a certain genius in Thoreau's mix of "a low tone" and large views, yet he deplored "the eternal Loneliness" this work fostered. Alcott was more positive; early in November he said Thoreau's practicality had its generous, lasting effects: "Sane and salt, and will keep forever."

Channing simply did not understand Thoreau's business, even though he tried to imitate it. On November 9 Thoreau described how Channing would scrawl some notes and sketches, then criticize Thoreau for scribbling at greater length: "he confines himself to the ideal, purely ideal remarks; he leaves the facts to me." Thoreau replied that facts were only frames for his pictures, "material to the mythology which I am writing," rather than to any common purpose. Two days later he compared his work to the almanacs that local farmers studied; his book had a smaller audience and a larger, less material purpose: " 'Says I to myself' should be the motto of my journal. . . . Things must lie a little remote to be described."

The pleasure Thoreau took in writing his Journal now made him less eager to extract books or lectures from its pages. Preparation of a text about his 1850 trip to Canada left him irritable and restless: "what it took the lecturer a summer to write, it will take his audience but an hour to forget," he complained on November 16. Surveying was not a better alternative, for after a month of this work he had done little writing: "It seems an age since I took walks and wrote in my journal, and when shall I revisit the glimpses of the moon?"

The Journal was a tempting sanctuary, where he spoke only to a kindred mind, while lectures threatened him with public exposure. He was critical of other lecturers in December and January, finding neither Caroline Sturgis nor T. W. Higginson exactly to his liking. Channing was brilliant but disconnected: "There was no sloping up or down, to or from his points. It was all genius, no talent."

His own lecture on Canada had similar problems. After one public delivery he read parts on January 8, 1852, to Mary Moody Emerson, a stern old Puritan who queried his treatment of the Deity: " 'Is that god spelt with a little g?' Fortunately it was. (I had brought in the word 'god' without any solemnity of voice or connection.)" He omitted some irreverent passages, but Greeley said the essay version was too long and citified; on March 18 he advised cutting its historical extracts and making chapter divisions. Thoreau made these changes, too, but Greeley still had trouble selling the story because of its length. In November 1852 a new journal called *Putnam's Monthly* at last accepted the Canada essay and also agreed to read part of a manuscript on Cape Cod.

The editor at *Putnam's* was an old acquaintance, G. W. Curtis, who had lived at Brook Farm and in Concord during the 1840s. He had walked and boated with Thoreau in those days, then helped to raise the house at Walden Pond. Curtis scheduled "An Excursion to Canada" for five installments, beginning with the magazine's first issue of January 1853. But in January, after three chapters were set in type, Curtis and Thoreau disagreed about the need to revise what Greeley called "your defiant Pantheism." Thoreau refused, so only the first three chapters were printed. He asked for return of his manuscripts in March 1853 and got back all of Cape Cod—but only the early chapters of Canada. The fair-copy versions of his last two chap-

ters had disappeared, although he did have the working drafts in Concord. Channing used them to prepare the posthumous edition called *A
Yankee in Canada* (1866), which includes a few corrections and additions Thoreau made to his copy of the *Putnam's* text.

Perhaps because of this checkered history, Thoreau later spoke
disparagingly of his Canada story. In February 1853 he told Blake, "I
had absolutely no design whatever in my mind, but simply to report
what I saw." That estimate seems unduly severe. His skill as a reporter
does shape these experiences, and a spatial design lifts them above the
level of simple facts. Moreover, his Anglo-French heritage (*grandpère*
came from the Isle of Jersey) gave him a unique perspective on the
struggle between Britain and France from 1754 to 1763. Thoreau's story explores the aftermath of this conflict and dramatizes an apparent
change in his own views. Like previous excursions, this one depicts a
physical and mental transition: as he follows the St. Lawrence River
on its widening course to the sea, Thoreau moves from narrow prejudices to broader understanding. His progress is direct, not meandering
as in *A Week*, but more like one of his daily walks in Concord. Problems arise when he has to turn and go home once again.

In the early pages Thoreau establishes his firm Yankee independence from Canadian mores, but he also notes that the American's
prime virtue is self-improvement, "under all circumstances fully resolved to better his condition essentially" (YC, 9). This potential for
growth is in stark contrast to the Old World atmosphere of Montreal
and Quebec, where soldiers and priests so crowd the streets that Thoreau feels he is living in "a black-letter volume," a medieval text with
handwritten pages (YC, 24).

His mood brightens during a hike down the St. Lawrence, for
away from the cities he senses "you could see objects distinctly there
much farther" than in America (YC, 32). Contact with the natives,
the amusing difficulties of speaking French, the glorious river scenery
—all conspire to turn him from his early prejudices. This movement
peaks at Ste. Anne de Beaupré, the northern end of his hike. A shrine
in the village marks the site of an allegedly miraculous spring, but
Thoreau chooses to venerate a nearby waterfall.

Although other falls on the St. Lawrence are much higher, Tho-

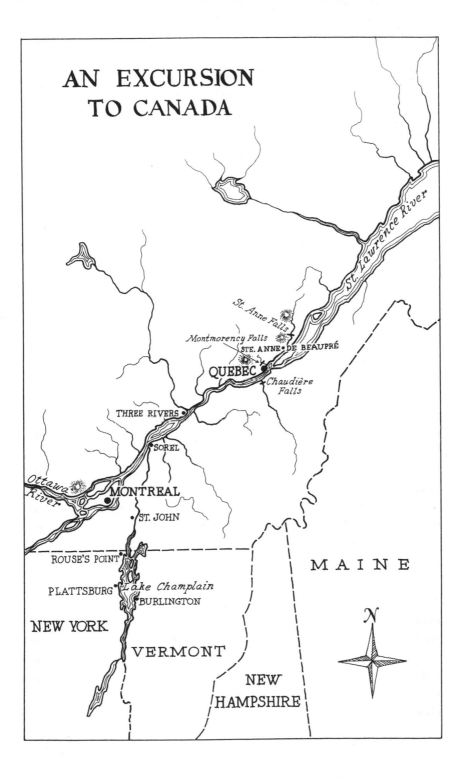

AN EXCURSION
TO CANADA

St. Lawrence River

St. Anne Falls

Montmorency Falls
STE. ANNE • DE BEAUPRÉ

QUEBEC

Chaudière Falls

THREE RIVERS •

• SOREL

Ottawa River

• MONTREAL

• ST. JOHN

ROUSE'S POINT

MAINE

PLATTSBURG • *Lake Champlain*
• BURLINGTON

NEW YORK

VERMONT

NEW
HAMPSHIRE

N

reau focuses on one—"called after the holy Anne"—because of its distinctive form: three streams merge and fall into a "large circular basin" below. From this lower spot he can see a fourth "tributary stream" falling from the summit, which has a deep cleft that resembles "*a black streak*" (YC, 50–51). Italics give unusual emphasis to this detail, for the scenery here is in strong contrast to the "black-letter volume" of Canada's cities.

The waterfall inspires a long meditation on the history of North America, set down as Thoreau retraces his steps along the great river. In early days three distinct races—Indian, French, British—settled here, the savage and exploratory spirit of the first two "gradually disappearing in what is called the Saxon current" (YC, 62). But certain tributaries continue to flow into this mainstream, for the survival of a French-speaking minority in Canada assures the Canadian of a "greater equality of condition" than is possible in America. In his diverse world the Canadian works and earns less, but "he possesses those virtues, social and others, which the Yankee lacks" (YC, 63).

The *Putnam's* text ends here, just as Thoreau has fulfilled his promise that a Yankee traveler knows how to better his condition. But in the remaining chapters he steps backward many paces, returning to cities that break this positive frame of mind. Repeated descriptions of greed and brutality, as well as rude gibes at "soldiery and the priesthood" (YC, 78) leave a cluttered impression of the trip's purpose. His closing description of the St. Lawrence, "the most interesting object in Canada to me" (YC, 82), is dry and factual; at the end he can only promise to make a future journey to "the wilder parts" of outer Canada, "*Iter Canadense*" (YC, 93).

Some of the problems in those last two chapters may have been less glaring in the version Thoreau lost at *Putnam's*, but in fact the editors did him a favor by cutting the story short. The text badly needed trimming, as Greeley had warned; its frequent puns and jests resemble the very style of lecturing Thoreau distrusted; and like Channing, he had failed to slope up to or down from his points adequately.

The dispute with *Putnam's* was a significant episode in Thoreau's career, the first of several quarrels he would have with editors of his work. This stand against censorship was reasonable, but it also masked

his anxiety about the need to publish. Greeley had complained in November 1852 that the story was "not so fresh and acceptable" because
of its long delay in reaching print. Other problems were less obvious:
"An Excursion to Canada" runs counter to many of Thoreau's
achievements in the Journal since 1850.

The Journal had taught him patience, the power of analogy, the
wisdom of traveling at home; but "Canada" has a crabbed and peckish
humor, clumsy interpolations of guidebook lore, and a didactic air.
Most of this story was excised from his 1850 volume, and since then
"Canada" had grown up separately, less affected by changes in the
Journal's form and contents. Certainly, by 1852 he was no longer so
defensive about his solitary ways, so hostile to the mores and manners
of others. In previous excursions he had turned homeward successfully, having struck at least a partial truce with social conventions.

Not here. The Canada story has some mean-spirited elements,
which a fledgling magazine could ill afford to print. Greeley had said
that *Putnam's* objected to the story's "Pantheism," probably meaning
its anti-Catholic bias. With "Know-Nothing" Protestants gaining
strength (they won the Massachusetts elections in 1854) the liberal
stance of *Putnam's* might have been jeopardized by Thoreau's irreverence. His judgment, in February 1853, that the narrative was "not
worth the time to tell" acknowledged his own mistiming. In February
1859 he visited one evening with Reverend Grindell Reynolds, who
remembered years later that Thoreau was not impious, but "told his
Canada story far better than in his book."

A book with a much stronger ending was now in progress, for early in
1852 Thoreau had resumed work on his fourth version of *Walden*. On
March 24 he sent two short excerpts to Greeley, who quickly placed
them in the *Union Magazine*, where "Ktaadn" had appeared. These
pieces were more marketable than "Canada" and more representative
of the writer Thoreau had become, a lyrical symbolist. His method of
composition had also changed, for now he consistently copied Journal
passages into separate, multiple drafts—where all the cutting and re-

vising occurred. He thus preserved the Journal's ongoing story of his growth, while *Walden* became its approximation on a smaller scale.

The Journal was a story with an organic design, like the house at Walden, which he described on January 11 as "gradually grown from within outward, out of the old character and necessities of the in-dweller and builder, without even a thought for mere ornament." His book should evolve in a similar fashion, but how? If he merely de-scribed growth, the effect would be illusory, an imitation of life rather than its actuality.

He often commented on this difficulty in the Journal that month, as he worked on *Walden* and prepared to deliver sections in lectures. A farmer, observed hauling muck from the river to his com-post heap on January 19, "is doing like myself. My barnyard is my jour-nal." The new soil was fertile, yet torn from its natural origins. Three days later he had a more complimentary image of this work: by bring-ing old thoughts together he tried to create "a frame in which more may be developed and exhibited. Perhaps this is the main value . . . of keeping a journal." If so, the normal vagaries of his record were less useful: "In thy journal let there never be a jest!"

This conflict between natural and artificial order reflected the problem common to both *A Week* and early versions of *Walden*: "Thoughts of different dates will not cohere." The Journal had its own coherence, for there he could suppress his opinions and enter descrip-tions with only "the colors of the thing reported." *Walden* must not become another Pythagorean cube; it should have a natural and more continuous form: "thoughts written down thus in a journal might be printed in the same form. . . . It is more simple, less artful."

Some of these comments also reflect difficulties he had in late January when revising "Canada," which was overly jocular and opin-ionated, a poor fit between his original travels and later ideas. A Jour-nal that was no longer simply a workshop made him see defects in its products: "Men have written travels in this form, but perhaps no man's daily life has been rich enough to be journalized." So he worked on in February, happiest when "engaged in recording my thoughts" in the daily record, hoping that *Walden* might acquire a similar integrity. If its facts were made sufficiently analogous, "I should need but one book of poetry to contain them all."

Soon the Journal resolved the problem of form, as Thoreau began to see how the seasons regulated his entries. In February he summarized the winter's progress since November, concluding: "Other
epochs I might find described in my Journal." The year seemed to
have its consistent chapters: "Might not some of my pages be called
'The Short Days of Winter'?" By mid-March, near the end of volume
IX, he was looking ahead to spring as the beginning of a new year, and
a month later he announced this fact: "For the first time I perceive
this spring that the year is a circle."

In previous writings Thoreau had shaped circular excursions that
began and ended at the same place, and he had used parts of the seasonal round. But he had not put these elements together in a single
cycle, leaving and returning within a year. This "discovery" gave him
a rationale for both the structure of *Walden* and the annual contents of
his Journal: to "make a chart of our life . . . know why just this circle
of creatures completes the world." From this point on, the two books
became closely related, developing apace in their year-long orbits.

The world outside his Journal knew little of his achievement.
One friend (probably Channing) cursed his habit of note-taking on
April 4; but Thoreau knew that ceasing would destroy his imagination, "and my journal no longer yield me pleasure nor life." Even the
river's waterline told the history of its seasons; "in this respect, too,
nature is self-registering." He needed that private assurance, for two
days later he lectured unsuccessfuly on *Walden* in Boston: a snowstorm
diminished the paying audience to a mere handful, and some recruits
obtained in an adjacent reading room either fell asleep or continued to
read their newspapers.

Silence, or at least the secrecy of a Journal, seemed a better alternative for his brand of writing. The fiasco in Boston and the difficulties Greeley had in selling "Canada" suggested to Thoreau on April 16
that he should lead "a more interior life. . . . Nobody ever advised me
not to print but myself." "Says I to myself" was the unpublished motto
of his Journal, where the audience was small but always wide awake.
His entry for April 19 gave him an analogy for this situation: he sat in
a barn during a rainstorm, hearing "an inexpressible dry stillness . . .
such stacks of quiet and undisturbed thought . . . the hay makes silence audible."

Silence, privacy, the inner life: these qualities he could see reflected in the Journal's daily log. On April 24 he read that the artist Giorgione, challenged to depict four sides of a figure in one painting, surrounded it with reflections: "So I would fain represent some truths as roundly and solidly . . . so that you may see round them." In writing the Journal this problem affected his depiction not of space but of time, as he noted on May 15: "I succeed best when I *recur* to my experience not too late, but within a day or two."

In volume XI he pursued this goal by writing about a series of walks in June and July, while keeping a chart of seasonal progress. Both kinds of entries revealed to him circles in time, the faithful correspondence between his living and writing. Entries on morning walks were effusive—morning was "the most glorious season of the day"; but the passages on moonlight walks were sober and analytical, with "a peculiar dusky serenity." Locales also affected his entries: a "cross-lots" ramble and a "fluvial walk" produced entirely different themes and prose rhythms. Finding the order of a season took more work; on May 17 he had to reread entries on wild flowers to mark the line between spring and summer, then followed a month later with careful notes on fruit to anticipate the fall.

On July 2 he wrote that his friends were "also more devoted to outward observation" this year, but in fact they were clinging to familiar ways. Channing tried to make some notes on plants in June, but Emerson twice laughed him out of this "affectation," and by late July Channing had agreed that "these forms of Diary" might be useless. At the same time Emerson could write in his journal a shrewd estimate of character: "Thoreau gives me, in flesh & blood & pertinaceous Saxon belief, my own ethics. He is far more real, & daily practically obeying them, than I." But while Emerson saw their differences, he did not attribute them to Thoreau's Journal. Those field notes and entries gave his ethics daily practice, as Thoreau wrote on June 21: "With our senses applied to the surrounding world we are reading our own physical and corresponding moral revolutions."

The Journal also captured emotional revolutions, the high and low points of Thoreau's days. As in 1851, his birthday coincided with the end of a volume (XI), and again this year he was dejected by these

"The vivid greenness of the tips of the sedge just pushing up out of its dry tussocks in the water."

approaching rites of passage. On June 25 he reviewed the superb entries of 1851 on moonlight walks, which seemed more "thoughtful" than his current ones. His writing now did not seem to equal the powers of nature. In early July he saw some hummocks near the Assabet River, a "natural graveyard" that seemed superior to his work: "The stream keeps a faithful and a true journal of every event in its experience." His own course seemed less true: "I am older than last year; the mornings are further between; the days are fewer."

Then, abruptly as it began, the depressive mood was over. He went back to the Assabet on his birthday (July 12) and took a long "fluvial walk" in its cold, racing current, studying not graveyards but the living trees that lined its banks. By the next day this excursion had restored his confidence in the account he was keeping: "A journal, a book that shall contain a record of all your joy, your ecstasy."

These cycles of alternating hope and despair were common in Thoreau's middle years, and some readers have seen only one side or the other of his ambivalence. But much earlier he (and Emerson as well) had seen that "undulation" is a common pattern in nature. He might write to Sophia on July 13 that he had "become sadly scientific," yet his Journal for the next month was full of poeticized facts: the river meanders in order to fertilize both its banks; sunset is a promise of

". . . a river, instead of flowing straight through its meadows, meanders from side to side and fertilizes this side or that, and adorns its banks with flowers."

the dawn to come. His daily habit of walking and writing, seeing and recalling, made him deeper and more divided, aware of "a certain doubleness by which I can stand as remote from myself as from another."

This sense of duality may have intensified in late August as Thoreau prepared a wedding gift for Harrison Blake. Blake, a teacher and former minister from Worcester, had been a friend and frequent correspondent since 1848. He was a dedicated philosopher, rather grave and sententious in manner, and he inspired the same tendencies in all the letters Thoreau sent him—including these two brief essays, titled "Love" and "Chastity and Sensuality." Emerson apparently thought this bachelors' friendship was not entirely wholesome. In his journal for October 14 he said Blake seemed "to ask his husband [i.e., Thoreau] for leave to marry a wife."

Whatever his motives, Thoreau's celibate status hardly disqualified him from writing about sex and marriage. His parents were not priggish; their firstborn (Helen) arrived five months after the wedding, and they could hardly conceal the facts of life from children who helped to raise chickens, pigs, and cows. In his home and elsewhere, Thoreau had seen many different models of married life. He was by no means contemptuous of human love; if anything, he may have held it in too high esteem.

The two essays are in a style characteristic of Thoreau's letters to Blake, using rapid and often illogical shifts of metaphor to convey lofty notions. Many passages come from the 1845–50 Journal—after that date he put such moralizing directly into his letters. Blake often read them aloud to friends invited for breakfast, which may explain Thoreau's frequent use of morning images, and why Blake later said the letters "may well be regarded as addressed to those who can read them best."

Thoreau had thus written not just a private confidence to Blake but an announcement to the philosophers of Worcester— friends like Theophilus Brown, T. W. Higginson, and David Wasson. He was not satisfied with the two texts, saying in September that they were "disconnected fragments" and promising "a completer essay" later. The division was significant; he did not see how to place his ideal of Love within the physical bonds of Chastity and Sensuality.

In their separate and preliminary states, the essays ask a question that remains intriguing: Why do the higher forms of life have two sexes? Thoreau's answer uses the metaphors of his Journal: woman is "a fairer flower and sweeter fruit," man "a string of an Aeolian harp" (EE, 268–69); she is flesh and he is spirit—their polarities give life its undulating, rhythmical structure. The sexes are a physical embodiment of higher laws, and for that reason Thoreau rates imagination above passion in a love affair.

This idea of love came largely from his experience as a writer, the one form of devotion he knew best. He accepted the belief, not uncommon among males, that sex depletes an artist's energy, while abstinence fires his imagination. This notion had also occurred to Hawthorne: in *The Blithedale Romance* (1852), a bachelor narrator spins wild fantasies about the sexual conflicts of other characters. For Thoreau, love endures best when it remains secret and unrequited. Who knew what passions he had felt yet never expressed? The Journal was a partial confidant, a record of his private joy and ecstasy, but largely unpublished. Even to Blake, Thoreau could not describe the Journal directly, only intimate its inner purpose: "What a difference whether, in all your walks, you meet only strangers, or in one house is one who knows you, and whom you know?" (EE, 273).

Those knowing partners I and Myself had guided the Journal for the past two years, through ten volumes of writing that gradually became an honest mirror of Thoreau's life and character. If his thoughts on sexual intercourse were "among the most fleeting and irrecoverable" in his experience (EE, 277), the pages of his Journal made a permanent record of things he could safely love, the "hieroglyphics which my eyes behold" on late August afternoons.

At its base Thoreau's sexuality was largely autoerotic, devoted to an ideal of love in which partners fuse into a single identity. The Journal told the story of his love because he was *both* its author and its best reader. Yet this mirror image of himself was not secure. Beyond it he glimpsed the outline of another identity, emerging from the recesses of his uncertain future: "I pine for one to whom I can speak my *first thoughts*. . . . I know of no one to whom I can be transparent instinctively."

5
A FAITHFUL RECORD

It is surprising how any reminiscence of a different season of
the year affects us. When I meet with any such in my
Journal, it affects me as poetry, and I appreciate that other
season and that particular phenomenon more than at the
time. . . . You need only to make a faithful record of an
average summer day's experience and summer mood, and
read it in the winter, and it will carry you back to more
than that summer day alone could show.
                                        —OCTOBER 26, 1853

As volume XIII began in September 1852 a slow and almost impercep-
tible change also came to the Journal. Thoreau's entries on birds and
plants became more precise and detailed, less fanciful in his reading of
their metaphysical significance. The entries also began to turn from
personal to more external concerns. In a sense, the Journal grew more
"scientific"—rigorous and methodical—with a consequent de-empha-
sis on lyrical mysticism. He was similarly occupied in his "Fact book,"
entering many passages from botanical or zoological texts.

Thoreau saw this change coming; on September 13 he wrote "Be
not preoccupied with looking. Go not to the object; let it come to
you." He feared the increase of technical knowledge, but he also knew
that his early views of nature were imprecise and complacent. This
ambivalence gave him distorted perceptions; often he would chide

himself for lacking imagination—in lines of witty, vigorous prose. With his interpretive faculties diverted from easy conclusions, the Journal increasingly became a repository for data in which he did not see clear patterns.

The contents of entries were now shaped less by his design and more by the spontaneous unfolding of natural events. He could write entries about hunting bees or chasing loons in September and early October, but he failed to note any parallels between these ingenious winged creatures. Nor did the Journal obviously nurture his publications. In November and December he wrote entries about the fish and the subsurface geology of Walden Pond, but only later did he see that they could be used in the winter chapters of *Walden* (now in its fifth version). The Journal's order remained intact; *Walden* was growing in accord with the seasonal round. Melville had described a similar experiment in *Pierre, or the Ambiguities* (1852), in which his hero tries to fit the "horological" order of reality to the "chronometrical" pattern of an idealized story. Unfortunately, Melville and Thoreau never met to exchange ideas, not even when Melville paid his sole visit to Concord on December 2, 1852. (He came to see Hawthorne; Thoreau was on the river all day with Channing.)

Many entries in the Journal had no bearing on *Walden*, for Thoreau's larger book allowed him to lead other lives. In the late months of 1852 he wrote about climbing Mount Monadnock in New Hampshire, the autumnal tints of October, an ice storm that transformed the Concord landscape. The Journal was open to recording life's accidental moments, even a spectacular explosion at the Acton gunpowder mill on January 7, 1853. But accidents have a long chain of causes; the workers had struck a few sparks in one building, the owners had thoughtlessly placed all the buildings too close to each other. Thoreau's chilling conclusion: "Put the different buildings thirty rods apart, and then but one will blow up at a time."

For all the apparent lack of connection in his "aimless life," as he had called it on November 4, Thoreau still believed that his thoughts and the world were one. In late December he concluded that patience was the better part of wisdom: "to appreciate a single phenomenon . . . you must camp down beside it as for life . . . and give yourself utterly to it. It must stand for the whole world to you, and [be] symbolical of all things."

"To appreciate" can mean either "to esteem" or "to increase in value"; in the Journal Thoreau could both collect and interpret his natural history data. Since mid-1852 he had been entering cross-references—as footnotes or marginalia—that compared facts from different entries. Some of these discerned new relationships: on April 23, 1852, he saw that birds migrate when fruits appear, and that feeding on them helps to distribute their seeds. This conclusion was imaginative but solidly based on facts. For similar reasons he began in January 1853 to name Concord locales according to their natural features, for example, "Yellow-birch Swamp." These epithets affirmed his imaginative hold on the landscape, which he had begun to see as a microcosm: "The sight of these trees affects me more than California gold."

Despite his growing command of natural history, Thoreau was never a scientist. He responded to nature as an artist, with moods that swiftly fluctuated from joy to melancholy. The Journal was like the echo he described on February 11; it revealed that nature was generous, "sympathizing with the better part of me . . . one degree, at least, better than talking with one's self." When a group of scientists inquired as to his interests, he wrote on March 5 (at the end of volume XIV) that they would never understand him: "The fact is, I am a mystic, a transcendentalist, and a natural philosopher to boot."

Fellow transcendentalists understood him little better. Emerson heard Channing joke about Thoreau's ability "to maximize the minimum" when taking notes; this mockery concealed Channing's own frustration over keeping a journal. In January 1853 he complained to its pages (as he had the previous summer), "nothing can be more barren than such notes. I can see no hope of putting them into book form." Thoreau was more optimistic about his own notes; on March 21 he sensed that his entries were consistent enough to survive distillation: "Might not my Journal be called 'Field Notes'?" Perhaps he wrote some entries that spring with publication in mind, for they are carefully planned as stories and run to extraordinary lengths—the one for March 29 surpasses 7,000 words.

This entry, which describes Thoreau's discovery of some underground frost crystals, seems to unfold as an exact rendition of the day's sequence as it occurred. The discovery is wholly unforeseen; he accidentally breaks open a muskrat nest and in the interior finds "frost crystals of a rare form," which at first look like daggers or "bodkins." A closer look modifies that image; the daggers become "clear crystalline dew in almost invisible drops." Then an incredulous third view reveals "minute white threads or gossamer" that form a rootstalk for the drops.

The more he studies these crystals, the more complex they become. His report describes not only a thing, but also the phenomenon of thinking, the series of inferences that eventually lead to insight. And he does not begin with his conclusion, as a scientist might; the entry rehearses his *process* of learning, to show its incremental nature. The images, although insufficient singly, gradually accumulate into a truth, that nature has the power to grow invisible, subterranean forms: "We are acquainted with but one side of the sod." Thoreau possibly framed this thought before writing, but the form of his entry seems unpremeditated.

Did he intend to put this episode in *Walden*? Probably not, for phenomena described in the book—like the "sand foliage" of spring —mainly illustrate the seasonal cycles of a year (Wa, 306). Underground frost crystals are irregular; they need special conditions of temperature and moisture to form. He did not understand the causal pattern exactly; in this case the muskrats' exhalations probably condensed and then froze on the cold upper surface of the lodge. But cause and effect were not his main concern: this entry explains how patience allowed him to *appreciate* the natural world.

Another possibility is that he wrote the entry for Channing. In April Channing had renewed the hope of printing his own field notes "in forms of some kind or another," and by May he had persuaded both Thoreau and Emerson to join this project. Channing outlined his plan: he would copy extracts from their three journals and arrange them in book form. On May 4 Emerson told a correspondent that Channing had proposed twenty chapters, under the mock title of "Walking in Addlebury, or Musings on the Piddlededees." The actual title became "Country Walking," and this work occupied Channing's time for several months.

Thoreau agreed to this scheme, a sign that both he and the Journal had evolved beyond the insularity of earlier years. But he had doubts about his collaborators. In late May he wrote that Emerson assumed "a false opposition" in their talks (Emerson would say this of Thoreau in 1856); while Channing behaved rudely to anyone who crossed his yard. Thoreau preferred the company of his daily accounts, where he invented "tropes and symbols" to describe his life: "all nature will *fable*, and every natural phenomenon will be a myth."

Often his entries were becoming poetic fables, in contrast to the data he had gathered. On May 22 he described a tiny kitten that saved itself from drowning, and then an incident "far more allegorical than actual," his discovery on May 31 of a rare pink azalea in bloom.

I am going in search of the *Azalea nudiflora*. Sophia brought home a single flower without twig or leaf from Mrs. Brooks's last evening. Mrs. Brooks, I find, has a large twig in a vase of water, still pretty fresh, which she says George Melvin gave to her son George. I called at his office. He says that Melvin came in to Mr. Gourgas's office, where he and others were sitting Saturday evening, with his arms full and gave each a sprig, but he doesn't know where he got it. Somebody, I heard, had seen it at Captain Jarvis's; so I went there. I found that they had some still pretty fresh in the house. Melvin gave it to them Saturday night, but they did not know where he got it. A young man working at Stedman Buttrick's said it was a secret; there was only one bush in the town; Melvin knew of it and Stedman knew; when asked, Melvin said he got it in the swamp, or from a bush, etc. The young man thought it grew on the Island across the river on the Wheeler farm. I went on to Melvin's house, though I did not expect to find him at home at this hour, so early in the afternoon. (Saw the wood-sorrel out, a day or two perhaps, by the way.) At length I saw his dog by the door, and knew he was at home.

He was sitting in the shade, bareheaded, at his back door. He had a large pailful of the azalea recently plucked and in the shade behind his house, which he said he was going to carry to town at evening. He had also a sprig set out. He had been out all the forenoon and said he had got seven pickerel,—perhaps ten (?).* Appar-

* Thoreau's query.

ently he had been drinking and was just getting over it. At first he was a little shy about telling me where the azalea grew, but I saw that I should get it out of him. He dilly-dallied a little; called to his neighbor Farmer, whom he called "Razor," to know if he could tell me where that flower grew. He called it, by the way, the "red honeysuckle." This was to prolong the time and make the most of his secret. I felt pretty sure the plant was to be found on Wheeler's land beyond the river, as the young man had said, for I remembered how, some weeks before this, when I went up the Assabet after the yellow rocket, I saw Melvin, who had just crossed with his dog, and when I landed to pluck the rocket he appeared out of the woods, said he was after a fish-pole, and asked me the name of my flower. Didn't think it was very handsome,—"not so handsome as the honeysuckle, is it?" And now I knew it was his "red honeysuckle," and not the columbine, he meant. Well, I told him he had better tell me where it was; I was a botanist and ought to know. But he thought I couldn't possibly find it by his directions. I told him he'd better tell me and have the glory of it, for I should surely find it if he didn't; I'd got a clue to it, and shouldn't give it up. I should go over the river for it. I could smell it a good way, you know. He thought I could smell it half a mile, and he wondered that I hadn't stumbled on it, or Channing. Channing, he said, came close by it once, when it was in flower. He thought he'd surely find it then; but he didn't and he said nothing to him.

He told me he found it about ten years ago, and he went to it every year. It blossomed at the old election time, and he thought it "the handsomest flower that grows." Yarrow just out.

And so on. Although factual, this entry reads like a Yankee version of medieval romance, with Thoreau the knight errant who must endure a succession of trials (eight different informants!) leading to a final encounter with the flower's guardian, crafty George Melvin. After their garrulous debate, nicely imitated in dialogue, Thoreau is finally led in triumph to the captive flower, which proves to be "conspicuously beautiful" and possibly "an undescribed variety."

Early June brought more spells of enchantment. The fogbound river became Cape Cod, Wachusett on the horizon was Atlantis, his own footsteps a "Pilgrim's Progress" into history. A brooding night-hawk reminded him of Saturn, the Sphinx, and Prometheus Bound. He decided to call the great woods north of town, inhabited a century ago, "the Easterbrooks Country," and reeled off a litany of his private names: Boulder Field, Yellow Birch Swamp, Black Birch Hill, Laurel Pasture, White Pine Grove.

Thoreau had become the town's most original proprietor, an authority on its varieties of life and land. Hunters brought him specimen birds; farmers sought his advice on the weather. As Emerson noted in June, many of the local boys believed "that Mr. T made Concord." In the Journal Concord was remaking his imagination, as the town became a miniature of the world. His entries for late June describe the Pyramids of Egypt, the Black Hole of Calcutta, the rivers of Damascus, all suggested by local places. Some of his analogies came from travel books, others from local topography: the three Eastern sites occurred to him on walks to Nawshawtuct and Fair Haven, hills from whence he could look farther east.

These daily journeys proved more reliable than Channing, who was still compiling the "Country Walking" project. Early in July he wanted to add entries from Alcott's diary to the manuscript, but Emerson had seen enough of its "old learning and fresh wit" to conclude that it would not merit publication. In October Emerson paid Channing for his work, which never saw print until 1873, when some sections appeared in his biography of Thoreau.

With the onset of hot summer weather both Thoreau and the Journal changed. Heat and humidity gave him severe headaches, draining his energy, and the daily entry often lapsed into a mere listing of botanical notes, as on July 11: "White vervain. Checkerberry, maybe some days. Spikenard, not quite yet." These entries do not mean that his life had dried up, only that he was writing less. Moncure Conway, a young Virginian with literary aims, met Thoreau on July 28 and later recalled that his face "shone with a new light" in the woods, where he gave eloquent explanations of the things they saw. Thoreau's entry for that day is flat and unemotional; it barely mentions Mr. Conway.

After a long, soaking rain his Journal could revive. The myth-making resumed on July 30, as he considered the names of plants—"that Adam that names things is always a poet"—and the spotless purity of a fresh tobacco-pipe, "a daughter of Tellus and Caelum," or Earth and Air, who would soon lead her on to decay. In nature he thus saw the cycles of his own imagination. At the heart of Thoreau's maturing vision was an implicit metaphor, consciously expressed on May 23: "The poet must bring to Nature the smooth mirror in which she is to be reflected." This idea was Emersonian, like the sentiment of August 7, "The objects I behold correspond to my mood," but Thoreau used it to justify his own leisurely inclinations. In early August, a season of "small fruits," he was content to ripen something "which will communicate my flavor to my kind."

"the distant shadow of our shadows,—first on the water, then the double one on the bank bottom to bottom, one being upside down"

As he wrote the last entry of volume XV, on August 18, a brief premonition arose about his future course. The season of harvest was upon him—and this year he had a sense of foreboding: "What have we done with our talent? . . . The year is full of warnings of its shortness, as is life." As a writer he felt a need to publish, which now contradicted the goals of this private book. The Journal was life; a lecture or essay had the taint of decay—dead leaves written for silent, unseen readers.

He calmed himself by accepting the season as a metaphor for his own life. On August 23 he saw that the year's changing foliage was like a diurnal cycle: silvery in "the dewy dawn" of spring, dark green in summer's "forenoon and afternoon," yellow-red in the fall "sunset," and brown-black when the winter "night" set in. At the age of thirty-six, Thoreau took a melancholy view of this round: "Perhaps after middle age man ceases to be interested in the morning and in the spring." In *Walden* his story climaxed in spring, but after 1854 he increasingly attended to the fall.

This fall was therefore a promise to him of ripening and fruition, "the emblem of a successful life, a not premature death." He would continue to make a faithful record of the year's turnings, and his published works would reflect that model honestly. In the smooth surface of the river on September 1 he saw "a mirror uncracked, unsoiled"—that was the clearest sign of his obligations.

From September 16 to 27 Thoreau made his third trip to Maine, a journey on the Penobscot River (West Branch) lying northwest of Katahdin. This river and its banks were not an unsoiled mirror, as in Concord. In Maine he often saw cleared forest and logging camps, some already fallen into ruins. The Indians he met had lost many of their native ways. While he studied plants, his two companions went hunting for moose. Their major kill: a female moose, still suckling her calf. When Thoreau tried to measure the carcass, he got its dimensions hopelessly confused.

Still, he managed to keep his usual "minutes" of the trip, which he converted to Journal entries back in Concord. During the late fall he prepared a lecture called "Moosehunting" for delivery at the Lyceum on December 14. He did not try to publish this work until 1858, and then its appearance was marred by another fight with an editor, James Russell Lowell—who had made nearly the same trip in August 1853.

The Journal entries* for Thoreau's trip reflect both the joys and problems his current methods of writing created. Composed in retrospect, the entries are not always exactly chronological (September 15, 12, 16, for example), and they include many details he never used in the lecture—like an exact description of moose dung on September 17. He added afterthoughts freely during his initial writing, then almost immediately went back over the text, in ink and then pencil, to revise its style heavily. During November his entries on Concord were perfunctory as this work proceeded, and some contained additional passages on Maine.

*Not published in the 1906 text.

But he could not ignore the fall entirely, and in late October a series of handsome entries on "the subject of fallen leaves" became a reminder of his difficult task. The leaves fell to earth, decayed to feed a new crop of seeds, and through a "subtle chemistry" rose again in the sap of young trees: "They teach us how to die." Perhaps the Journal leaves would follow the same cycle and be reborn in the process of his writing and revising. The latest issue of *Putnam's* (Thoreau was still a subscriber) did not encourage this hope: in Melville's new story, "Bartleby the Scrivener," a copyist turns from writing to silence and death, his past forever an enigma to the loquacious narrator.

Thoreau believed that the Journal was keeping his past alive and unambiguous. On October 26 he looked over entries of previous seasons and saw more "poetry" now than on the original occasions. To preserve the highest value of a day, "You need only to make a faithful record" and its meaning will endure. This attitude affected his draft of "Moosehunting" and the latest version of *Walden* (the sixth), for they also were faithful records of ideas and experiences entered in the concurrent Journal.

A reminder of past failure, when he used the Journal much differently, only confirmed this new aesthetic. On October 28 Munroe & Co. returned the unsold copies of *A Week*, 706 from a printing of 1,000, but Thoreau joked about this addition to his library and turned to writing his daily entry "with as much satisfaction as ever." In retrospect his failure might have seemed a blessing: it had postponed *Walden*, assured his privacy, left him free to grow into a different kind of writer.

His decision to stay fixed in Concord, as he wrote on November 12, "to study and love this spot of earth," was also fortunate, for through the Journal he had found that Concord was his unique subject. By late November he was considering a book "entitled October Hues or Autumnal Tints," with pictures as well as texts. But his view of the town had definite boundaries. When the Channings separated in mid-November and a storm of rumors ensued, Mrs. Thoreau felt obliged to make a legal deposition about Ellery's marital faults. (Channing never forgave her for this interference; in later years he always painted her as a malicious gossip.) Henry held his tongue, or at least he wrote nothing of these troubles in the Journal. Its anecdotes were only mildly critical, as when he noted on December 8 that Emerson absentmindedly drove his own calf out of the yard and into a passing herd.

After sending an article of fifty-seven pages—possibly part of *Walden*—to a new (and still untitled) antislavery magazine on December 2, Thoreau completed his work on the lecture draft of "Moosehunting." On a worksheet he had prepared an index of Journal entries about his trip, arranged in chronological order. He also had added to the index later thoughts and revisions, as though they had occurred on the journey. The index became his outline for the lecture: from Bangor to Lake Chesuncook, then returning to Concord. He next copied the entries onto separate sheets, making further revisions. Thus he left the Journal intact but pulled a similar chronicle from its pages. The lecture was an artful distillation of its source, more concentrated and forceful, as the subtle chemistry of writing worked its way.

As usual, Thoreau was uneasy over the prospect of delivering a lecture, saying on December 10 that only "what I write about at home" was clear and natural. He made the same argument to Emerson, yet tried to convince twelve-year-old Edith Emerson that this lecture was not "an old philosophical thing." The lecture was moderately successful, but he was not satisfied with the return for his invested time. On December 5 he learned that his fifty-seven-page article had been returned because the new magazine was indefinitely postponed. He made no plans to publish "Moosehunting" for a while, and thus his autumnal work yielded little profit. Surveying brought him more cash, he wrote on December 18, even though few others could "lecture as well as I on my themes." Perhaps a book would change this pattern.

When Thoreau wrote the fifth and sixth versions of *Walden* in 1853, he at last broke the manuscript into titled chapters. It looked like a book, but he was still not eager for publication. He had *Walden* in mind when he wrote to Blake on December 3 about finding some clamshells in a muskrat lodge: both structures had heavy exterior layers, "a great pile of doing," around a hidden central core. In the Journal entry for December 3 he described one shell as "a splendid cenotaph to its departed tenant." The handsome inner lining was visible, but its creator was dead. He hoped that *Walden* would survive him, yet revising its pages was a tedious, painful expenditure of life:

whatever he wrote cost him "so many months, if not years, and so much reluctance to erase," he noted on December 27.

By now he had begun negotiations to publish *Walden*, but the memory of *A Week* and its debt was not encouraging. At the year's end he wrote, "How can a poet afford to keep an account with a bookseller?" Throughout January 1854 he tried to balance Journal accounts against the constant expense of *Walden*. Some entries—on snowdrifts, art history, ice "foam"—contributed nothing to the book, while others—concerning a new coat, town records, Walden's ice—became significant episodes in its winter chapters. The Journal was growing as *Walden* cooled and hardened into a cenotaph, but their parallel structures imparted a similar lesson: "It is for man [that] the seasons and all their fruits exist."

As volume XVI ended in mid-February he began the seventh version of *Walden*. In the Journal he found an event to bridge winter and spring, the "sand foliage" produced by thaw on the banks of a railroad cut. On February 5 he wrote an imaginary view of the scene, then on March 2 a view based on actual observation. In his draft version the sand became an emblem of the art that lives within nature (Wa, 304–309). Soon art came to the fore, however, after he finally reached an agreement with Ticknor & Fields to publish *Walden*.

In early March he began the last version of his book, a fair copy for the printers. Revising went on; as he "purified the main body" of text he could easily reinsert previously discarded passages. His friends made various demands: Greeley wanted him to collect his earlier essays into a volume; Channing often tempted him into "harsh, extravagant and cynical expressions concerning mankind." Emerson was more helpful; for several weeks he tried, unsuccessfully, to find an English publisher for *Walden*.

As with *A Week*, Thoreau and the publisher worked on small batches of copy and proof, so he could revise later chapters with the printed ones in hand. The proofs revealed flaws not visible in manuscript; reading them in late March his critical sense "breaks the ice and comes to the surface." Life and art were elaborately related: he was alluding to the current spring thaw, to a chapter just frozen in print, and to his volatile feelings about publication.

Releasing a book that he had so long withheld was painful; he delayed this process on April 8 by indexing the draft "to recall it page by page to my mind" and by using a survey job "to take new points of view." He added notes from the Journal as late as April 27, and then *Walden* was at last out of his hands. As he turned to describing spring in the Journal on May 5, he saw that the writer's obligation to man-kind was "in some shape or other to tell the story of his love."

———

For many of its readers, *Walden* is Thoreau's only great book. Robert Frost said it contained "part or nearly all" of what Thoreau had to say; Wright Morris believed that after *Walden* "he had finished with his life." Thoreau's feelings were quite different. *Walden* summarized much life and thought, but far more writing was to come: in his re-maining eight years the Journal doubled its length, while *Walden* was set, a life caught in amber. And he could not have written *Walden* without the Journal, since its entries gave him a narrative plan, the seasonal round that is also a history of his mind.

In *Walden* Thoreau wrote an enormously suggestive book, and thus readers have developed strongly conflicting versions of its mean-ing. Early critics were obsessed with *what* Thoreau says; more recently *how* he says it has become the main issue. Detailed analyses of the style and structure have been advanced, suggesting that few words in the book are misplaced or redundant. (A notable disputant of this view is B. F. Skinner, author of *Walden Two* [1949], who prefers to read Tho-reau by dipping for sentences here and there: "It does not much matter what preceded or will follow.")

If Thoreau had not cared about the book's order, he would not have taken so long to write it—nor reduced his two years at the pond to one "for convenience" (Wa, 84). In fact, the single year of his story embraces even larger cycles of time: the fifteen years of drafts and Jour-nal entries, memories that go back to his childhood, and allusions to literature or history from current times back to the ancient Vedas.

He arranged those references to match both the annual and the diurnal cycles: his early chapters depict early stages of time—youth, morning, spring, "the heroic ages" of ancient Greece and India. These

are the earliest chapters he wrote, from 1846 to 1848, and in later revisions he preserved their youthful, auroral character: they *begin* his
story by locating readers in a succession of historical beginnings.

As the story advances, its temporal references shift from afternoon to evening, fall to winter, youth to maturity; and the allusions
move forward to modern authors like Gilpin, Champollion, and Webster. He wrote those chapters in later draft versions, from 1852 to
1854; they derive for the most part from the Journal for those years,
and thus reflect his own maturity as a thinker and writer. Thoreau had
reduced all of history to one year, the solar cycle that shapes all measured time. His story is an autobiography, but on a large scale: it uses
one life as a metaphor for the entire course of human growth.

The pattern Thoreau saw in his life since 1845 became the story
of *Walden*: youthful ambition, and failure, conflict with the values of
elders, rebellion and a retreat to solitary ways, emergence as a free
man who can live in society again. The movement is from error to
wisdom, imitation to originality; and Thoreau sees its resemblance to
the progress of America from colonial dependency to violent revolution to emergence as an independent nation. Autobiography is thus a
form of symbolic history, narrated by an "I" that sends this account
"to his kindred from a distant land" (Wa, 4).

The "I" who tells Thoreau's story plays a double role in another
sense, as a character who reenacts past events and a narrator who tells
the tale now: "When I wrote these words . . . I lived alone in the
woods. . . . At present I am a sojourner in civilized life again" (Wa,
4). These two figures are the I and Myself of his Journal; at the beginning of *Walden* (1845) they are widely split in time, but by the end
(1854) they have reunited. Their attitudes early in the story are sharply different; then gradually youthful anarchy yields to a mature sense of
communal needs. *Walden* is a tale of reconciliation, merging its author, character, and readers on a retrospective journey into time.

To give a faithful record of his development, Thoreau has to begin with an honest appraisal of youthful attitudes. Unfortunately, that
becomes the burden of his long first chapter, "Economy," which takes
up one-fourth of the text and has often antagonized readers by portray-
ing him as a vitriolic hermit.

Written principally from 1846 to 1849, "Economy"—like "Resistance to Civil Government"—demonstrates Thoreau's belief in action from principle. The chapter states his doctrine of economic simplicity, then tests it by recounting how he built his house. The two subjects, finance and architecture, provoke sharply different responses from his "I" persona: one harsh, vindictive, and simplistic; the other more tolerant and complex. Part of the "I" advocates saving, a niggardly retention of money; part makes a counterclaim for spending, the expressive act of construction. The "I" is virtually two different persons, a Miser and a Builder; their thematic conflict dramatizes Thoreau's separate roles as character and narrator.

The younger and more radical character is scornful of his elders; he speaks with exaggerated irreverence, often in puns and paradoxes that subvert conventional language. He upends the material terms of commerce—"cost," "profit," "balance"—giving them spiritual meanings; thus poverty becomes a form of wealth, while success is a sign of failure: "What my neighbors call good I believe in my soul to be bad" (Wa, 10). But this hostility betrays the insufficiency of his rhetoric, for he is perpetuating the very language and ideas that he hopes to subvert. Like the local farmers, he is "endeavoring to solve the problem of a livelihood by a formula more complicated than the problem itself" (Wa, 33).

The narrator is an older, conciliating voice who wants "as many different persons in the world as possible" (Wa, 71), because he knows that the young radical will later change, becoming more satisfied with "the present condition of things" (Wa, 16). Instead of providing simple answers, the older voice raises complex questions about change, growth, the passage of time: "It is never too late to give up our prejudices" (Wa, 8). His rhetoric features not paradox but images, often of ascension and metamorphosis. In the riddle of his lost hound, bay horse, and turtle-dove lies the mystery of unceasing change, as every traveler that he meets is "as anxious to recover them as if they had lost them themselves" (Wa, 17).

Seen from this perspective, the building of a house at Walden Pond is a positive, constructive act that liberates Thoreau from youthful solipsism. He borrows his tools, recycles old materials, builds from a foundation upward. The house is an ascending form; it begins in March and grows in stages that are persistently faithful to the indweller's character. His past and future selves are not contradictory, they fulfill each other: "We belong to the community" (Wa, 46).

"Economy" poses a difficult obstacle for readers, yet it is a necessary beginning for Thoreau's story. Beyond that spring of 1845 he is free to subdue his early didacticism and describe the larger views that emerged. The later story, written from 1850 to 1854, unfolds a legendary year spent at Walden Pond, observing the cycle of four seasons. By drawing this temporal pattern from his Journal, he condensed personal history into an archetypal sequence. By placing the story beside a woodland pond, he gave his philosophy an exact physical form.

The story begins in summer, when he takes up residence on Independence Day, and its first seven chapters ("Where I Lived . . . " through "The Village") sketch his progress toward maturity: "I grew in those seasons like corn in the night" (Wa, 111). Like a plant he requires nourishment and cultivation, which come from books and rigorous self-discipline. These controls help him tolerate both solitude and visitors, whom he greets as a reborn Squanto, the Indian who taught the Pilgrims how to plant New World crops (Wa, 154). In his own bean field he learns that a planter can tend growing things but not control them, and that spirit of trust guides him safely through the woods at night: "not till we have lost the world, do we begin to find ourselves, and realize . . . the infinite extent of our relations" (Wa, 171).

During the summer of growth Walden Pond helps him to find those relations. The pond at first seems like a mountain pool, "its bottom far above the surface of other lakes" (Wa, 86), and it provides him with an image of the ground he must find, "a hard bottom and rocks in place, which we can call *reality*" (Wa, 98). The pond is a companion in his solitude, for the legend of its unmeasurable bottom confirms that "there might be men of genius in the lowest grades of life" (Wa, 150).

The four chapters Thoreau devotes to fall ("The Ponds" through "Brute Neighbors") are an account of ripening and harvest. No longer in a prescriptive mood, he sees in this season of plentiful fruits that dietary rules are less important to life than one's imaginative appetite. A recent immigrant from Ireland is a case in point: he circumscribes his life with Old World food and regulations, instead of seeing that in America "you are at liberty . . . to do without these" (Wa, 205). Like his foraging animal neighbors, Thoreau agrees to harvest whatever the earth provides.

One of its richest provisions is Walden, which he harvests in the fall as an emblem of himself. In an extended analogy the pond's literal attributes ripen into metaphors for the human spirit: no visible inlet or outlet, lying between heaven and earth, its water of crystalline purity, the levels rising and falling mysteriously (Wa, 175–82). To a modern geologist these details describe a "kettle" lake, formed by a chunk of melting glacier, fed by underground springs, and lined with a watertight bottom. Thoreau personifies aspects of the pond to make a symbolic point—the shorelines are lips, where no beard grows; the trees and surrounding cliffs are eyelashes and brows: "It is earth's eye, looking into which the beholder measures the depth of his own nature" (Wa, 186).

Walden is a smooth mirror, reflector of the character's "eye" at its surface and concealer of the older "I" in its hidden bottom. Throughout the fall he does not measure its depth, only studies the surface before him. A floater on this enigmatic plane, he admires a wily loon that eludes his pursuit by forever diving for "the deepest part" (Wa, 235).

Winter comes and goes in four chapters ("House-Warming" through "The Pond in Winter"), telling of dormancy and life retarded. The cold and snow prompt him then to gather fuel and build a chimney, to sustain his lonely hours with thoughts of former inhabitants of the woods and present animal neighbors. The season teaches humility and patience, the acceptance of necessary alterations. After plastering, his house is less handsome but more comfortable; old driftwood for his fire remains solid and combustible at the core. The lowest creatures, "nearest allied to leaves and to the ground" (Wa, 281), are best able to endure this season.

The pond also withdraws in winter, its "eye-lids" closed beneath a cover of snow and ice (Wa, 282). But its frozen surface provides a

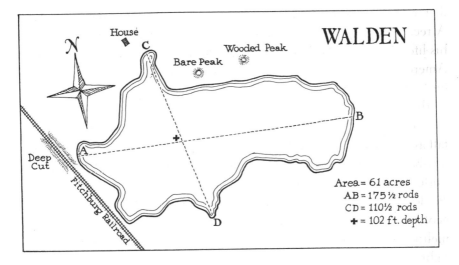

solid base for his plumb line and stone, allowing him at last to "recover the long lost bottom of Walden Pond" (Wa, 285). Of course its depth is measurable, 102 feet at the deepest point, but a momentous discovery follows: on his survey map the lines of greatest length and breadth intersect at this same point. The visible surface and unseen bottom are coequals, and so are the separate halves of his identity. When thaw brings puddles to the ice, Thoreau sees at last the image of an integrated self, "a double shadow of myself, one standing on the head of the other" (Wa, 293).

Spring swiftly follows this climax, in two chapters ("Spring" and "Conclusion") expressing the year's symphonic renewal. The signs of resurrection are all cohesive and reconciliatory: the "sand foliage" in the railroad cut is a "hybrid product" shaped by man and a supreme Artist (Wa, 305–306); the uprising grass is fed by last year's dead crop. With his own inner division healed, Thoreau can see that self-improvement is also an act of social fidelity: "Through our own recovered innocence we discern the innocence of our neighbors" (Wa, 314).

The end of Walden is therefore implicit in its beginning; Thoreau becomes a sojourner in civilized life again. But he promises to keep alive the questioning spirit of his reborn life, exploring the wild meadows and forests that lie at the edges of town. Life there is open-ended, an unceasing progress in which we "witness our own limits transgressed" (Wa, 218), and thus he urges that his story be accepted as a metaphor, not a program, for self-discovery; "Our voyaging is only great-circle sailing" (Wa, 320).

The pond is also transformed in spring, melting again into the fluid state: "Walden was dead and is alive again" (Wa, 311). In that resurrected form it resembles the pond of old; but Thoreau gradually expands its borders to suggest a larger identity, "the Atlantic and Pacific of one's being alone.—" (Wa, 321). Despite this change of scope, the integrity of his discovery at Walden will hold: "There is a solid bottom every where" (Wa, 330).

Walden is an extraordinary achievement in literature, a many-figured story that richly deserves the acclaim it has won. Thoreau's book articulates the "search for identity" that has long characterized American culture, a moral burden concomitant with the privileges of democracy. His message is both critical and hopeful, as he warns against arrogance and rigidity, while celebrating humility and growth. At the heart of his story is a simple paradox, difficult for an ambitious nation to accept: that success may spring from the bitter trial of defeat.

Yet for all its merits as a public statement, *Walden* was also a compromise with Thoreau's private notions of his art. In the Journal since 1852 he had evolved new goals for his writing: to appreciate the myriad phenomena of nature, to replicate its processes, to distill from its order an exact but suggestive fable. After years of tedious revising and editing, little of this natural spontaneity survived in his text. His story urges readers to submit to the force of time; yet he himself had forcibly drawn the circle of this imaginary year.

In his final chapters, heavily revised in 1854, Thoreau urges readers to look beyond the arbitrary realm of his book. He is especially fearful of literalists who will see him as advocating a scheme for social reform, and thus he urges a larger vision, transcending even the limits his metaphors have imposed. On a private level, he is also willing to grow beyond *Walden*. In the sand foliage he sees earth's "living poetry" as superior to the compacted sediment of "dead history, stratum upon stratum like the leaves of a book" (Wa, 309). Now he seeks expansion, advancement, other lives to lead; and in them he can see only indefinable shapes, quite unlike the solid house built in *Walden*: "The volatile truth of our words should continually betray the inadequacy of the residual statement. Their truth is instantly *translated*; its literal monument alone remains" (Wa, 325).

Two fables at the end of *Walden* emphasize his desire to transcend its boundaries. Reversing his early account of housebuilding, these stories depict metamorphosis in the act of tearing down layers of wood. In one story, the artist of Kouroo whittles a staff for eons of time, and when finished it stands as "a world with full and fair proportions." But the heap of shavings at his feet also says that his invested time "had been an illusion" (Wa, 327). In the other story, a bug that lays its egg in a "green and living tree" later has to gnaw its way out of a table, "the semblance of its well-seasoned tomb," to reach its destiny in a "beautiful and winged life" (Wa, 333). Thoreau looks for the same progression in his craft: "Say what you have to say, not what you ought. Any truth is better than make-believe" (Wa, 327).

The audience for *Walden* was small in 1854; that era of Manifest Destiny and rising personal wealth had little interest in poverty and inner exploration. Popular tastes favored sensation and sentiment, as in T. S. Arthur's *Ten Nights in a Bar-Room* (1854), the sort of book Thoreau said was properly labeled "Little Reading" (Wa, 104). Nor did iconoclasts understand him: two of Melville's later stories— "Sketch Ninth" of "The Encantadas" (May 1854) and "The Apple-Tree Table" (May 1856) are parodies of the solitary life and the hope for resurrection, inspired either by *Walden* itself or by conversations with Hawthorne.

But Thoreau's friends were joyous over the book's publication. During August Alcott pored over it repeatedly and predicted in his diary that *Walden* would bring its author fame. It was widely reviewed, even as far away as San Francisco, but judgments were mixed. Newspapers usually paraphrased "Economy" and quarreled with it; the most favorable notices, in December 1854 by Lydia Maria Child and in January 1856 by George Eliot, appeared in journals of small circulation. The sales of *Walden* were not impressive: 80 percent occurred within four weeks of publication; half were limited to the Boston area. In Thoreau's lifetime barely 2,000 copies were sold.

Once the proofs left him in early May of 1854, Thoreau turned to other concerns. A new occasion for writing was suddenly provided by political events: on May 26 an abolitionist mob in Boston attempted to prevent the Commonwealth of Massachusetts from returning a fugitive slave to his southern owners. The slave was delivered, but only after U.S. Commissioner Loring had secured the protection of federal and state troops. Thoreau heard eyewitness reports from friends, read newspaper accounts, and by May 29 his Journal had erupted with dark, apocalyptic threats "to blow up earth and hell together." Late in June he assembled an address to be read on Independence Day at an antislavery convention in Framingham; on July 21 "Slavery in Massachusetts" was printed in W. L. Garrison's *Liberator*.

Garrison burned a copy of the Constitution during his speech at Framingham; Thoreau's address is less theatrical but still uncompromising. Passage of the Kansas-Nebraska Act by the U.S. Senate had touched off the riot, and in his text Thoreau depicts this western extension of slavery as a threat to the entire body politic. Using the symbolic logic of *Walden*, he argues that one locus is indivisible from them all: "There is not one slave in Nebraska; there are perhaps a million slaves in Massachusetts" (RP, 91). These "slaves" are ostensibly free citizens, held in bondage by politicians and the popular press, who successfully mold the public mind. He attacks the enemy with crude sarcasm, even using a barnyard simile, "like the dirt-bug and its ball," to describe Daniel Webster (RP, 97).

The political ideal of Thoreau's address is at the same time an artistic credo, that the highest duty is to deliver "a true opinion or *sentence*" (RP, 98), and in that respect he feels the press has badly failed. His own development as a reporter and writer makes him contemptuous of journalists who manipulate popular opinion and tastes. Newspapers have become "the only book which America has printed, and which America reads" (RP, 100), and their success arouses a sour irony: "events of the past month teach me to distrust Fame" (RP, 104).

His radical faith in solitude is badly shaken, for events also suggest that the quiet pursuit of a literary vocation is futile—as though he had built a small villa, surrounded with pictures and a garden, and then discovered that the site is in hell: "do not these things suddenly lose value in your eyes?" (RP, 107). And his recently completed book, whatever its merits, could hardly remake the world it was about to enter: "I walk toward one of our ponds, but what signifies the beauty of nature when men are base?" (RP, 108). This discussion of authorship is candid, yet also secretive, for Thoreau had addressed a public issue that would hardly suggest other meanings to his audience.

After his first printed copy of *Walden* arrived on August 2, he tried to lift the depression by finding new lecture topics in his Journal. On August 28 Emerson told one of his correspondents that Thoreau was "in a tremble of great expectation over *Walden*," but in fact he was compulsively turning to several new projects, largely ill-conceived. He hoped to put together a series of lectures for a tour in the Midwest, and his first thought was to revise "Walking, or The Wild" by splitting it in two. He compiled a list of relevant Journal passages from 1851 to 1854 that might be added, but apparently he never used them.

Near the end of volume XVII, on September 2, he next settled on writing about his "moonlight walks" of 1850 to 1854. This project at once threatened to become larger than *Walden*: he compiled elaborate indexes, outlines, and notes, and his apparent plan was to use the Journal in an entirely new fashion. Working solely with volumes written since he had moved to the house on Main Street in 1850, he would lift from their unexcised pages a composition that summarized these years of growing independence.

On September 4, early in volume XVIII, he expressed a concern that reflects on the new project: "The artist changes the direction of Nature and makes her grow according to his idea"; for he planned to copy entries and arrange them in twelve lunar months, thus creating a nocturnal version of the *Walden* calendar. But he also wanted to imitate the Journal directly; although his transcripts came from various years he arranged them in a daily order: July 4, 7, 8, 11, et cetera. In this sequence, with their style further polished, they resembled the Journal but had changed direction and grown according to his idea.

Thoreau gathered more than 100 pages of these monthly transcripts, far more than he could read in a single lecture. From them he could have organized his ideas into a pattern governed by time, location, or topics. Repeatedly the transcripts emphasize inversion, not just of daytime scenes but of Thoreau's entire milieu. In the long nights of winter he roams far from the comfort of village hearths: "The scenery is wholly arctic" (February 3, 1852). * The shorter nights of spring are less welcome; "ours is to be henceforth a daylight life" (April 3, 1852).

Summer nights, which take up half the transcripts, become a brief interval in vegetative growth, symbolized by the virginal moon—this despite Thoreau's assertion in *Walden* that he grew "like corn in the night" (Wa, 111). Fall moves through the season of harvest to a tranquil acceptance of death, "those islands of the blessed in the evening sky" (September 7, 1854). One of the transcripts records several pages of memories about boating at night with his brother, and his thoughts of the oncoming winter are elegiac as "the horns of the new moon" bring on another year (December 20, 1853).

He finished the transcripts early in September, but time never permitted him to use them extensively. On September 17 he agreed to give an October lecture in Plymouth, and in his rush to prepare a text he set all the preliminary work aside. His first page is titled "Moonlight (Introductory to an Intended Course of Lectures)," and the lecture's surviving fragments indicate that it had the simple form of a local excursion, from Bear Garden Hill to Baker Farm, returning past Fair Haven Cliff to the village. Each locale suggests a similar mood: reverent, pensive, muted—in sharp contrast to the recent antislavery address. At Fair Haven, the highest elevation in Concord, the lecture's climax is subdued: "no great comedy or tragedy is being enacted," and his return path is "comparatively barren."

"Moonlight" is not impressive; it falls short of the ambitious plans suggested by Thoreau's preliminary work and never emulates the form or style of recent Journal entries. The entries ceased entirely during his last five days of composition, and in the end his audience at Plymouth was a tiny circle of friends like Alcott, whose diary for October 8 says only that he heard "an admirable paper." Thoreau never published the lecture; his posthumous editors culled from the papers a text they called "Night and Moonlight" (Ex, 307–19).

---

*Dates are of the original Journal entries; quotations are from the transcripts.

"There is the moon in the south, with one bright star beneath it."

Undaunted, Thoreau pushed ahead with his third lecture since *Walden*, a manuscript called "Getting a Living" (printed posthumously in a different form as "Life Without Principle"). After trips to Philadelphia—where he read "The Wild," first composed in 1851—and New York, he delivered "Getting a Living" in Providence. His reception was dismal, probably because he railed at the audience and its common notions of business and art: "If you would get money as a writer or lecturer, you must be popular, which is to go down perpendicularly" (RP, 158).

Thoreau himself was going downhill, regressing to earlier ideas and modes of writing. Having long ignored the Journal, he fumed on December 6 that lecturing was a waste of time and art. He preferred a silent and unseen audience: "I would rather write books than lectures." Possibly he thought that the "Moonlight" papers would yield a book, but he also had an old "course of lectures" on hand, the manuscript about Cape Cod that he had offered to *Putnam's* in 1852.

Perhaps the best place to write was in the ongoing book of his Journal, where the audience suited him well and the work more honestly reflected his latest ideas and skills. He set aside "Moonlight" at this time and never returned to it. This imitation of the Journal's calendar was defective; like many of his published writings, it contradicted the current state of his art. He would keep instead this faithful record of days and months spent in nature, where a sudden winter thaw on December 14 was a cherished experience: "The river is open almost its whole length. It is a beautifully smooth mirror within an icy frame."

The Book

Here is self-registered the flutterings of a leaf in this twisted, knotted, and braided twine. So fickle and unpredictable, not to say insignificant, a motion does yet get permanently recorded in some sort. Not a leaf flutters, summer or winter, but its variation and dip and intensity are registered in THE BOOK.

—JANUARY 24, 1855

6
A CERTAIN GREENNESS

The charm of the journal must consist in a certain
greenness, though freshness, and not in maturity.
                                    —JANUARY 23, 1856

In the winter of 1855 Thoreau worked on revising his Cape Cod lectures for publication. He had built them from Journal accounts of two trips to the peninsula in 1849 and 1850; since then he had compiled many historical and geographical facts about the Cape in other notebooks. Now his task was to make a single, coherent story. The sight of a wire-rolling mill in Worcester on January 5 was suggestive, for its raw materials were odd scraps of metal, like "many a piece of composition, which . . . mere compression would weld together into a homogeneous mass."

Coherence was a problem not just in his projected book but also in the Journal. In January its entries had become dense with factual data, such as a simple enumeration of oak-leaf types, with cross-references to his concurrent "book of facts." Late in the month he tried to curb this tendency by watching for "the hue of heaven" in his daily treks, and—looking again at some oak leaves—he found in their wind-braided stalks an emblem for his work: "Not a leaf flutters, summer or winter, but its variation and dip and intensity are registered in THE BOOK."

The figure of *liber naturae*, nature as a book, is an ancient metaphor for the sacred design of Creation; for Thoreau this analogy expressed a function that had overtaken his Journal. No longer just an autobiographical mirror, the Journal had become more external and comprehensive, taking in a larger image of the world lying around him. He was now recording facts more precisely, often without evaluating or summarizing the data. On February 5 he entered his first notes on the daily weather, explaining that such simple details "in a journal . . . cannot be unimportant to remember."

The Book he was reading had discernible "characters" on its pages; the snow tracks left by animals or other walkers in late January revealed stories of previous action. In mid-February he said the tracks were "like some mystic Oriental symbol," but they also told exactly how the animals moved, ate, or adapted to the cold. To pursue this theme he trapped several small animals over the next two months and wrote anatomical descriptions in the Journal, recording even the length of a mouse's "longest mustachios." He then compared these notes with authorities, compiled a list of Concord's quadrupeds, and traded forepaws with a fellow trapper.

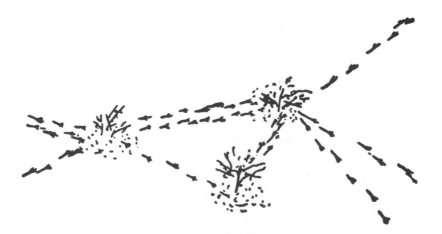

". . . a flock of snow buntings . . . feeding extensively on . . . Roman wormwood."

"The impression of the foot a little like this, but not so much spread: They have but four toes on the fore feet, with rudiment of a thumb."

The actuality of these specimens interested Thoreau more than any "impression" he got from books or even from his own imagination. More empirical now than transcendental, the Journal became a record of vigorous outdoor activity. Throughout February he often wrote of skating, enjoying it so much that he thought this should "be called the winter of skating." But skating was also instructive; on February 3 he noted variations in the ice and admired the snow blown across its dark surface, "braided of a myriad streaming currents."

The "braided" oak leaves and snow currents suggested that patterns were everywhere in his Book, even if he did not always see them at first. His knowledge of Concord accumulated, one fact leading to others: the ice patterns helped him to predict floods and the formation of meadows on the Sudbury River later on in February and March.

This growing absorption in Concord made Thoreau reluctant to look beyond its horizons. Readers of *Walden* wrote flattering letters, urging him to travel abroad, but his usual response, as on February 1, was "I have a real genius for staying at home." He made only two lecture trips that winter, then remained in Concord with his chosen tasks until summer. Emerson could not comprehend this attachment to one town; years later he reportedly said that Thoreau's purpose "was not to be seen, or even anticipated. . . . though dwelling in Concord, he lived in a far country."

His country was actually close at hand, in Concord's homely and visible realities. On March 8 he saw on some cut logs tiny crystallized drops of turpentine that caught the sunlight, reflecting the world with "perfect sincerity," seemingly liquid but actually firm: "And is this that pitch which you cannot touch without being defiled?" The figure is reminiscent of Melville's Encantadas, where giant tortoises have both bright and black sides. Like Melville, Thoreau had begun to see with the perfect sincerity of an unsentimental observer.

His imagination remained strong in these years, but it found new avenues of expression. The man who had mourned the loss of a turtle-dove in *Walden* now rejoiced in finding a dead duck. Early in April he skinned and stuffed the bird, described it exactly for the Journal, even studied the anatomy of its anal vent. His constitution was less sound than his imagination. At the age of thirty-seven he knew that his eyesight had weakened; by April 16 he was using a telescope to study water birds.

Aging turns men into realists. That spring Thoreau developed an illness that persisted for several months. Weak in the legs and generally lethargic, he may have contracted a mild form of tuberculosis. He wrote little in the Journal about his ailment, but its effects were apparent in the perfunctory lists and miscellaneous facts he set down in early May "without regard to the time when they began." On June 11 he fell into a self-pitying depression, writing "no friend appears, and perhaps none is dreaming of me." In fact, the Emersons were trying just a week later to have him convalesce at their home. Thoreau declined, but in September he added a footnote to the June entry, saying his "months of invalidity and worthlessness" were over.

———

During those months he did not neglect his career. In April he looked after his books, trying unsuccessfully to have Ticknor & Fields reissue the old sheets of *A Week* and contracting with *Putnam's* for serialization of the chapters on Cape Cod. As with the aborted Canada story, his editor was again G. W. Curtis, who still objected to religious irreverence. On April 13 and 20 Thoreau agreed to a few changes in the early chapters, which Curtis scheduled to commence in June. Thoreau was to send more chapters that summer; he went to the Cape in July partly to gather some fresh material.

Four chapters appeared from June to August, and he sent copy for at least two more on August 8. Meanwhile a dispute had arisen. Curtis had told the printers to make several unauthorized revisions; the two men also disagreed over Thoreau's fee and his plan to print the chapters later as a book. As before, Curtis suspended publication in *Putnam's* and sent the unprinted chapters back to Thoreau. In Concord he thus had a complete book of ten chapters, three in working draft and seven with notes added from his July trip. Over the next few years he made further revisions, some as late as 1861, but they did not change the book's structure or tone. The manuscript Ellery Channing edited and published as *Cape Cod* (1865) was essentially complete in September 1855.

An abrupt departure from the positive message of *Walden*, *Cape Cod* has a somber tone that reflects Thoreau's changing cast of mind: "I did not intend this for a sentimental journey" (CC, 71). Filled with images of violent destruction, *Cape Cod* is a solemn trek into a dark world of drowned bodies and rotting fish, thrown up from "a vast *morgue*," the sea that pounds relentlessly against this barren spit of land (CC, 173). Some of this tragic realism may have appeared in the original Cape Cod lectures, but Emerson described them in a letter on February 6, 1850, as mostly humorous. The more likely source of Thoreau's bleak vision lay in the disappointing months after *Walden*, when he abandoned several projects, trapped and skinned animals, struggled with his undiagnosed malady. He had accurately set down these plain facts, yet hoped to find some homogeneous braiding in the Book of his Journal.

Although *Cape Cod* includes material from all three of his trips, Thoreau wisely melded them into a single story. The main outline follows his 1849 trip, when he traveled along the Cape's entire length, from Sandwich to Provincetown. The form of this peninsula, a long "bared and bended arm" (CC, 2) that curves out and then back toward the mainland, gave him a suggestive pattern for his story.

Thoreau did not know the geological history of Cape Cod, the eons of glacial and ocean deposit that built its armlike shape, the erosional tides and waves that carved its massive cliffs and sand banks. Yet his book describes the effects of those forces, for he knew they

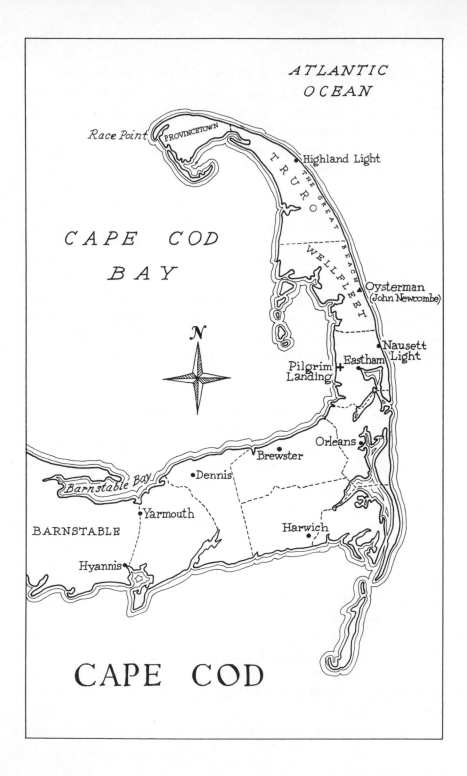

expressed the dynamics of physical change. As he walks along the Cape, an arm forever "boxing with northeast storms" (CC, 2), he also grapples with the tough reality of a nature that endlessly builds and destroys, indifferent to man's presence in the scene.

At the same time, his many notes on the history of Cape Cod suggested a temporal pattern to braid into this spatial movement. Cape Cod was a landfall for the early explorers of North America, including Bartholomew Gosnold in 1602. The Pilgrims first touched the New World in November 1620, near the later site of Provincetown. Other villages on the Cape were founded in the early eighteenth century; most had changed little since then.

To walk north toward the fist of Provincetown is to "take Time by the forelock" (CC, 4), reversing normal chronology and challenging the supremacy of popular myths. *Cape Cod* reexamines the old legends of exploration and discovery; it ends at the place where a national story began. *Walden* also ends with a search for new beginnings, but in *Cape Cod* the mood is more aggressive: Thoreau now seeks not reconciliation with the past but a bout with its claims.

The thematic burden of his story is to reinterpret the Pilgrim dream of America as a new Eden, where men of the Old World can reclaim their lost innocence by founding a community of saints. In post-Revolutionary times this myth survived in the secular vision of America as a land of Manifest Destiny, the open frontiers and rising cities that await new generations of pilgrims.

Walden challenges this materialism; now Thoreau wants to expose its historical sources. *Cape Cod* opens with a ghastly description of shipwreck and drownings, the aftermath of a storm near Cohasset that killed hundreds of Irish immigrants who were "coming to the New World, as Columbus and the Pilgrims did," but a mile from shore "emigrated to a newer world than ever Columbus dreamed of" (CC, 11–12). Unlike the old Pilgrims, who prudently created a civil body politic when the *Mayflower* lay a mile offshore, these Irish newcomers represent a bitter truth about material ambitions: "It is hard to part with one's body, but . . . easy enough to do without it . . . once it is gone" (CC, 10).

Thoreau's ensuing chapters offer a radical paean to death, exalting the very force that immigrant dreams sought to deny. He wants to remind his readers that death is a dynamic principle in history; that it shapes the very movement of time. The Pilgrims had evaded this fact in their millennial theology and social polity, and their descendants on Cape Cod continue the struggle to survive in an "exceedingly barren and desolate country" (CC, 22), where trees cannot grow and even the saltworks have gone to decay. These people stubbornly resist death: they build fences out of whale ribs, plant crops in a soil that can barely nourish weeds.

Thoreau believes that the Pilgrim Fathers are the source of this dogged materialism. They imposed upon a free land the alien concept of ownership, taking up property near Eastham that the Indians said "not any" owned. "The Pilgrims appear to have regarded themselves as Not Any's representatives" (CC, 38). The ministers of their Calvinist successors were equally privative, terrorizing congregations with physical and mental abuse. (G. W. Curtis had objected to this scornful treatment of preachers; not having read the later chapters, he could not anticipate the changes to come.)

As Thoreau reaches the Great Beach and begins to walk north, his vision of the past expands to match this world of broad horizons. The sights he encounters are lessons in moral relativity, drawn from the hypostatic union of this "savage ocean" and "Promised Land" (CC, 51). An old beachcomber, who lives by picking the dead bones of shipwrecks, "may have been one of the Pilgrims—Peregrine White, at least" (CC, 53), an allusion to the firstborn (and first orphaned) English child in New England. This example suggests that the Pilgrims were in fact no strangers to death and decay—unlike their descendants, who erect survival huts for shipwreck victims but fail to provide supplies or furniture. Thoreau peers into one gloomy hut and concludes: "It was the wreck of all cosmical beauty there within" (CC, 70).

At the midpoint of his story Thoreau places a chapter describing his overnight stay with a Wellfleet oysterman, a living witness to the American Revolution whose stories are "a strange mingling of past and present" (CC, 84). Thoreau doubts his host on the dangers of eating clams, then later becomes thoroughly ill, and discovers that passengers on the *Mayflower* suffered the same misfortune: "It brought me

". . . a round clam or quahog alive, with a very thick shell, and not so nearly an isosceles triangle as the sea clam,—more like this: with a protuberance on the back."

nearer to the Pilgrims to be thus reminded by a similar experience that I was so like them" (CC, 86).

On the beach again his judgment of the present seems to become more rigorously neo-Pilgrim. Out of the ocean comes debris, tossed ashore to feed scavenging men and animals. America is not simply a place of rebirth, "the sacred abode of our first parents," but of decadence and atrophy, processes that form "the dry land [that came] out of the water on its way to the heavens" (CC, 117).

In Truro he turns west to explore the Cape's interior, discovering barren stretches of poverty-grass, "as wild and solitary as the Western Prairies—used to be" (CC, 125). The inhabitants follow an anomalous mixture of old and new ways; they thriftily patch their homes with bits of sea wreckage, but slaughter black whales and leave their carcasses to rot on the beach.

At the Highland Light he sees more evidence of modern confusion. Built to save the lives of mariners, the lighthouse—standing on an eroding sand bank—is unable to prevent the frequent wrecks and drownings that form the "annals of this voracious beach" (CC, 150). Later, the lighthouse-keeper describes his futile struggle "to keep his light shining before men" (CC, 157), but the light is its own worst enemy, for it draws insects or forms condensation that makes the lantern beam invisible. Destruction is an essential condition of life; the sea washes ashore headless corpses but also cargoes of seed that give new plants "to a continent's stock, and prove on the whole a lasting blessing to its inhabitants" (CC, 153). The New World arose out of this old law, and present inhabitants can ill afford to ignore its workings.

Near the land's end, with the sea widening before him, Thoreau at last ponders the full meaning of the discovery of America. Looking east into the past, he sees a dark intimation of future history. Like the Hesperides, America was once deemed beyond the reach of men. Yet explorers came west: Vikings in the eleventh century (with names like his: "Thorwald," "Thor-finn," and "Thorall") who launched "the ante-Pilgrim history of New England" (CC, 210–11); then came Dutch, Spanish, and French expeditions, the true beginnings of continental discovery. The English Pilgrims arrived much later, staying timidly on the coast and inventing legends about the interior. Their successors have forgotten this history. "If America was found and lost again once, as most of us believe, then why not twice?" (CC, 231).

By the end of his journey Thoreau has challenged prevailing myths about the Pilgrims, even pounded at them with his surging rhetoric; but he cannot destroy their influence. At Provincetown he sees "barrenness and desolation" where the Pilgrim writers recalled fertile land—yet facts alone cannot displace legends: "the Pilgrims were pioneers and the ancestors of pioneers in a far greater enterprise." Behind their will to survive lie the origins of American character, "the force of *Alpha privative*, negativing all the efforts which Nature would fain make through them" (CC, 238).

His tone is more resigned than reconciliatory. Unlike the agreeable return to society in *Walden*, the ending of *Cape Cod* has a note of bitter melancholy. The cultural institutions of Boston and Concord seem merely "accidental" after his trip, and he foresees the day when "this coast will be a resort." In its raw and undeveloped state the Cape is closer to his idea of Eden: "A man may stand there and put all America behind him" (CC, 252).

Cape Cod is an orderly book, but its reading of history has been too negative and idiosyncratic to have drawn many appreciative readers. Thoreau's quarrel with American myths succumbs to at least one of their virtues, that they give a nation of diverse immigrants a sense of common heritage and purpose. The Pilgrims are a useful fiction, and no amount of debunking is ever likely to destroy their influence. As Thoreau himself wrote to a correspondent in late July of 1853, the seashore is a common home, where "we pilgrims all landed not long since," only to wander inland and "lose ourselves, and the savor of our salt."

Other flaws mar his narrative, similar to the "faults" he listed on the inside cover of his latest Journal volume: paradoxes, ingenuity, puns, clichés, and "Want of conciseness." The historical extracts in *Cape Cod* are too long, his tone too macabre to attract readers. His air of persistent gloom accords with that of Melville's recent stories in *Putnam's*, "Israel Potter" and "Benito Cereno" (1854–55), which also attacked the historical naïveté of Americans—and were also unpopular.

———

By failing to publish *Cape Cod* in 1855, Thoreau struck the pose of withdrawal that became habitual in his later years. Increasingly he grew more secretive about his daily living and writing. His values became defiantly provincial: after reading about Australian gold diggers on October 18 he wrote, "Is not our native soil auriferous?" If his walk on October 29 yielded only the bitter taste of a wild apple, he insisted that it was "a sort of triumph to eat and like it, an ovation."

He was secretive, yet longed for ovations; he wrote copiously in the Journal but would not mine its gold. The habit was compulsive but also prudent; he gathered waterlogged firewood in November because no one else valued this resource: "The pleasure, the warmth, is not so much in *having* as in a true and simple manner *getting* these necessaries." The Journal encouraged this idea of his vocation, for it so shaped his writing habits that now *getting* a work—through endless notes, entries, drafts—was more pleasurable than *having* it set before an audience. In Amherst the same mechanism was beginning to work in young Emily Dickinson, a poet whose morbid aversion to fame makes Thoreau look almost gregarious.

Thoreau's intellectual concerns had also shifted, away from philosophy toward applied forms of knowledge. After a friend sent him a handsome library of Oriental scriptures, Thoreau wrote a gracious note of thanks on December 1, but he rarely consulted these books in later years. For provender he looked to the Journal, where he could write on December 11 that winter was "not an evil to be corrected" but a proper subject for his art.

His studies, now grown increasingly factual, made him more aware of imprecision in his entries. On December 11 he longed to "daguerreotype" thoughts or feelings rather than write them; in the final week of 1855 (and the last pages of volume XIX) he reviewed the Journal and said it was a "true history" but lacked the solid details of a biography: "the most important events in my life, if recorded at all, are not dated." With his mother's help he therefore wrote a summary of his life, including all dates and places of residence.

In its simple and purely functional prose, this listing outlined the changes that had come to Thoreau and his Journal in recent years. He had aged, grown more set in his solitary ways, and gravitated in his writing from the ideal of mystery to that of truth. The Journal had therefore grown fuller and denser, shaped less by his ideas than by the facts he brought to its pages. But its "science" was self-taught, rarely set down as systematic field notes. And although Thoreau was no longer the poet of his youth, he still sought a spiritual reality that lay beyond these observations of the physical world.

In volume XX, headed "The Long Snowy Winter" on January 4, 1856, Thoreau began to put more drawings into his entries. These rough sketches made him think more about the actual shapes of natural objects, leading to rapt descriptions of nature's creative genius—as in this entry for January 5:

> The thin snow now driving from the north and lodging on my coat consists of those beautiful star crystals, not cottony and chubby spokes, as on the 13th December, but thin and partly transparent crystals. They are about a tenth of an inch in diameter, perfect little wheels with six spokes without a tire, or rather with six perfect little leafets, fern-like, with a distinct straight and slender midrib, raying from the centre. On each side of each midrib there is a transparent thin blade with a crenate edge, thus:
>
> How full of the creative genius is the air in which these are generated! I should hardly admire them more if real stars fell and lodged on my coat. Nature is full of genius, full of the divinity; so that not a snowflake escapes its fashioning hand. Nothing is cheap and coarse, neither dewdrops nor snowflakes. Soon the storm increases,—it was already very severe to face,—and the snow comes

finer, more white and powdery. Who knows but this is the original form of all snowflakes, but that when I observe these crystal stars falling around me they are not just generated in the low mist next the earth? I am nearer to the source of the snow, its primal, auroral, and golden hour [of] infancy, but commonly the flakes reach us travel-worn and agglomerated, comparatively without order or beauty, far down in their fall, like men in their advanced age.

As for the circumstances under which this phenomenon occurs, it is quite cold, and the driving storm is bitter to face, though very little snow is falling. It comes almost horizontally from the north. Methinks this kind of snow never falls in any quantity.

A divinity must have stirred within them before the crystals did thus shoot and set. Wheels of the storm-chariots. The same law that shapes the earth-star shapes the snow-star. As surely as the petals of a flower are fixed, each of these countless snow-stars comes whirling to earth, pronouncing thus, with emphasis, the number six. Order, Κόσμος.

On the Saskatchewan, when no man of science is there to behold, still down they come, and not the less fulfill their destiny, perchance melt at once on the Indian's face. What a world we live in! Where myriads of these little disks, so beautiful to the most prying eye, are whirled down on every traveller's coat, the observant and the unobservant, and on the restless squirrel's fur, and on the far-stretching fields and forests, the wooded dells, and the mountain-tops. Far, far away from the haunts of man, they roll down some little slope, fall over and come to their bearings, and melt or lose their beauty in the mass, ready anon to swell some little rill with their contribution, and so, at last, the universal ocean from which they came. There they lie, like the wreck of chariot-wheels after a battle in the skies. Meanwhile the meadow mouse shoves them aside in his gallery, the schoolboy casts them in his snowball, or the woodman's sled glides smoothly over them, these glorious spangles, the sweepings of heaven's floor. And they all sing, melting as they sing, of the mysteries of the number six,—six, six, six.

By implication this entry describes Thoreau's creative genius as well. Like the snowflakes, his account is transparent but also fashioned, an appreciation of completed forms and an inquiry into their origins. The snow becomes his metaphor for all natural shapes, from stars to flowers, heaven to earth, and for his destiny as an artist: the man of expanded consciousness, an eloquent spokesman for life's dumb phenomena, unrecognized by other minds yet faithful to the mystery of their common source.

His entries for the rest of January included statistical tables, sometimes added up incorrectly (as on January 12), but often with imaginative effects. On January 18 he saw that shadows on the snowdrifts were not always black: "I am turned into a tall blue Persian from my cap to my boots." After a lengthy computation of an elm tree's dimensions he wrote a eulogy to "this old citizen of the town," which had grown so steadily throughout its history. The botanical components of trees, their radicals (roots) and heartwood, suggested an analogy for citizenship: "They combine a true radicalism with a true conservatism. . . . They take a firmer hold on the earth that they may rise higher into the heavens."

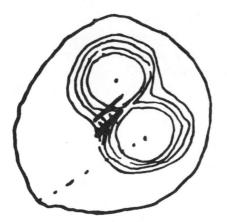

"They have cut and sawed off the butt of the great elm at nine and a half feet from the ground, and I counted the annual rings there with the greatest ease and accuracy."

His factual entries had a similar purpose, to accumulate in rings of constant growth, assuming a form—like snowflakes and elm trees —consistent with that function. Clearly the Journal's contents had changed; on January 24 he defined its new shape as "a record of experiences and growth, not a preserve of things well done or said. . . . The charm of the journal must consist in a certain greenness, though freshness, and not in maturity." This "greenness" explained both the vigor and the incompleteness of *Cape Cod* and his private Book, where each daily event, as he wrote on January 31, was "a new leaf of Nature's *Album*."

Growth also had its human dimensions, as Thoreau noted in a series of January and February entries about the past. He visited with Mary Moody Emerson, who showed great vitality of mind and spirit for a woman of eighty-one years. He studied Concord's early buildings and records, and found them a useful resource for his current studies. Understanding antiquity was a means of staying alive, if not young; old Journal entries changed his ideas about willows, which he described on February 14 as "emblems of youth, joy, and everlasting life." Once he had mocked Alcott's interest in genealogy, but on February 23 he wrote out the Thoreau family history with no apologies.

Old friends were less easy to understand. That winter Thoreau's relations with Emerson declined sharply, for reasons not clear to the older man. Emerson was his usual bustling self, so busy on a western lecture tour that he had written Thoreau on December 26 and asked him to proofread the last chapters of *English Traits*. In January Thoreau read the chapter on Stonehenge, in which Emerson said that he had never known "a man of sufficient valor" to resist government policy, and that the English landscape made America seem "a great sloven continent." From local friends Thoreau also heard strong praise of Emerson's February lectures; this in a season when Thoreau was delivering none.

When their conversations resumed Thoreau surprised Emerson, according to the latter's journal, by quarreling with "some weary captious paradox," or by delivering a report of his thoughts, "quite inattentive to any comment," then abruptly departing. Thoreau wrote of similar grievances in his own Journal. On March 4 he described two unidentified friends: one (probably Emerson) was patronizing, formal; he never returned visits or accepted favors. "Our relation was one long tragedy." The tragedy lay in their silences, peculiar for two men who were so articulate. Thoreau's reticence in personal matters was obsessive. The other friend (Channing?) had been too obtuse to understand a certain "fact" that Thoreau still would not specify.

In early March Thoreau briefly considered leaving Concord and living with the Greeley family near New York, but then he decided to stay put. Emerson may have settled the issue by encouraging him to go, for in the Journal on March 11 Thoreau defended himself against a critic who did not see that "the commonest events, every-day phenomena" of daily walks and talks were his best inspirations.

In fact much excellent writing went into the Journal, with no apparent publication in mind. He was not invited to lecture that winter, he wrote Blake on March 13, "So you see I am fast growing rich." His entries drew profit from the slightest incidents: three people who took bad falls (trying to help a fallen fourth) became characters in a mock-heroic story for March 19, titled "What Befell at Mrs. Brooks's." The next day he described the results of several weeks of collecting and boiling sap. His father thought the experiment a waste of time, but Thoreau had the pleasure of learning and writing: "I felt as if I had been to a university."

His study of antiquity—and his own aging—now made Thoreau more conscious of losses. Old books about Concord told of wild animals that no longer inhabited the area, reminding him on March 23 that the present town was "an imperfect copy," like his early Journal: "my ancestors have torn out many of the first leaves and grandest passages, and mutilated it in many places." As he had predicted years earlier, spring was a less welcome season in middle age; at the end of April his notes on leafing and blooming had a casual, obligatory air.

Thoreau saw these changes in himself and the Journal, but he accepted them as evidence of growth. His entry for April 24, the first in volume XXI, gave a positive emblem of his work: dead vegetation at the bottom of a pool did not cloud its water, for "through this medium we admire even the decaying leaves and sticks at the bottom." The medium of his daily record would sustain him by inspiring a more philosophic life, its structure like the pure melody he described on April 30: "you will hear more of it if you devote yourself to your work."

Thoreau's fieldwork seemed rigorously scientific to his less informed friends, for now he carried a spyglass and measuring tape, stored plants in the "botany-box" of his hat, and brought home specimens for his growing collections. He wrote field notes on the backs of old business letters; many of these jottings became entries with little alteration. In his journal for May 21 Emerson said Thoreau kept a "breast pocket diary" of plants due to bloom, like a banker waiting for bonds to mature.

His methods seemed calculating, but in fact they attracted him to subjects he had previously ignored. In early June he began to focus on sexual reproduction in plants and animals. For the first time he speculated that the alternating generations of pines and oaks in local woodlots might be caused by animals dispersing the seeds. He told Emerson that the river possessed a "male and female bank," one side propagating the other with willows; he spent several hours on June 10 observing the slow, tedious egg-laying of a painted tortoise. These events reassured him of his own continuing creativity, through the patient accumulation of knowledge.

"The nest . . . shaped like a short, round bottle with a broad mouth."

The greenness of his studies ruled against harvesting them prematurely. When Blake invited him to lecture in Worcester, Thoreau replied on May 21 that he had not yet put his thoughts together, or even thought sufficiently about the facts he had gathered: "I am still a learner, not a teacher." To another correspondent on May 31 he reported "nothing new in the book form. I am drawing a rather long bow."

If he had a book in mind, it was possibly *Cape Cod*; for in late June he gathered materials for its text during a tour of the South Shore. But his published writings had never brought him much satisfaction—or understanding from his readers. On July 12, his thirty-ninth birthday, he received a note from Mary Moody Emerson, who said his books were witty and thoughtful, but unclear as to "motive and end and infinite responsibility of talent."

She did not know of his private Book, where Concord had become an infinite realm. His entries for July and early August depicted
—in local places—Algerian deserts, Honduran rain forests, "Olympian fruit." He made ordinary scenes and events seem extraordinary: the
escape and recapture of his father's prize boar on August 8 became a
brilliant picaresque in miniature, 2,000 words on the animal's superior
cunning and his own foolish nature lore. Here is a brief excerpt:

> Once more he [the pig] glides down the narrow street, deliber-
> ates at a corner, chooses wisely for him, and disappears through an
> openwork fence eastward. He has gone to fresh gardens and pastures
> new. Other neighbors stand in the doorways but half sympathizing,
> only observing, "Ugly thing to catch." "You have a job on your
> hands." I lose sight of him, but hear that he is far ahead in a large
> field. And there we try to let him alone a while, giving him a wide
> berth.
>   At this stage an Irishman was engaged to assist. "I can catch
> him," says he, with Buonapartean confidence. He thinks him a
> family Irish pig. His wife is with him, bareheaded, and his little flib-
> bertigibbet of a boy, seven years old. "Here, Johnny, do you run
> right off there" (at the broadest possible angle with his own course).
> "Oh, but he can't do anything." "Oh, but I only want him to tell
> me where he is,—to keep sight of him." Michael [the Irishman]
> soon discovers that he is not an Irish pig, and his wife and Johnny's
> occupations are soon gone. Ten minutes afterward I am patiently
> tracking him step by step through a corn-field, a near-sighted man
> helping me, and then into garden after garden far eastward, and fi-
> nally into the highway, at the graveyard; but hear and see nothing.
> One suggests a dog to track him. Father is meanwhile selling him to
> the blacksmith, who is trying to get sight of him. After fifteen min-
> utes since he disappeared eastward, I hear that he has been to the
> river twice far on the north, through the first neighbor's premises. I
> went that way. He crosses the street far ahead, Michael behind; he
> dodges up an avenue. I stand in the gap there, Michael at the other
> end, and now he tries to corner him. But it is a vain hope to corner
> him in a yard. I see a carriage-manufactory door open. "Let him go

in there, Flannery." For once the pig and I are of one mind; he bolts in, and the door is closed. Now for a rope. It is a large barn, crowded with carriages. The rope is at length obtained; the windows are barred with carriages lest he bolt through. He is resting quietly on his belly in the further corner, thinking unutterable things.

Now the course recommences within narrower limits. Bump, bump, bump he goes, against wheels and shafts. We get no hold yet. He is all ear and eye. Small boys are sent under the carriages to drive him out. He froths at the mouth and deters them. At length he is stuck for an instant between the spokes of a wheel, and I am securely attached to his hind leg. He squeals deafeningly, and is silent. The rope is attached to a hind leg. The door is opened, and the *driving* commences. Roll an egg as well. You may drag him, but you cannot drive him. But he is in the road, and now another thundershower greets us. I leave Michael with the rope in one hand and a switch in the other and go home. He seems to be gaining a little westward. But, after long delay, I look out and find that he makes but doubtful progress. A boy is made to face him with a stick, and it is only when the pig springs at him savagely that progress is made homeward. He will be killed before he is driven home. I get a wheelbarrow and go to the rescue. Michael is alarmed. The pig is rabid, snaps at him. We drag him across the barrow, hold him down, and so, at last, get him home.

Despite this story's merits, Thoreau apparently had no thought of publishing it. In February 1857 he did write a shorter version, titled "How to Catch a Pig," but even then his motive was apparently just the sheer pleasure of narration.

———

Although *Walden* was slowly spreading Thoreau's fame, he kept to himself. The sight of some flowering desmodiums on August 19 justified this course: "They are outsiders, few and far between, . . . exercising their dry wit on the race of man." And the days of late August, once his slowest season, stirred a blaze of fine entries on humble sub-

". . . a box tortoise, the first I have found in Concord . . . A beak like any Caesar's."

jects: the rattlesnake plaintain, "prettiest leaf that paves the forest floor"; the painted tortoise again, whose eggs slowly hatched after incubating all summer—"Be not in haste; mind your private affairs."

By recording these moments of epiphany the Journal taught Thoreau to live in constant expectation—not of eternity, but of each present moment. He could never anticipate which experiences were useful; only his entries confirmed their lasting value. If cranberrying on August 30 at first seemed a waste of time, in the Journal account (ca. 3,500 words) he could sort out his botanical discoveries, exclaim over the neglected riches of remote Beck Stow's Swamp, and expand the thoughts suggested by this outing. "I would fain improve every opportunity to wonder and worship, as a sunflower welcomes the light."

Although his later methods were exacting, Thoreau's purpose remained philosophical. His merging of the actual and the ideal qualified his early romanticism, brought him nearer to the realism of Walt

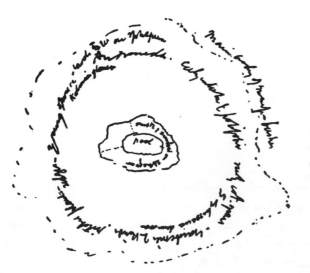

"I improve the dry weather to examine the middle of Gowing's Swamp."

Whitman, whose *Leaves of Grass* (1855) Thoreau had read by now. Yet the odd mixture of fire and ice in Thoreau's character set him apart from any mentor. His behavior was unpredictable: he could refuse to take a friend boating on August 31, then abruptly invite himself to visit Alcott in Walpole, New Hampshire, on September 1. A day later the Journal resolved these contradictory moods, which sprang from the same impulse: "My expectation ripens to discovery. I am prepared for strange things."

Alcott had promised "a tour of talk" in Walpole, but Thoreau's main purpose was to "botanize" in a northern latitude, where he could see the effects of higher elevation on plants also found in Concord. His days there ripened beyond that expectation; the Journal account from September 6 to 11 (which opens volume XXII) describes missed train connections, chance meetings with other botanists, and first sightings of new plants. Concord had prepared him for these surprises; returning home on September 13, he professed to see there "a more interesting horizon, more variety and richness."

This idea continued to vex Emerson, who knew that Concord was clearly not the world. Important figures like James Russell Lowell wanted to dine in Boston with the author of *Walden*, but Emerson could not persuade Thoreau to come. Correspondents found that he refused most social invitations, as he did on September 23, with a frank explanation: "I am engaged to Concord & my very private pursuits by 10,000 ties, & it would be suicide to cut them."

Like Whitman, Thoreau saw that his own time and place were the most congenial materials for his imagination. Homely phenomena were therefore most stirring, and Concord was an ample world to explore. In late September he found two of the plants first seen in Vermont, and on October 16 he came across something truly strange, "a rare and remarkable fungus" that resembled an erect human penis.

Thoreau's description of the *Phallus impudicus* (common stinkhorn) verifies several themes he had recently developed in the Journal: gather facts, control inferences, temper expectations. He makes an exact drawing* of the fungus, notes its form and dimensions, then

---

*Omitted from the 1906 edition.

"It may be divided into three parts, pileus, stem, and base,—or scrotum, for it is a perfect phallus."

takes it home—and discovers that it decays rapidly, smelling "like a dead rat in the ceiling." He is offended, saying nature has put herself "on a level with those who draw in privies," yet he follows up with more details on the plant's rotted appearance.

Some readers think this entry expresses deep sexual neuroses, yet its tone is remarkably controlled and unemotional. Emerson was amused by the finding (although in 1865 he complained about seeing "this very undesirable neighbor" under his study window). Thoreau was disgusted not by the stinkhorn's form but by its swift deterioration —all the more appalling because it resembled human flesh. On October 18 he wrote that nature had surprised him, yet he had not evaded her lesson: "Man is all in all, Nature nothing, but as she draws him out and reflects him. Give me simple, cheap, and homely themes." Two days later he pursued this analogy in a letter, saying his spirits were "as indifferently tough, as sluggishly resilient, as a dried fungus."

In that letter Thoreau also wrote of his great interest in the American West, calling it "the road to new life and freedom"; but his own travels soon took him south, on business. A surveying job in New Jersey became an opportunity to revisit his New York haunts of the 1840s, including Broadway and Barnum's Museum. His employers in Perth Amboy were members of a lapsed commune, now reorganizing their joint property into private lots. Paradise was not to be regained by the old Reform methods, after all. He met several aging radicals, including Elizabeth Peabody, who had published his "Resistance to

Civil Government" in 1849. Then, on the morning of November 10, he and Alcott went to Brooklyn to meet Walt Whitman.

The shock of recognition was not instantaneous. In his diary Alcott said the two men circled each other like wary beasts, not knowing "whether to snap or run." Their habits and ideas differed sharply, but Thoreau sensed that they were members "of the scribbling gentry." They also had a common problem in Emerson. He had written a flattering letter to Whitman in 1855, then was stunned when Whitman published it as a testimonial in the next edition of Leaves of Grass (1856). Writing to Blake on November 19, Thoreau told Whitman's version of the letter incident, which threw "the burden of it—if there is any, on the writer," meaning Emerson.

Whitman later recalled that he differed with Thoreau about newspapers, politics, and the average man: "He couldn't put his life into any other life." Thoreau was more sympathetic than Whitman realized. He saw in the new poet a vigorous antidote to the waning age of Reform and told him (according to Whitman) that he would have "immense significance." The value of this other life was not lost on Thoreau: his letter to Blake said Whitman was "the greatest democrat the world has seen."

Thoreau carried home to Concord a copy of the new Leaves of Grass, read it closely, and recorded its impact in the Journal for early December. His faith in democracy was more easily cultivated in the village, where he found "kindred of mine" in the "humble, reserved countrymen" he had known for twenty years but never fully befriended. Whitman was a *Phallus impudicus* of a poet, surprisingly erotic and suggestive even to a New England bachelor. Thoreau saw a short, gnarled tree full of unreleased leaves, an image of himself, and mused, "There was a match found for me at last. I fell in love with a shrub oak."

Two of Whitman's poems were special favorites, the ones later titled "Song of Myself" and "Crossing Brooklyn Ferry." In their celebration of ecstasy and the present moment Thoreau saw a principle his Journal had also caught, that life is ultimately congruent: "I have never got over my surprise that I should have been born into the most estimable place in all the world, and in the very nick of time, too."

In a letter to Blake on December 7 Thoreau both praised and

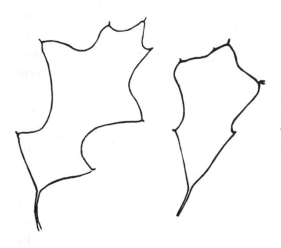

". . . these leaves still have
a kind of life in them. . . .
Their figures never weary
my eye."

censured *Leaves of Grass*, identifying with it as a sympathetic reader. If
the eroticism was shocking, "whose experience is it that we are reminded of?" If the interminable catalogues—when the poet threw in
"a thousand brick"—were dull, Thoreau knew he shared that fault.
He also sensed that the central metaphor, "Myself," represented all of
humanity: the book had no "brag or egoism. . . . He is a great fellow."

Whitman had become an analogue for Thoreau's own vocation.
Leaves of Grass did him "more good than any reading for a long time,"
he told Blake. The Journal entry for December 6 described a clump of
decayed leaves as an emblem for his own writing: "Not merely a mat-
ted mass of fibres like a sheet of paper, but a perfect organism and system in itself, so that no mortal has ever yet discerned or explored its
beauty."

But taking his leaves before the public verified all too certainly
how few mortals saw their merits. After his lecture "Walking, or The
Wild" was poorly received at Amherst, New Hampshire, he suspended
all talk of democracy, fuming in an entry on December 18 about the
"stupidity of most of these country towns." Then he decided to revise
the lecture extensively. Although he had compiled an index of additional passages in mid-1854, Thoreau did not use them in the new version—its latest material came from an entry in February 1852.

The Journal dwindled appreciably in late December, as the rewriting process created several problems. He thought also of writing on "Dry Leaves," especially of the shrub oak, yet was pleased to think how this species "serves no vulgar purpose." Blake wanted him to speak in Worcester, but Thoreau wrote on December 31 that his new thoughts had "not taken the shape of lectures" and the old ones were unsatisfactory.

The shape of "Walking, or The Wild" troubled him also, for it was virtually two lectures in one, as its title suggested. Half of the text described the pleasures of rambling in the local countryside; half, the joys of roaming far afield from civilization. His walk on January 7, 1857, was an attempt to get Concord out of his head, yet his description of the woods persistently used images of town. His thinking seemed as divided as the lecture; the same day he recalled a persistent childhood dream of two flat surfaces, one "Rough" and horrifying, the other delicious and "Smooth." He felt the two symbolized his waking life: "In other words it is Insanity and Sanity."

In less dramatic terms this dichotomy represented wilderness and society, the two elements that had not fused in his current lecture. By mid-January he was greatly depressed over the state of his career. Lectures would never make him popular; the Journal entries were satisfying but completely unknown. His situation resembled the snow cave Eddy Emerson had just built. Thoreau paid a visit on January 20, admired the cave's interior, but saw one major defect: "we might lie in that hole screaming for assistance in vain, while travellers were passing along twenty feet distant."

On February 3 he lectured in Framingham (on an unspecified topic) and felt like "a mountebank pretending to walk on air"; then he noticed that these good citizens rarely walked anywhere: around their town ran a single footpath in the snow, barely six feet wide, from which no one diverged throughout the winter. What force could "Walking, or The Wild" have on such narrow, circumscribed lives? Moreover, he had delivered an abridged version of this lecture in Worcester a few years earlier; when he finally accepted Blake's invitation on February 6, Thoreau was careful to say that he now had a longer, two-part text: "You may call it 'The Wild'—or 'Walking' or both —whichever you choose."

The lecture Thoreau read in Worcester on February 12 brought this phase of his career to an ambiguous close. He was persistently muddled about the text, saying on April 26 that he could not copy "my essay on the wild" because it was only prepared "for lectures." In March 1862 he finally revised it for the *Atlantic Monthly*, telling the editors that a "natural joint" at the center would allow printing it in two installments. This manuscript had only minor changes, mostly firming up parallels between the two halves, and in print it appeared under a single title. The posthumous version of "Walking" (June 1862) was not greatly altered from the lecture Thoreau delivered in February 1857.

"Walking" strongly resembles *Cape Cod*, for this excursion also considers the meaning of America's discovery and settlement. It unfolds in four movements: a brief opening "word for Nature"; two contrasting segments, on "the art of Walking" and "in search of the Wild"; and a synthesizing conclusion, "with regard to Nature I live a sort of border life" (Ex, 161, 185, 207). The form is circular but not as symmetrical as the calendar of *Walden*; in "Walking" Thoreau describes "a parabola" that has a narrow axis but a long horizontal line, "like one of those cometary orbits which have been thought to be non-returning curves" (Ex, 176).

The curvature in "Walking" lies between the poles of Freedom and Order, a duality that had vexed Thoreau for the past year. Whether his entries were green or ripened, their stories of turtles, pigs, fungi, and dreams repeatedly sought a point of balance between unconscious impulse and conscious design. As a child he was frightened by the alternation of Rough and Smooth, but in this essay he made them congruous at last.

The opening declaration for "absolute freedom and wildness" thus modulates at once into gentle sauntering, a going out and coming back "to the old hearth-side" of home (Ex, 161–62). Thoreau's claim, familiar in the Journal pages, is that discovery in America is not material but spiritual; that it can occur even on an old abandoned road (Ex, 172–74). With some exaggeration he says that his favorite walks in Concord are to the west, where he sees unbroken forest and "no towns nor cities" (Ex, 176). In fact, the west quarter was well settled in his day, and he often walked elsewhere to avoid the factories at Acton and at Damon's Mills.

At a deeper level Thoreau wants to challenge the myth of western settlement—celebrated by both Emerson and Whitman—by posing a radical paradox: that America's Manifest Destiny is not to go on living forever but to die. From classical mythology he draws a geographical trope: Americans have crossed the "Lethean" Atlantic, forgetting their Old World ways, and the "Lethe of the Pacific" is "perhaps one more chance for the race left before it arrives on the bank of the Styx" (Ex, 177). The demise of America is written in its orientation: in the west lies a bright place on the horizon—where the sun inevitably goes down.

Sunset becomes Thoreau's metaphor for the life-in-death that he sees as America's destiny. The bountiful fertility of western lands is a source of pride, but he thinks this material wealth obliges the nation to evolve a higher form of culture: "Else to what end does the world go on, and why was America discovered?" (Ex, 183). The movement of a walker is *sauntering*, toward a Holy Land (*Sainte Terre*) that comprises all previous nations.

The driving force in this parabolic orbit is not civilization but the Wild, which Thoreau calls "the preservation of the World" (Ex, 185). The Wild is both primordial and millennial, the origin of all life and the state to which it ultimately returns. Thus men are instinctively drawn from cultivated fields to remote swamps and forests: "There is the strength, the marrow of Nature" (Ex, 190) and of their humanity as well. This relationship obliges men not to exploit the world but to nurture and preserve it.

The argument has implications for artists as well as pioneers: "uncivilized free and wild thinking" is the basis for a culture rooted in the living earth, not in dead traditions (Ex, 193). Thoreau recognizes that mythology is the primal source of human art, "the great dragon-tree" that thrives on "the decay of other literatures" (Ex, 195), and that figure confirms his sense of America's transitory role in history: "Perchance, when, in the course of ages, American liberty has become a fiction of the past . . . poets of the world will be inspired by American mythology" (Ex, 195–96).

Thoreau's eschatological view of the West arises from Eastern sources, especially the Hindu doctrine of reincarnation, which holds that destiny unreels in successive cycles, the parabolas of life and

death. By conserving its vast wilderness areas America can slow this
process but not avoid it, "preparing a mould against a distant future,
by the annual decay of the vegetation which it supports" (Ex, 202).

He thus depicts human destiny as transience, a ceaseless journey
over permanent ground, and he concludes by advising the nation—
through his own example—to live "a sort of border life, on the confines of a world into which I make occasional and transient forays
only" (Ex, 207). He gives three examples of forays in the Concord
area: first to a fictitious "Spaulding's farm," where the family lives in
"cohabitancy" with its natural surroundings; then to a tall pine tree,
whose topmost branches hide superb flowers, well out of most men's
sight; and finally to a hillside meadow to watch "a remarkable sunset,"
the closure of day becoming the promise of new mornings to come. In
this last epiphany all shadows stretch eastward, the western sides of
objects gleam "like the boundary of Elysium, and the sun on our backs
seemed like a gentle herdsman driving us home at evening" (Ex, 213).
The parabola has closed; oncoming darkness is a Holy Land toward
which all walkers saunter, there to find "a great awakening light, as
warm and serene and golden as on a bankside in autumn" (Ex, 214).

"Walking" illustrates many of the changes that came to Thoreau's writings after *Walden*. In this lecture-essay, as in *Cape Cod*, he
moves away from problems of self-definition toward broader issues of
history and culture. His gaze had turned outward, to Concord and the

". . . a bow about the sun
became quite distinct. . . .
But higher up was an arc
of a distant rainbow. . . .
Is this what is called a
parhelion?"

larger world its landscape represents. Preserving that world had become his major concern, and his role as artist was to emulate the *vates* or prophetic bard that Whitman had defined. Thoreau was anticipating the continental vision of Whitman's poem "Passage to India" (1871): *Cape Cod* explores the beginning of America on its East Coast; "Walking" foresees its end in the Far West.

Yet for all their eloquence and formal integrity, both works betray the "greenness" that also characterizes Thoreau's Journal for this period. The language in "Walking" is often inconsistent, ranging from a somber clarity to rough stretches of puns, paradoxes, and forced analogies. The fanciful play on *saunter* and *Sainte Terre*, so important to "Walking," is contrived, and his use of conventional religious terms (*grace, redemption, sin,* and *penance*) is ambiguous, suggesting doctrines quite alien to Thoreau's Oriental views. And, perhaps most distressing, he alters some natural facts—about "actinic" or ultraviolet rays —in order to make baroque moral points (Ex, 202).

These flaws contradict the essay's praise of a natural style, words nailed "to their primitive senses" (Ex, 194). Rarely does he strike the pungent brevity of his best Journal entries on animals: "The partridge loves peas, but not those that go with her into the pot" (Ex, 162). Perhaps the fault lay with Thoreau's preparation of "Walking," for the changes he made after 1852 were largely formal and intellectual, rather than stylistic: he built a stronger design but neglected to accumulate fresh contents.

In the Book of his Journal he had been preoccupied with growth rather than maturity; hence he neglected to mend this early piece completely. All of his later essays developed rapidly from the Journal; they more clearly measured its emerging concerns and achievements. When a correspondent requested a copy of "Walking," Thoreau declined on April 26. A finished work was less satisfactory than one in progress, still green and alive: "you are turning a broad furrow among the books, but I trust that some very private journal all the while holds its own through their midst."

7
THE ACCUMULATING GRISTS

I trust there will appear in this Journal some flow, some
gradual filling of the springs and raising of the streams, that
the accumulating grists may be ground.

—OCTOBER 26, 1857

By early 1857 Thoreau's studies in Concord had turned from detailed natural facts to the broader subject of community. In mid-February he was writing about local antiquities, the cellar holes of houses that dated back to Concord's founding. His personal life was now more governed by social relations. On February 22 he expressed his unhappiness over a "neighbor, who was once my friend," for whom he felt both contempt and affection: "While I think I have broken one link, I have been forging another."

The solitary was learning to accept his place in society. In early March Alcott described a growing mood of gentleness in Thoreau, still sly in conversation but given to boyish whistling when he left the parlor. Instead of writing about his intellectual friends Thoreau preferred to describe his rude, practical neighbors: a muskrat trapper like John Goodwin worked outdoors in all weather, consuming little fuel; Emerson sat at his desk and burned many cords of wood. On March 20 Thoreau dined at the Emersons' and talked of fish and turtles with the famed naturalist Louis Agassiz, but four days later the Journal gave more space to a similar dialogue with Humphrey Buttrick, a local hunter.

Thoreau attributed these preferences to his collecting habits. A first report of a conversation, he wrote on March 24, lacked its "picturesque and dramatic points"; it therefore should be considered later "from many points of view and in various moods." He had often said this about his studies; the concern for accurate reports about conversation and perspectives was new. Although writing about facts, he was beginning to incorporate the fictive elements of character and dialogue into his daily narratives. The Journal enhanced his memories; he could write, look back over previous entries, and write of them again—as on March 27: "The men and things of to-day are wont to lie fairer and truer in to-morrow's memory."

A clear sign of changing values was his decision in early April to observe the arrival of spring at New Bedford. Thoreau's later account of this trip emphasizes human relations. At the outset he recalls being "touched with compassion" by an incident in Concord, when an elderly vagrant was treated rudely by a tradesman. He is pleased to meet Alcott, Channing, and Blake on the trip, but he records none of their evening talks (unlike Alcott). Instead, a lively outdoor scene of villagers fishing for smelts catches Thoreau's eye on April 11, and he also writes several long entries on the character of his genial host, Daniel Ricketson.

Ricketson had first sought out Thoreau after reading *Walden* in 1854, and their friendship had slowly warmed through letters and visits. Although not acute, Ricketson was quick and merry; he played Sancho Panza to Thoreau's graver mien. On April 10 Thoreau describes at length Ricketson's "Shanty," which he saw as a metaphor for his cluttered, sentimental friend: "I found all his peculiarities faithfully expressed." Thoreau obviously enjoyed his trip, yet the Journal says little about his own behavior. In a letter on April 7 Alcott detected a "solitary & sad-seeming" air in the quips and jokes that Thoreau and Channing exchanged, but Ricketson later recalled a jovial evening when Thoreau entertained the company with songs and antic dances, even tromping on Alcott's toes for comic effect.

At home Thoreau continued to think and write about the people he had met at New Bedford. On April 23 he described a twenty-year-old Irish-American schoolteacher named Kate Brady. Young women rarely appear in the Journal, and Thoreau's picture of Kate is so attractive that some readers think he may have been in love. That seems unlikely. His tone is neutral; mostly he stresses Kate's vigorous, independent ways. She led an outdoor life, loved nature as he did, planned to run a farm without family or servants. Here was an original woman, "not professedly reformatory," and he admired her instinctive freedom from conventional roles. Kate was an equal, one who shared his affections: "All nature is my bride."

His tolerance for others was growing. On April 26 and 27 he wrote two more accounts of Ricketson, sympathizing with his fear of lightning and of death. On the latter date he wrote to a correspondent who had asked him to explain the story of the lost hound, bay horse, and turtle-dove in *Walden*. Thoreau replied, "How shall we account for our pursuits if they are original? We get the language with which to describe our various lives out of a common mint."

This generosity also reflects his changed social status in Concord. The years had transformed his early reputation for shiftlessness; as he noted on April 16, people now spoke of him and his friends, the "Walden Pond Society," as a respectable alternative to church. Surveying had also helped; he was widely admired for his accuracy and honesty. He ran all the lot lines, laid out most of the town's new streets and buildings. Surveying made him part of Concord's social machinery; it also provided field notes for his private work in the Journal.

Visitors to the Thoreau house in these years describe how Henry presided at the family table, listening courteously to his talkative mother at one end, addressing quips to his smiling (and slightly deaf) father at the other. His daily stint of writing made him active and happy; it gave him a high level of confidence. A trip on the Sudbury River on Sunday, May 3, seemed to him naturally blessed, for he could imagine this voyage going even farther south, to the Caribbean and beyond: "All isles seem fortunate and blessed to-day; all capes are of Good Hope."

Probably Thoreau had not read Melville's *The Confidence-Man* (published in April 1857); yet this entry exactly counters the novel's theme and form—a river journey that heads south into increasing darkness and despair. Melville's bitter travesty of "confidence" includes caricatures of Emerson and Thoreau, in Chapters 36–40; he drew the profile of Thoreau from suggestions in A *Week* and *Walden*, ironically contrasting their themes of friendship and solitude. Here was the liability of publishing, for by now Thoreau had grown beyond those works. Readers could infer a stereotype from his publications, but he had a private Book for recording his days of good hope. Melville himself lacked this resource: his early books created a popular image of "the man who lived with cannibals," which obscured the achievements of his later, darker years.

Thoreau's Journal was no longer a hermitage; it had become an open history of his people and land. His subjects in early May ranged from toads to trousers, but each of these disparate accounts sanctioned the integrity of his work: "I hear these sounds, have these reminiscences, only when well employed . . . doing something from a sense of duty, even unconsciously."

At times he could still be difficult, even with friends of long standing. In late May Ricketson paid a return visit to Concord, despite Thoreau's discouragement. During this period he complained to the Journal about "notional nervous invalids" who would not travel outdoors. Emerson was a better companion; his journal for May 20 said Thoreau had "perfect magnanimity" on their walks and made no secret of his rare birds or plants. Edward Hoar, who shared Thoreau's love of botany, later recalled that long hikes and boat rides were his way of testing: "If you flinched at anything, he had no more use for you."

Even when the Journal celebrated being alone, Thoreau's values were less egocentric. A long entry (2,700 words) for May 29–30 described being caught in a heavy shower and taking refuge in a cave. Reversing Plato's allegory, Thoreau looked out and saw the substance of reality. At first he felt secure, but then a new storm roused his fear of lightning. In a second report Thoreau recalled that he sang "Tom Bowling" in the cave, "and the dampness seemed favorable to my voice."

Again he had found an advantage in collecting a second view of events. "Tom Bowling" was his favorite song because it reminded him of John; its sentimental verses tell of a young sailor—manly, jovial, friendly—who once worked hard below and above decks, "But now he's gone aloft." This song, with all its connotations of friendship and nostalgia, had ended his rift with Ricketson, who had sent him the sheet music for "Tom Bowling" only two weeks earlier.

By the same token, Thoreau could exclude society from the Journal when he preferred. Before the rainstorm he had also walked with Emerson, but the entry did not say so. In his own journal Emerson praised the "idleness" of their stroll, which suited his complacent view of Thoreau: "Our young men have nothing to do. . . . Their friends like them best if they do nothing new or important."

In fact, Thoreau was busy in early June preparing for a fourth trip to Cape Cod, in search of material for his unpublished book. As a companion he wanted Channing, who liked to travel incognito, dressed as "a common man." But Channing reneged at the last minute, so Thoreau went alone to the Cape. He was there for ten days, June 11 to 21, after which he wrote a 15,000-word account in the Journal, adding data from reference books and keying passages to previous entries. In July he also entered some final notes in a "Fact book"; yet *Cape Cod* includes none of this material, probably because it did not fit the themes and narrative form he had built in early 1855.

Although this trip moved in the same northerly direction as its predecessors, Thoreau stayed inland instead of walking the beach. He took "retired" roads away from the shore, looked at ponds and forests, avoided houses by walking "across lots," as was his custom in Concord. He was in a retiring mood himself: though he told one host some

---

"I go along a sandy road . . . between slight gray fences . . . looking agreeably loose and irregular."

stories of the Viking discoveries, he evaded a direct question as to the meaning of the hound, bay horse, and turtledove passage in *Walden*, saying only, "Well, Sir, I suppose we have all had our losses."

In the Journal Thoreau wrote that walking "by solitary sandy paths" through remote areas was the main attraction of his trip. The few people he met were not inspiring, and he could say little positive of villages that seemed "as strange as if I were in China." *Cape Cod* stresses the hospitality of villagers; on this trip he found people too wary of strangers to answer their doors. His appearance may not have helped. At Truro he picked up a dead sea petrel and tied it to his umbrella, then slung it over his shoulder like a rifle: "they may have taken me for a crazy man."

On June 20 he revisited scenes described in *Cape Cod* but found them changed: the bare remains of an old shipwreck, a well-provisioned survival hut, improved communications at Highland Light. The only similarity to his previous trips was consistently foggy weather. On his last night at Provincetown he had one useful experience, for the beds at Pilgrim House were infested with bedbugs, the rooftops with prowling cats: "Such is your *Pilgerruhe* or Pilgrims'-Rest." But Thoreau used nothing from this trip; it was a sojourn at odds with his book—and his prevailing mood of sociability. After returning home he quickly invited his friends from Worcester to come sailing in Concord, "this quite *Mediterranean* shore."

———

Although Thoreau told a correspondent on July 8, "I like a private life, & cannot bear to have the public in mind," he was already planning another trip for literary purposes, this time to Maine. Recently he had discovered several errors in maps of Cape Cod and Concord; since those for Maine were quite primitive, he had to plot his intinerary cautiously. His initial plan, described in a letter on July 11, was to make a great west-to-east circuit, starting at Moosehead Lake and going north along the Penobscot and Allagash rivers into Canada, then home "by whatever course we prefer," probably the St. John River.

The final plan was shorter but still circular, and it passed through

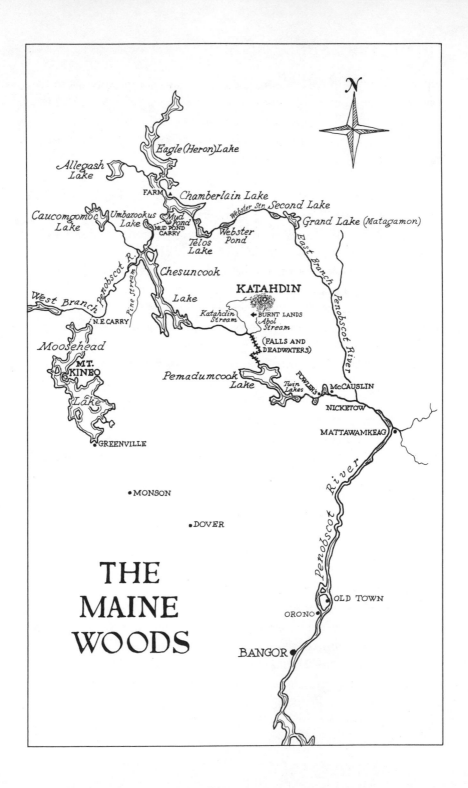

THE
MAINE
WOODS

deep wilderness country. Thoreau and his two companions, Edward
Hoar from Concord and Joseph Polis, an Indian guide from Oldtown,
spent eighteen days in a bark canoe, going from Moosehead Lake to
the Penobscot River (West Branch), then through a series of lakes
—Chesuncook, Umbazooksus, Mud Pond—into the Allagash waters
of Chamberlain and Heron (now Eagle Lake). Instead of going north
along the Allagash they turned south on Chamberlain, passing
through more lakes—Telos, Webster, Matagamon—to the Penobscot
River (East Branch) again.

Their itinerary followed a route created by loggers in the 1840s to
link Bangor and the distant north woods. On his trips in 1846 and
1853 Thoreau had retraced short loops, against the river current for
half of each journey; this time he made one continuous circuit, from
west to east, always moving downstream—"a very important consideration," as he told a correspondent on January 28, 1858.

The trip was an arduous undertaking for a forty-year-old man.
Thoreau paddled for days on the great open lakes, fighting headwinds
and high waves. He packed heavy supplies over long carry paths; he
endured the summer conditions of Maine, where the weather is fickle
and the insects eternal. The food was monotonous, but not his companions: Polis was the best source of Indian lore Thoreau had ever
met, and Hoar shared his passion for collecting rare plants. Twice
Hoar got lost on the carries, first with Thoreau at Mud Pond, and then
by himself on Webster Stream. The whole journey was an exciting adventure, captured by Thoreau as it occurred in his habitual packet of
notes.

After the trip he began to write up the notes as Journal entries,[*]
setting aside pages both in volume XXIII and volume XXIV while he
continued to write current entries about Concord in August and September. The entries on Maine began as an uncensored account, with
both Hoar and Polis clearly identified, not always in a flattering light.
On July 26 Polis had rejected some fish as inedible, saying they were
Michigan, "(& that Michigan means 'shit.' I remembered that it was
the name of the lake where the Les Preants dwelt)." (*Preant* means

[*]Omitted from the 1906 text.

"stench.") Soon Thoreau began to shape the entries into a story, changing the names Hoar and Polis to "my companion" and "the Indian," making the itinerary clearer, polishing his style with revisions. As he told Ricketson on August 18, the best writing in nature always came "simply & directly, as a stone falls to the ground." After finishing the entries he revised them for consistency and decorum. Again, scatology was a problem: Joe Polis's persistent diarrhea on August 2 became a euphemistic "colic."

On August 29 (misdated "July") Thoreau commented in the Journal on this work, saying he wanted to create "an indistinct prospect, a distant view" of Maine rather than a strictly literal one: "The most valuable communication or news consists of hints and suggestions." Some hints he found throughout September by studying the trees in Concord. On September 25 one sight was especially suggestive. A young ash, sprouted from an old stump, had grown into a shape as handsome as the original: "The tree thus has its idea to be lived up to and . . . fills an invisible mould in the air." In a similar fashion his Maine story was a recasting of the Journal, filling its mold yet providing new hints and suggestions. The story thus emulated many entries he had written in the Journal since February; reports about houses, trappers, sailing, and hiking that gained clarity and drama through repetition. Although faithful to the facts, his narrative could become a fictive circle, bringing a larger meaning to its themes, events, and characters.

In keeping with these plans, Thoreau used the Journal in late September as a place to write entries on Concord and draft passages about Maine. Emerson grew weary with the wilderness theme, saying in his Journal that "Henry avoids commonplace, & talks birch-bark to all comers, & reduces them all to the same insignificance." But repetition was important to Thoreau; in early October he was rereading entries and drafting inserts about Maine in the same order, catching up loose ends in the story without changing its circular structure. At the same time, some new inserts came from his current entries: meditative descriptions of Concord's autumn foliage, written on October 6 to 12, provoked a severe critique of lumbering practices in Maine.

In the inserts Thoreau made "the Indian" a fuller and more representative spokesman for his race, a role suggested by conversations with George Minott, a local farmer who told stories "with fidelity and gusto to the minutest details," like a village Herodotus. Thoreau wanted his landscape descriptions to be equally accurate, for during October he read most of Ruskin's *Modern Painters* and later said its ideas were "singularly good and encouraging, though not without crudeness and bigotry." He shared Ruskin's distaste for sentimental personification, the "pathetic fallacy" that ascribes human feelings to natural forms and events. Ruskin said the best poets control this tendency, seeing always in a flower its "plain and leafy fact." In his story Thoreau, too, wanted a balance between facts and feelings.

Some of the Journal entries that fall were leading him away from Maine. In mid-October he wished to summarize again the progress of autumnal tints, a subject conceived as a literary project in 1853. The materials had accumulated each fall, but as yet he had no structural plan for them. Such long-deferred works were natural in his career; they encouraged him to learn and grow each day without postponing the rigors of composition: "Is not the poet bound to write his own biography? Is there any other work for him but a good journal?"

This ideal matched the day-to-day progress of Thoreau's travel story, but unfortunately it also justified his dilatory pace. By late October he should have been extracting a draft from the Journal, for—like the town's rivers—it was flooding its banks: "I trust there will appear in this Journal some flow, some gradual filling of the springs and raising of the streams, that the accumulating grists may be ground."

The source of his problem lay in that dual metaphor, for the Journal was both a continuously flowing stream and a pile of raw materials that needed processing and refinement. He admired the native properties of his Book, but his responsibilities as an artist demanded that some productive work emerge from it: "The perfect correspondence of Nature and man, so that he is at home in her!"

As an artist his practical solution was to arrange man and nature in complementary patterns. By mid-November he was going over his Maine woods passages with a pencil, making further revisions, keying them to slots in the trip's chronology. He worked for expository effects rather than historical accuracy, playing down his role as navigator of the canoe party in order to stress Joe Polis's skill at orientation. In the current Journal for early November he noted similar instances of nature's artistry: reflections that framed landscape pictures, thimbleberry shoots with a coat of bloom: "It must be invested with a similar bloom by the imagination of the reader."

With that hope—and latent fear—in mind, Thoreau at last began to write a separate draft, at first titled "The Allegash and Webster Stream East Branch" (MW, 364). Although James Russell Lowell, now editor of the *Atlantic Monthly*, was expressing interest in the story, Thoreau held off responding until his draft was complete. In this version "Allegash" (Thoreau's spelling) grew more compact, the desired effect of his tedious revising. As he told Blake on November 16, that was the main burden of writing: "Not that the story need be long, but it will take a long while to make it short."

Compacting the wilderness, grinding its grist for civilized readers, was difficult. In late November he mused in the Journal about this work. He had spent forty years in Concord "learning the language of these fields" and would have happily spent more on its swamps and ponds. The entry that spanned volumes XXIV and XXV intimated his fear of extracting a story from the Journal's flow: "how much, from the habit of regarding writing as an accomplishment, is wasted on form."

After finishing a long draft in early January 1858, he decided to read only part as a Lyceum lecture, telling a correspondent that he was uncertain as to "how soon I shall print it." This story was his first attempt to announce in public the changes that had occurred since "Walking": the patient accumulation of facts, new interests in social and cultural themes, a concern for depicting human character. Yet Thoreau was a secondary figure in "Allegash": its main focus was on another life and personality—not Raleigh, Carlyle, or the doubled self of *A Week* and *Walden*, but an Indian who spoke "out of a peculiar remoteness" from the worlds of Concord and Boston (MW, 158).

That figure seemed to discourage him from printing the story at all. On January 23 Thoreau told Lowell that "Allegash" reported Polis's words and deeds "very faithfully" and that because he was likely to read the *Atlantic*, "I could not face him again." Thoreau offered instead his old "Moosehunting" lecture, based on the 1853 trip to Maine, which would take a month to prepare for publication.

This concern for Polis's feelings was a flimsy pretext. Polis was rarely identified by name in "Allegash," and little there would have embarrassed him, for Thoreau had suppressed several unflattering details and enhanced others to make "the Indian" representative. Polis's literacy and civilized values were important issues in "Allegash," and surely Thoreau had not built a rationale for suppression upon one of the story's main features. No, the reasons for delay were probably less generous: Thoreau trusted neither his portrayal of "the Indian" nor the editor who had solicited this work.

Thoreau and Lowell had not been on friendly terms since the summer of 1838, when Lowell decided that Thoreau was aping Emerson. He made this taunt public in A *Fable for Critics* (1848), later wrote a mixed review of A *Week*, calling its digressions "snags," and he never reviewed *Walden*. In taste and temperament he was Thoreau's exact opposite, an elegant and witty urbanite whose notion of the wilderness was expressed in his essay "A Moosehead Journal" (1853), a satirical burlesque about the same country Thoreau had described in "Moosehunting."

During February Thoreau turned to revising that old lecture, which he now called "Chesuncook." He also made changes in "Allegash" and spliced elements of both works together. He was too busy to write much in the Journal that month, and on February 22 he advised Lowell that "Chesuncook" would take another two weeks to complete. In private, Thoreau was anxious. On March 2 he complained that few magazines shared his themes, of "life and death and good books"; then three days later he attended a lecture by an Indian whose companion was the brother of Joe Polis—a small world, indeed, among these literate savages! The lecturer spoke of an Indian's "far off" life, and the audience laughed rudely at his English. Thoreau wanted protection: that same day he had turned in the first eighty pages of "Chesuncook," retaining an option "to publish it in another form" and asking specifically to see the magazine proofs. Lowell scheduled the essay to run in three segments, June through August.

Although he had to copy only fifty more pages of "Chesuncook," Thoreau dawdled at this task nearly ten weeks. Often he was drawn back to the Journal, where the flow of entries was a welcome alternative to grinding public grist. As he wrote on April 2, "It is not important that the poet should say some particular thing, but should speak in harmony with nature."

This year was "a remarkable spring for reptile life," and Thoreau spent many weeks in April and May following the reproductive cycle of frogs, from spawn to tadpoles. He was fascinated by the stages of their metamorphosis, a slow, barely discernible progress that counseled the same pace to his work: "You conquer them by superior patience and immovableness." Frog-watching also had its comical results: on April 28 a farmer saw Thoreau standing motionless for hours and came to help, thinking this was "his father, who had been drinking some of Pat Haggerty's rum, and had lost his way home."

The reptilian ways were leading Thoreau away from his work on "Chesuncook." Frogs and toads were "perfect thermometers, hydrometers, and barometers," he wrote on May 6, not mechanical instruments but elements of an organic cycle. A few days later he argued this issue with Emerson, comparing his involvement in his new studies to the life of a hermit he had seen in Maine. Emerson had a mechanical response for his journal: "a man was not made to live in a swamp, but a frog."

In early May Thoreau saw in his entries a sound barometer of Concord; he could identify a farmer by the sound of his voice, or the origin of a tree by the grain in some freshly cut planks. Millwork at the *Atlantic Monthly* was far less constructive. After Lowell wrote an urgent "Bulletin" demanding the missing copy, Thoreau icily replied on May 18 that he was still waiting for the June segment of proofs. Of course he wished "that the paper be disposed of soon"; the remaining pages were sent that morning. When the proofs for July arrived his suspicions were confirmed: several sentences had been canceled. He restored them with a marginal "Stet."

Before the July issue appeared he had time to visit New York City and then Mount Monadnock, in southern New Hampshire. One highlight of the latter trip was seeing on June 4 a virgin forest of white pines, "so round and perpendicular that my eyes slid off." Late in the month he saw that Lowell had cut down one pine in "Chesuncook." Despite Thoreau's "Stet" this sentence had been deleted: "It is as immortal as I am, and perchance will go to as high a heaven, there to tower above me still" (MW, 122). He sent Lowell a blistering letter

"the white spruce has its branches retraced or turned downward"

on June 22, denouncing his "mean and cowardly" act as the suppression of "a sincere thought," and flaying the mismanagement of his journal: "Is this the avowed character of the Atlantic Monthly?"

Thoreau's letter made valid points, but he was not being entirely rational. The omission may have been accidental, one of those lapses that can occur between an editor and his printers. Lowell was certainly not an orthodox bigot; other pantheistic sentiments in "Chesuncook" had passed unchallenged. (In one of his own poems, "To a Pine Tree," published in 1845, Lowell expressed a similar veneration for a tree on Katahdin, "who towerest / From thy bleak throne to heaven.") If Lowell deliberately suppressed Thoreau's sentence, the grounds could have been stylistic: it appeared at the end of two long paragraphs on the pine tree's "spirit," its soul / sap, and this final apotheosis made rather much of the conceit. These are plausible defenses; Lowell apparently never made his own.

In Lowell Thoreau had found a scapegoat, thus safely diverting anger that might otherwise have turned against himself. This specter of outside interference justified the delays and anxieties that accompanied his long struggle to separate "Allegash" and "Chesuncook" from the Journal. The very charges hurled at Lowell could describe Thoreau's working methods: in the stories he, too, had deleted sentences, "put words into my mouth," suppressed opinions and details. Meanwhile the Journal had flowed on, patiently recounting the lives of frogs and his city or mountain journeys. Its character held, but he had lost touch by venturing into a marketplace that would never satisfy his private needs.

Moreover, by publishing "Chesuncook" instead of "Allegash" in

1858 Thoreau again gave to the public an example of outmoded work. Although he did finally prepare "Allegash" for print in early 1862, the changes made then were not extensive. The essay published as "The Allegash and East Branch" in *The Maine Woods* (1864) was essentially the lecture he gave in early 1858, before revising "Chesuncook."

————

Thoreau had stressed the virtues of his circular, downstream itinerary, but that plan did not tell him how to end his story satisfactorily. On April 23, 1862, he told Channing it was "in a knot I cannot untie" and two weeks later he died with the words "Moose—Indian" on his lips. "Allegash" almost precluded closure, for it described a deep wilderness country that seemed infinite, outside the bounds of historical time.

Despite Thoreau's misgivings, much of "Allegash" works as a handsome replica of his Journal entries: the story moves in its geographic arc, through days that cycle from light to dark, storm to clearing, and these patterns frame rounded and recurring observations by the author. Many images reinforce this motif: caribou and black dippers that circle while feeding, a ring of foxfire found in the woods (MW, 162, 166, 179). They complement the canoe party's steady progress across the lakes, never in a direct course "but a succession of curves from point to point" (MW, 186).

Thoreau reminds readers of his downstream course by noting how difficult even a brief reversal was (MW, 196) and how easily they could have followed the Allagash into Canada, as Polis suggested (MW, 232). But staying on the Penobscot loop has two natural advantages: it takes the party into wild, unsettled country, and the downstream current constantly moves them along (MW, 243). Edward Hoar becomes lost for many hours when he walks downstream ahead of the others, but eventually the current reunites them (MW, 261). Thoreau also notices that the area's land forms follow the direction of flowing water (MW, 271), just as the journey alters its pace according to the rate of current—slow in fast or "strong water," swift in the calm "dead water."

The story covers fifteen days, four each on the approach and departure, a full week in the center for the wilderness trip from West to East Branch. The central chapters vary in length and intensity, linked by the rhythms of loss and discovery: finding foxfire, getting lost on Mud Pond Carry, losing and then finding Hoar. This pattern suggests a compensatory force at work in the wilderness, rounding each day into regular cycles. Joe Polis is most in touch with this power: "No use, can't do anything in the dark; come morning, then we find 'em" (MW, 260).

Certain refrains punctuate the daily round: the trees, moose, and insect pests accompany all forward motion, even serving as crude measurements of time and space. Mosquitoes are active from dusk to midnight, then quiet till dawn; some lakes are too wide for them to cross, "and this, perhaps, will serve to distinguish a large lake from a small one" (MW, 231).

Some rhythms Thoreau invents, using expository devices to cluster information at useful points. He gives lists of plants, arranged "in the order of their abundance" (MW, 176); makes synopses of common routines, like how the party crossed lakes or established camps (MW, 189, 197); and provides firelight meditations on the day's experiences (MW, 240). He also inserts editorials or historical asides, based on later research but tied to the journey: a long condemnation of logging dams erupts when he first sees how rising water has killed trees along the shore of Lake Chamberlain (MW, 227–30).

Thoreau creates a formal congruity in "Allegash" by setting these cyclical patterns around the inner circle of his two main characters, "the Indian" and himself. Although he did not have a novelist's flair for portraiture, Thoreau had learned—in the Journal—to report action and dialogue accurately, and these effects reinforce the larger implications surrounding the two men, who quickly agree to share their ways: "I would tell him all I knew, and he should tell me all he knew" (MW, 168).

The character of Joe Polis is not entirely positive, which may explain why Thoreau later made him semi-anonymous. As presented, Polis is a man of strong contradictory traits. He is extremely reserved, even more than Thoreau, but eventually he talks freely about private matters. He never addresses Thoreau by name, only refers to "you and I." His "strange remoteness" from the white man expresses itself in silence or brief utterances, yet his peculiar English has a "wild and refreshing sound," and he can imitate animal calls with amazing fidelity (MW, 158, 167–68).

As a surveyor, Thoreau admires Polis's ability to find his way without a map and compass. Instead he reads natural signs, understanding them intuitively: "He does not carry things in his head . . . but relies on himself at the moment" (MW, 185). This knowledge is not magical, but subrational, and Thoreau's stress on that side of the Indian's character allows him to avoid the stereotype of the Noble Savage. Polis carrys an ax and a rifle; he walks the perimeters of an encircled life: "He understood very well both his superiority and inferiority to the whites" (MW, 197).

Yet to a surprising extent this Indian accepts the bourgeois values of civilization. He wants regular meals and a rest on Sunday, thinks it polite to pay calls at the dwellings they pass. Among the Penobscots he is an aristocrat, worth over $6,000 in property. He has been a political leader—important enough to confer with Senator Daniel Webster—and he prefers to hire whites for labor "because 'they keep steady, and know how.' " (MW, 174).

Thoreau is amused by these attitudes, which he has often satirized in white men. Other aspects of the Indian's character seem more indigenous, and possibly suggestive of the race's historical fate. At the base of this "steady and reliable" figure (MW, 158) is a phlegmatic temperament, little given to experimenting in his life and thoughts. Polis is superstitious about climbing Mount Kineo, he prefers familiar canoe routes, and he will not eat wild vegetables—even after his heavy meat diet gives him a miserable "colic." He takes little interest in Thoreau's knowledge, whether of the stars or the merits of mosquito-wash. This creature of fixed habits belongs to the wilderness because he is most like its unchanging realities.

In his own self-portrait Thoreau stresses opposite attitudes, yet with a similar impartiality. Throughout the story he maintains the chatty enthusiasm of a good tourist, finding novelty in experiences that Polis ignores or takes for granted. Thoreau identifies arrowheads

"There is scarcely a square rod of sand exposed, in this neighborhood, but you may find in it the stone arrowheads of an extinct race."

and hornstones for the Indian; he uses a map to describe geological forces that shaped the region. Polis says that Thoreau deserves the title of "great paddler" (MW, 295) and compliments him with a challenge race over one of the carries. Thoreau's persona is adaptable, curious about variables that the Indian either suppresses or ignores.

But the tourist has his inadequacies. Unfamiliar sounds he describes with urban analogies: waterfalls become mills, wind-tossed trees are railroad cars. His civilized background makes him an alien in the wild, which leads to many foolish mistakes. Getting lost on Mud Pond Carry takes some doing; Polis finds Thoreau and Hoar after locating an informant who "could better understand the ways of white men" (MW, 217). The white men are not just erroneous but fearful: each of the carries seems a difficult obstacle to them, and hiking cross-country in this dense forest (as Polis once had) seems an impossible feat: "It made you shudder" (MW, 279).

That sense of alienation contrasts with the Indian, who is confident that he can reach his home in three days by walking cross-country: "It reminded me of Prometheus Bound. Here was travelling of the old heroic kind" (MW, 235). When Hoar is lost on Webster Stream Thoreau becomes furious with the Indian's stoicism, yet after their reunion he sees the transience of his own emotions: "The beauty of the scene may have been enhanced to our eyes by the fact that we had just come together again after a night of some anxiety" (MW, 264).

The two characters in Thoreau's story have a natural density and complexity because they do not conform to racial stereotypes. His report of the story's wilderness setting is equally unconventional, for Thoreau qualifies many sentimental descriptions with rational afterthoughts: "It was a perfect lake of the woods. But this was only a transient gleam, for the rain was not quite over" (MW, 175). Conversely, he knows that "monster" waves and slopes that "gnaw at his heart" are largely psychological, examples of Ruskin's pathetic fallacy at work: "Generally speaking, a howling wilderness does not howl: it is the imagination of the traveller that does the howling" (MW, 219).

His attitude is persistently ambivalent: the best places in Maine are on a middle ground, rough homesteads that lie at the edge of wilderness. He criticizes loggers for not improving the land by clearing and planting it, "but leaving it a wilderness, as they found it" (MW, 228). Yet Chamberlain Farm, the northernmost outpost he visits, seems "a cheerful opening in the woods," where the inhabitants "walked about on Sundays in their clearing somewhat as in a prisonyard" (MW, 240).

Thoreau was ambivalent, too, about "Allegash," a strong piece of writing that he could not agree to release. The story was incomplete; it needed a closing statement to follow his farewell to Polis. On February 22, before his single public reading, he told Lowell, "I shall not hesitate to call names," but then he set aside "Allegash" and prepared "Chesuncook" for the *Atlantic*. After its publication he promised G. W. Curtis on August 18, "I have another and a larger slice to come," but the postponement proved to be permanent: Thoreau never saw "Allegash" reach print.

"Moosehunting" had been a popular lecture, something Thoreau could read to family audiences in Concord and Perth Amboy. From January to March 1858 he recopied much of the text on fresh paper, revising mostly for style, and incorporating one passage on logging from "Allegash" (MW, 364). He told Lowell that the main subjects were "the Moose, the Pine Tree, & the Indian," apparently ranked in that order of importance. In its published form "Chesuncook" is briefer and more polished than "Allegash," but far less ambitious.

The itinerary is casual, at times accidental, and it does not enhance Thoreau's narrative structure. The initial plan is to go north through a series of lakes and connecting streams, then to return over the same route. Going out, the paddling is all downstream, but the party stops earlier than expected because of poor moosehunting; then they have to return against the current.

The story is not clearly divided into daily units, and its swing of action is irregular. Thoreau spends many pages describing two days of travel from Monson to Pine Stream, where a moose is killed. The trip to Lake Chesuncook is anticlimactic, although the lake is the turning point of his travels, and his return journey along an identical route provides little new material—except for an appended account of his later visit to Oldtown, the Indian village near Bangor.

"Chesuncook" derives its form less from Thoreau's artful control of time and space than from the historical order of events. In 1853 this mode of writing had been a new step for him, closely imitating his Journal, but more recently—in *Cape Cod* and "Walking"—he had learned to extract story patterns from the land. While the title "Chesuncook" attributes an importance to locale, Thoreau's emphasis is mainly on action, the moosehunting that provides his true climax.

He prepares readers for that event by some manipulations of context. An image of a school, "a sort of gallows for the pupils" (MW, 88) appears early in the story, although this idea actually occurred on the return trip of September 21, 1853. He gives foreboding tones to a description of hearing a tree fall, "a dull dry rushing sound, with a solid core to it . . . like the shutting of a door in some distant entry" (MW, 103). The killing of a moose is a "tragical business," for these animals resemble "gigantic frightened rabbits," and the victim ultimately proves to be a cow, first seen with her unweaned calf (MW, 110, 115).

In place of narrative logic Thoreau controls the story with firm moralizing: he writes a grimly visual account of the skinning process, in contrast to his auditory impression of the tree's fall. The tree's death is noble and ritualistic; the cow's is *contra naturam*: "it affected the innocence, destroyed the pleasure of my adventure" (MW, 119). The pathetic fallacy works overtime in these episodes, creating moral conflicts that later events do not resolve.

At Chesuncook Thoreau anticipates a higher revelation, and he approaches the lake "with as much expectation as if it had been a university" (MW, 122), yet all he finds there is a modest collection of log huts. On the return trip he spends a night talking with Indians, who appear to have many deficiencies: they are unclean, ignorant of Indian history, unable to translate their language into clear English. He feels they have too readily accepted modern ways, yet criticizes their lack of bourgeois standards: "the Indian is said to cultivate the vices rather than the virtues of the white man" (MW, 146).

Thoreau's condescending view of the Indians is also apparent in his portrait of Joseph Aitteon, the Penobscot guide who plays a supporting role in "Chesuncook." Although he employs an Indian in order "to study his ways" (MW, 95), Thoreau finds that Aitteon is too civilized to be distinctive. He dresses and talks like a white logger, and knows little about the old Indian customs. He is also illiterate and therefore cannot vouch for Thoreau's spellings of Indian words—even of his name, which Thoreau spelled as "Atean" in the 1853 Journal. Joe makes his share of mistakes in the woods, and he offends Thoreau's sense of duty by wandering off "on his own errands" (MW, 106).

This character confirms a wide cultural gap between Thoreau and the Indians; they are not the Noble Savages he expected to find. Most of his critical remarks rest on civilized notions of propriety or training that the Indians do not share, but he also rejects traits of theirs that are stubbornly indigenous. Again, many of his thoughts were five years behind his current values. In 1853 he was still a relative neophyte in his "Indian book" studies; by 1858 he had shed these cultural prejudices and was generally more responsive to human society. "Chesuncook" came from a Journal that was still serving as Thoreau's private mirror; hence his portrait of Aitteon is narrow and unsympathetic.

His own character in "Chesuncook" is that of a complacent lyric poet who offers no touristic advice on provisions or itinerary, and little data of practical import: even his measurements of the moose are wrong, as he found by examining other specimens on the 1857 trip (MW, 113). He is interested less in facts than the analogies he can make of them, "the truest use of the pine" rather than its physical properties (MW, 121).

This poetic sensibility is not a handicap, yet the trait separates him from the crudities of hunters and Indians. While they slaughter moose he collects wild flowers, dreaming of a "solitary and adventurous" year he might spend in the woods, "living like a philosopher" (MW, 101, 119). That motive clearly reflects Thoreau's pre-*Walden* years, but since then he had found other lives to lead and no longer romanticized the role of forest recluse.

In "Chesuncook" Thoreau does not acknowledge the limitations of subjectivity, and thus his vision of the wilderness is appreciative and sentimental, schooled by his reading of Gilpin rather than of Ruskin. Moosehead is "a suitably wild looking sheet of water" and a log house has its "very rich and picturesque look" (MW, 89, 125), notwithstanding his reverence for the uncut pine tree. These values reflect his contradictory aesthetics in the 1850s; he condemns the efforts of settlers to clear parts of the wilderness, yet is pleased to return to the "partially cultivated country" of Concord (MW, 155).

Thoreau's excuse for not submitting "Allegash" to Lowell—Polis's literacy—was revealing: Thoreau feared most readers, not just Polis—he was safer writing his Book than taking chances with an unseen public. That he should have quarreled with Lowell over a sentence about immortality was also significant, for Thoreau had converted that single pine tree into an emblem of his own spirit. As he wrote on June 22 to Lowell, "I do not ask anybody to adopt my opinions, but I do expect that when they ask for them to print, they will print them, or obtain my consent to their alteration and omission." Lowell had assumed the one prerogative Thoreau jealously guarded for himself. He alone would grind the accumulating grists of his Journal, even as it flowed on toward an uncertain destination.

Of Concord Life

It is easier far to recover the history of the trees which stood here a century or more ago than it is to recover the history of the men who walked beneath them. How much do we know—how little more can we know—of these two centuries of Concord life?

—OCTOBER 19, 1860

8
MY KALENDAR

This may not be an annual phenomenon to you. It may not
be in the Greenwich almanac or ephemeris, but it has an
important place in my Kalendar.

—OCTOBER 16, 1859

In June and July of 1858 Thoreau made two long trips to mountains in
New Hampshire: first Monadnock, then Washington and Lafayette.
He wrote long accounts in the Journal, stored them for future use, but
did not live to convert them into publications. In these later years he
continued to write with great energy and control, but with less enthusiasm for going into print. The Journal made a virtue of slow, patient
development: in the turning of its calendar years he seemed to find a
model for his life and work.

Both of his mountain trips gave Thoreau several incidents for
good travel stories. He had made two previous excursions to Monadnock, in 1844 and 1852, but his visit on June 2–4, 1858, was of a
different character: he built a strong shelter, made an exacting survey
of the summit area, and calculated the height of clouds in the valley
below. These events he reported to the Journal at considerable length
(about 9,000 words), building the story from his earliest impression to
a closing view of the mountain as a single, massive form. He ended
with a note to look again at his "last expedition to Monadnock," probably for comparisons with the new botanical data.

"Such springy mountain bogs . . . are evidently the sources of rivers. Lakes of the clouds when they are clear water."

The trip to the White Mountains was on a larger scale—seventeen days of travel with four companions (Edward Hoar, Harrison Blake, Theo Brown, and a guide named William Wentworth), into country Thoreau had not visited since his trip with John in 1839. Like the trips to Cape Cod, this was no sentimental journey; it was an expedition to a part of the White Mountains favored by alpine botanists like Edward Tuckerman. Thoreau's party approached Mount Washington via Pinkham Notch, climbed the bridle path to the summit, then descended by compass reckoning into Tuckerman Ravine, a deep glacial cirque. They had several mishaps: Thoreau tore his nails, and later sprained an ankle; Wentworth set a campfire that got out of control and burned several acres of forest. After four days they left the ravine, journeyed north and west to Franconia Notch, then climbed Mount Lafayette before turning south for home.

The Journal entries for this trip are about 18,000 words in all, and they provide an exhaustive account of mountain scenery and botany. While hiking and camping Thoreau had fresh experiences, but on the whole he did not find as much novel material as he had in Cape Cod or Maine. The story he told had familiar trappings: descriptions of "elevating" mountain scenery on July 2 and 6, an excursional ascent and descent of Mount Washington on July 6–12; then a summary by topic (plants, animals, et cetera) of Mount Lafayette on July 14–16. Possibly he wanted to avoid repeating the Monadnock story pattern. He closed with more general summaries on July 19: lists of provisions, best views of scenery, and the vegetative zones on Mount Washington, from deciduous trees to lichens.

The last item was important, for Thoreau had confirmed (on both Washington and Monadnock) a relationship between altitude and plant distribution. After reading Darwin in 1860 he began to sense the ecological significance of these patterns. At the summit were earth's earliest, most primitive plants, the alpine flowers and lichens of the sub-Arctic north. On descending he could follow the stages of botanical succession to their natural climax, the broad-leafed forest. This lesson Thoreau later applied to the Concord woodlots, and he went to Monadnock in 1860 with the idea of eventually writing about mountain environments.

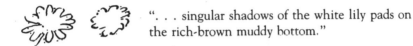 ". . . singular shadows of the white lily pads on the rich-brown muddy bottom."

Back in Concord he turned from mountains to the local rivers. His entries for early August became almost exclusively riparian, describing the patterns formed by water lilies and black willows, the play of light and shadow on the water's surface. Occasionally he muttered at others: a housewife bought two of his favorite river ducks from a hunter—"What if I should eat her canary?" A week later he wrote a satirical hearsay account of Emerson's recent trip to the Adirondacks, where his party mostly drank ale and fired rifles at the empty bottles.

For himself Thoreau attended to the good fortune of living in Concord. He no longer sought his early ideal of a Great Friend; now Concord and his daily entry were sufficient: "The writer needs the suggestion and correction that a correspondent or companion is. I sometimes remember something which I have told another as worth telling to myself, i.e., writing in my Journal."

This sentiment was not solipsistic, for Thoreau believed (as Emerson did) that individuals represent all of humanity. Concord—the very word means harmony, integrity—confirmed his faith that the One and the Many are identical. In its landscape of late August he saw

"The *Carex stricta* tufts . . . are like great long-haired heads, now drooping around the great tussocks."

the contours of his inner life: "If that place is real, then the places of my imagination are real." There was a companionable story in his Journal, one he expected someday to tell others: "My knowledge now becomes communicable and grows by communication."

As he had predicted in 1854, fall was the best season to study in his maturity. In September his entries on fruits and leaves greatly expanded, taking in new subjects, like wild grasses. *Gramineae* were a challenge to his expertise, for their apparent similarities masked subtle differences in structure and habitat—hundreds of species grew in Concord alone. Just as the grass was Whitman's metaphor for democracy, Thoreau saw in this common plant an emblem for the community of men. On September 6 the Indian grasses were first to turn red and die, a "representative of the race" that foretold the fate of all men.

Autumn was an elegiac season, the final beauty that brought all creatures to their demise. On a perfect fall day in mid-September the whole earth became a swollen fruit, ready for him "to put my knee on it, press it gently, and hear if it does not crack within as if ripe." Searching for wild fruits—and describing them for the Journal—promoted his own ripening. He did not seek the meaning of his days; they brought him passive understanding: "the forms and colors which adorn our daily life, not seen afar in the horizon, are our fairest jewelry."

Thoreau's view of autumn was not melancholy or foreboding; the stately movement of life toward death seemed full of natural pageantry. In late September wild flowers shifted from warm reds and oranges to "transcendent blue"; a few days later his cat hunted for sparrows in the weeds: "I saw her studying ornithology between the corn-rows." In mid-October he said that all growth was according to law, that decaying matter only fed that process. From the leaf mold arose saprophytes like the red pinesap, its color reminiscent of late sunset, "a sort of afterglow in the flowery year."

The season aroused in Thoreau a joyous, sensuous mysticism, but underneath his entries ran the firm current of empirical knowledge. Recognizing that "our mental reflections are more distinct at this season," he attributed the cause to improved reflections on water surfaces, the product of cooler air and increased sunshine in the bare forest. The dying leaves brought more light into his life, revealing a transcendent clarity and purity "in this twilight of the year."

He also looked for the human implications of autumn, seeing in the village's great sugar maples a living institution, "ministering to many generations of men." On October 24 he discovered a parable for the aging process: all plants had distinctive tints that grew brighter before death, and these tints followed a regular progression, from deep, rich hues to the cooler, silvery ones—comparable to the sky tints that changed from sunset to twilight: "as if the globe itself were a fruit on its stem, with ever one cheek toward the sun."

By late October Thoreau had decided to write a lecture on the autumnal tints, a phenomenon he saw as distinctly American but little described in "our literature." His work on this lecture over the next three months reflected a growing mood of certainty and generosity. The work had an avowedly social theme, and its composition aroused less of the anxiety that had troubled him in recent years.

Instructive parables abounded in his daily life. Concord's largest aspen had grown patiently through the years, waiting for him to find it on October 31: "Such is its fame, at last, and reward for living in that solitude and obscurity." A day later he celebrated one simple rite of village life, waiting with his neighbors for the evening mail:

> As the afternoons grow shorter, and the early evening drives us home to complete our chores, we are reminded of the shortness of life, and become more pensive, at least in this twilight of the year. We are prompted to make haste and finish our work before the

night comes. I leaned over a rail in the twilight on the Walden road, waiting for the evening mail to be distributed, when such thoughts visited me. I seemed to recognize the November evening as a familiar thing come round again, and yet I could hardly tell whether I had ever known it or only divined it. The November twilights just begun! It appeared like a part of a panorama at which I sat spectator, a part with which I was perfectly familiar just coming into view, and I foresaw how it would look and roll along, and prepared to be pleased. Just such a piece of art merely, though infinitely sweet and grand, did it appear to me, and just as little were any active duties required of me. . . . You cannot see anything until you are clear of it. The long railroad causeway through the meadows west of me, the still twilight in which hardly a cricket was heard,* the dark bank of clouds in the horizon long after sunset, the villagers crowding to the post-office, and the hastening home to supper by candlelight, had I not seen all this before! What new sweet was I to extract from it? Truly they mean that we shall learn our lesson well. Nature gets thumbed like an old spelling-book. . . .

And yet there is no more tempting novelty than this new November. No going to Europe or another world is to be named with it. Give me the old familiar walk, post-office and all, with this ever new self, with this infinite expectation and faith, which does not know when it is beaten. We'll go nutting once more. We'll pluck the nut of the world, and crack it in the winter evenings. Theatres and all other sightseeing are puppet-shows in comparison. I will take another walk to the Cliff, another row on the river, another skate on the meadow, be out in the first snow, and associate with the winter birds. Here I am at home. In the bare and bleached crust of the earth I recognize my friend. . . . A man dwells in his native valley like a corolla in its calyx, like an acorn in its cup. *Here,* of course, is all that you love, all that you expect, all that you are. Here is your bride elect, as close to you as she can be got. Here is all the best and all the worst you can imagine. What more do you want?

---

*Probably too cool for any these evenings; only in the afternoon. [Thoreau's note]

Writing a lecture about Concord demanded few compromises with these beliefs. The annual fall of leaves brought on a barren season of empty twigs and branches, but he was then more free to work on his accumulating papers. At the end of volume XXVII he wrote: "It is a great art in the writer to improve from day to day just that soil and fertility which he has . . . whatever it may be." Something occurred on November 16 to upset this equilibrium, inspiring one of his old Jeremiads against lectures and editors; but a day later he wrote that Concord had a similar alternation of moods and seasons: "Nature is moderate and loves degrees."

Confirmation of this principle lay in many directions: when a late November drought lowered the water table, he was able to gather some minnows that proved to be a new species of bream. In a season of dormancy, writing of dead leaves, he had found that Concord was still vital: "How wild it makes the pond and township to find a new fish in it! America renews her youth here."

"I think they are breams. Are they not a new species?"

He pressed on with the lecture in December, writing little in the Journal, unperturbed by a report from his publishers that neither *A Week* nor *Walden* had sold many copies that year. Again his friends wanted him to attend monthly dinners in Boston, but he preferred the obscurity of Concord, where he wrote near the year's end: "The man of genius knows what he is aiming at; nobody else knows."

His lecture, which dealt joyously with somber matters, gave him some problems of tone and style. He wanted a manner that was "vital and natural," he said on January 2, 1859, even if pedants and grammarians objected. Death was not a subject to be governed by academic rules. Even as Thoreau wrote, several persons were passing from him: Reverend Barzillai Frost, who had preached at brother John's funeral; and then John Thoreau, Sr., dying of consumption. Henry helped at the bedside vigil throughout January, nursing with a tenderness that surprised his mother. The Journal caught none of these moments; instead he noted that a remarkable hoarfrost made the woods "peculiarly soft and spirit-like, for there is no marked edge or outline."

The transformation expected any day for his father also drove the natural history of Concord. On January 22 an early thaw destroyed many caterpillars prematurely, but they became a food supply for starving winter birds: "Even these deeds of death are interesting as evidences of life, for life will still prevail in spite of all accidents."

A few days later, on February 3, Thoreau wrote: "Five minutes before 3 p.m., Father died." He left the rest of the page blank, perhaps as a silent tribute; then on succeeding pages he described his father's last days and his strong affection for Concord: "He belonged in a peculiar sense to the village street: loved to sit in the shops or at the post-office and read the daily papers."

Then he pressed on with the lecture, now in a late draft form. On February 7 he accepted Blake's invitation to read "an extract" in Worcester, and for the next two weeks he was busy and confident, experiencing on his winter walks "the sabbath of the year, stillness audible." Although the lecture required some tearing apart of old materials—much living to produce a small composition—he now accepted the writer's fate: "He makes, as it were, *post-mortem* examinations of himself before he is dead. Such is art."

One of the auditors at Worcester later recalled that Thoreau "fascinated every one of us," but he gave a different impression in his Journal for February 25–27. Someone told him that the audience knew more about leaves than he thought, and he was stung by the suggestion of arrogance: "Pay for your victuals, then, with Poetry; give back life for life."

Two readings at Concord did not raise his confidence. Alcott, in his diary for March 11, called the lecture a brilliant success, its author the "soul of soundness. He is rightly named *Thorough*"; but Thoreau was less certain. A week earlier he criticized both himself and his audience: "there can be no good reading unless there is good hearing also. It takes two at least for this game, as for love, and they must cooperate."

Uncertain of its merits, Thoreau did not move to publish "Autumnal Tints" at this time. Over the next two years he apparently worked on a longer project, called "The Fall of the Leaf," parts of which he drew from his lecture. The longer work was never completed, and little of its contents has survived. Thoreau kept a reading text of "Autumnal Tints," which he delivered as late as December 1860; then he prepared a version for the *Atlantic Monthly* in February 1862 with the help of his sister. The last text had some stylistic changes but it contained no Journal passage later than November 21, 1858, when he first began the lecture draft.

"Autumnal Tints" was a deliberate turn away from the literary excursions of 1855–57; it is a discursive essay that presents topics in calendar order. Thoreau's one previous effort in this vein, "Moonlight," was abandoned in 1854 after he compiled an elaborate calendar of entries, then put it aside to write a brief excursion. For "Autumnal Tints" he greatly simplified matters by drawing up an index of relevant passages, August to November, which became the working outline of his draft. Entries reached the draft with less revision, in an order approximating the Journal's original sequence. Most of Thoreau's later writings adopted this format, which reduced the problems created by his early "mosaic" methods of writing.

"Autumnal Tints" developed rapidly from the Journal, with half of its contents drawn from entries for August to November 1858. One-fourth came from 1857, and the remainder from previous years back to 1851. The 1858 entries gave his lecture its main themes and style; thus it clearly portrayed the current state of his mind and art. He had not drafted a lecture in the Journal, but extracted from it a representative season in Concord.

The lecture had another innovation: subtitled sections. The six sections, framed by an introduction and conclusion, present a foliage sequence (August to November) in various species, from "The Purple Grasses" to "The Scarlet Oak." This plan Thoreau took directly from his 1858 Journal, where he had written about the same species in that order. But the calendar has a secondary rationale, as it moves from the simple, widely distributed grasses to more complex and localized trees of the deciduous forest. He had seen this order in the mountains; "Autumnal Tints" imposed an evolutionary rationale on the natural history of Concord.

From the outset Concord represents a larger realm, as Thoreau boasts that its bright autumn foliage is a uniquely American phenomenon. (He was right; New England has a large variety of deciduous trees and a climate that changes their colors, two conditions duplicated almost nowhere else in the world.) No longer nourished directly by soil and water, the leaves go dormant and enter a "more independent and individual existence" as they prepare for their "late and perfect maturity" (Ex, 216). In "Walking" Thoreau had predicted that America would achieve this destiny; out of death comes the guarantee of survival through fruition and seeding. In projects beyond this lecture he would take up those later calendar cycles.

The sections of "Autumnal Tints" offer a reprise of American history, beginning with grasses, an emblem of the Indians who ripened early and now stand "for the most part unobserved" (Ex, 227). Red maples, "burning bushes" against the prevailing green of September, are reminders of the immigrants who followed the Indians: "I do not see what the Puritans did at this season, when the maples blaze out in scarlet" (Ex, 232). And the elms of Concord preach mortality to its present citizens, who ignore the "great yellow canopies" above them, "an *ulmarium*, which is at the same time a nursery of men!" (Ex, 233–34).

To remind these Americans that death is the destiny that men and nations "are all steadily approaching together" (Ex, 238–39), Thoreau places at the lecture's center a general description of fallen leaves. The many species of a forest gradually merge their separate identities on the "party-colored" forest floor, falling into mold, and by that "subtle chemistry" rising again to feed new generations of trees. The transformation of leaves is nature's most solemn lesson: "They teach us how to die"—especially for Americans "with their boasted faith in immortality" (Ex, 240–41).

Two final species, both turning color late in the year, are specific emblems of America's future. In Concord the sugar maples are an "in-

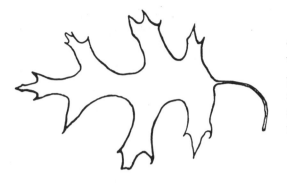

"The scarlet oak leaf! . . .
Your love of repose and
your spirit of adventure are
addressed, for both bays
and headlands are
represented."

stitution which needs no repairing nor repainting" (Ex, 250–51), a
model of governance for the New World. The scarlet oak leaf is a
physical talisman of the higher life within all earthly forms: its deep
lobes and sinuses make it the most "ethereal" of leaves, shaped by
"what is not leaf and . . . what is leaf" (Ex, 253), the flesh and spirit.
His reading of this leaf as "some still unsettled New-found Island" recalls the voyages of discovery that found America, bringing "late and
unexpected glory" to the world (Ex, 255). Saved for the last, his nation must be among the best, dying more slowly and gloriously than all
the others, "the ripest fruit of the year" (Ex, 259).

"Autumnal Tints" is a brilliant synopsis of Thoreau's later poet-
ics, its mystical vision firmly attached to a ground of solid facts. Perhaps he was mistaken to deliver the text as a lecture, for its imagery
and structure would not be apparent to a listener. As in the Journal,
his effects were strongly visual: he displayed a scarlet oak leaf to his
audiences and later insisted that its engraved outline appear in the *Atlantic Monthly* text.

———

With this composition Thoreau had entered the final stage of his career, in which he prepared from the Journal several works that announced a sacramental vision of "Concord," his home and emblem of
the earth's harmony. He now planned to describe the next phase of
the organic calendar, moving beyond leaves to fruits. Scientific ac-

counts of fruition did not get at its "evanescent and intangible" qualities, he wrote on March 7; this subject required "the genius of the poet
to pluck it."

But even as his sense of purpose became more focused Thoreau
still asked the Journal to help him lead a rich and varied life. All of
Concord was his theme, not just its seasons. He was fascinated with
the town's relics, studying in mid-March a seventeenth-century house
for evidence of "the Winthrops of that date." At the month's end he
wrote a long entry (1,800 words) on arrowheads, relics that could in-
spire "a course of lectures on human life" if he wished.

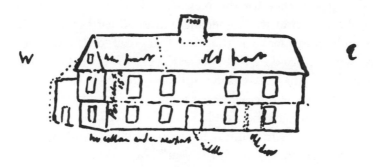

"The Hunt House, to draw from memory . . . looked like this."

Daily writing was an important outlet for his creative energies,
for the plumbago business had become an increasing burden. With his
father gone, Thoreau had to spend many hours in the shop, filling orders and keeping accounts. The customers took him from his true
work, and they were depressingly venal. On April 3 one person asked
about his lecture earnings: "I might as well, if my objects were mostly
pecuniary, give up the business." A few days later, writing at the end
of volume XXVIII, he snarled that in commerce it was "impossible to
keep one's skirts clean." Thoreau tried to suppress these reactions, but
they kept erupting over the next few months.

That spring he began to write summaries of previous Journal entries on seasonal phenomena, like the blooming and leafing of flowers, shrubs, and trees as of April 10. Many similar lists entered the Journal in later months, when he also began compiling separate inventories of "General Phenomena" for calendar months. These he gathered from entries written as far back as 1851, usually marking the item with an X or slash and then copying it on an appropriate list. His purpose was not fully defined; he wanted to learn more about seasonal progress—the science now called phenology—and to shape more consciously the rhythms of his daily life. Lectures or books were not his prime consideration, as he noted on April 24: "There is a season for everything. . . . There is no other land; there is no other life but this, or the life of this."

Plumbago took many hours from these pursuits, and surveying took even more. He spent eleven full days in May on surveys, including the plans for a new "factory village" on the Assabet. As he wrote on May 1, this work aligned him with the developers of Concord's wild land: "With our prying instruments we disturb the balance and harmony of nature." He was too busy to write much in the Journal, even about John Brown's antislavery lecture at the town hall on May 8. After a brief hiatus, surveying occupied him again in early June, when he was hired by a group of local farmers to make an extensive study of the Sudbury and Concord rivers.

The farmers needed evidence that their meadows were being flooded by grain mills downstream at Billerica, where the dams were set high to maintain hydraulic power. In the Journal Thoreau had years of notes on water levels, and he knew how to locate old maps and deeds to document his findings. The project had a commercial purpose, but it also tapped a higher need, as he wrote on June 18: "the water is lit up with a joy which is in sympathy with our own, while the earth is comparatively dead."

For the next six weeks he studied the rivers attentively, composing what limnologists now regard as a pioneer study of stream formation. His procedure was carefully inductive, working from elaborate tables of statistics* to logical conclusions, but he never ignored the

---

*Omitted from the 1906 text.

"At each bend . . . the more stagnant water has deposited mud and . . . a phalanx of bulrushes presents itself as you ascend."

moral significance of facts. On July 5 he saw that only careful probing revealed the deep places: "So perhaps it is with human nature." Nor did he confine his observations solely to the farmers' interests: between July 6 and 16 he explained the formation of meanders and meadows, their effect on river vegetation, and the striking differences between the Assabet and her more placid sisters.

Having begun this study as a matter of law, Thoreau found by late July that the rivers followed decrees of their own. Any object that impeded the current affected its depth, direction, and rate of flow. The rivers were not accidental forces, but sentient beings with a life of their own: "you can feel the pulse of our river only in the shallowest places. . . . you would presume it dead a thousand times, if you did not apply the nicest tests, such as a feather to the nostrils of a drowned man." If his employers could make little use of this poetry, Thoreau had turned it to his own profit. The river entries rescued his summer and taught him the fundamentals of Concord's ecology, which he applied to later studies of plant dispersal and succession.

After that peak of activity a slump was sure to follow, but the one that came surprised Thoreau with its intensity and duration. The "moral and physical sluggishness" of August almost brought his Journal to a halt, while his correspondence about plumbago orders quadrupled. Few of his entries were inspired, including one about blackberries on August 29, which prayed that "the fruit of my summer were hardening and maturing a little." His irritation with townsmen mounted in early September; he complained in the Journal of an incompetent cobbler, a miserly client, a muster of the state militia that made Concord "more uninhabitable than I knew it before."

Part of his frustration came from sluggish progress on a new lecture, which he called "Life Misspent" in a letter on September 5. This title aptly conveyed his feelings of the moment, when he was too vexed by his outer life to make the inner one coherent. Near the end of volume XXIX his prose grew violent and twisted, savagely attacking the "bloodsuckers," "hogs," and "promiscuous company" that interfered with his pursuits.

His father had always spared him the vexations of commerce, for Thoreau lacked the diplomacy of a good businessman. His sense of revulsion grew obsessive: on September 22 the mere sight of tobacco sprouts in an old cellar hole seemed loathsome, "As if what was foul, baleful, grovelling, or obscene in the inhabitants had sunk into the earth and infected it . . . symbols of . . . idiocy and insanity." This entry, although possibly drafted for "Life Misspent," was too bitter and raving for a public discourse. Two days later he recognized that only some swift, heroic action would improve his mood: "He has got to *conquer* a clear field, letting Repentance & Co. go."

Writing about ordinary matters did not help; the same entry degenerated into mad, whirling words, dotted with grotesque portraits and wild fantasies on the mundane:

> Road—that old Carlisle one—that leaves towns behind; where you put off worldly thoughts; where you do not carry a watch, nor remember the proprietor; where the proprietor is the only trespasser,—looking after *his* apples!—the only who who mistakes his calling there, whose title is not good; where fifty may be a-barberrying and you do not see one. It is an endless succession of glades where the barberries grow thickest, successive yards amid the barberry bushes where you do not see out. There I see Melvin and the robins, and many a nut-brown maid *sashe*-ing [sic] to the barberry bushes in hoops and crinoline, and none of them see me. The world-surrounding hoop! faery rings! Oh, the jolly cooper's trade it is the best of any! Carried to the furthest isles where civilized man

penetrates. This the girdle they've put round the world! Saturn or
Satan set the example. Large and small hogsheads, barrel kegs,
worn by the misses that go to that lone schoolhouse in the Pinkham
notch. The lonely horse in its pasture is glad to see company, comes
forward to be noticed and takes an apple from your hand. Others are
called *great* roads, but this is greater than they all. The road is only
laid out, offered to walkers, not *accepted* by the town and the travelling world. To be represented by a dotted line on charts, or drawn in
lime-juice, undiscoverable to the uninitiated, to be held to a warm
imagination. No guide-boards indicate it. No odometer would indicate the miles a wagon had run there. Rocks which the druids *might*
have raised—if they could. There I go searching for malic acid of
the right quality, with my tests. The process is simple. Place the
fruit between your jaws and then endeavor to make your teeth meet.
The very earth contains it. The Easterbrooks Country contains malic acid.

A letter to Blake on September 26 had similar excesses: images piled
upon each other, sudden non sequiturs and shifts of tone, lines over-
charged with kinetic energy. Yet Thoreau said that writing could end
this confusion: "But what a battle a man must fight everywhere to
maintain his standing army of thoughts, and march with them in orderly array through the always hostile country."

One of Thoreau's problems was that he could not put "Life Misspent" into order. Its materials were too dated, coming mostly from
the Journal for 1854, with a few more recent passages added, and its
theme was too negative. He had tried to temper his rhetoric, describing local farmers and tradesmen as "devoid of thinking & originality,"
when his true feelings were far more violent. Events also conspired
against him: on October 5 he lost an entire day in Boston, testifying in
court for his aunts about a petty dispute. When he lectured in Boston
on October 9, Thoreau read the old "Getting a Living" text, an appropriate choice because it denounced labor and wages. "Life Misspent"
was also time misspent; eventually he abandoned the project, and
most of its leaves were later scattered.

In the next few weeks he tried to recoup his losses. The relative
success of "Autumnal Tints" had prompted new work on fruits. On

sheets of paper headed "Miscellaneous" he gathered indexes of the May to September entries for 1850–59. His lists included fruits of shrubs and trees, but later he came to see nuts and pine cones as "seeds" and shifted those notes to another project. In mid-October he began to collect revised drafts of the old entries, while writing in the Journal on his current findings. Some entries were tentative drafts for a lecture, and they modified his recent antisocial humor by calling for the creation of public parks and forests: "A town is an institution which deserves to be remembered."

These calendar lists recorded the progress of Concord's natural history, which continued despite his aberrations, like the Journal. If the annual phenomena were not recorded in other books, he wrote on October 16, each had "an important place in my Kalendar. . . . There will be some reference to it, by way of parable or otherwise, in my New Testament." "Kalendar"—an allusion to the *Kalendaria* of early botanists such as Evelyn or Linnaeus—described the gospel he was writing, a chart of the seasons in one place and time. By October 18 he was ready to face the winter, full of "fresh and fragrant thoughts." Then news arrived in Concord of John Brown's raid on the U.S. Arsenal at Harpers Ferry.

Thoreau had met Brown and had heard two of his speeches, but he never wrote about him in the Journal until after Harpers Ferry. His only recollection was that Brown had wanted money but would not divulge his plans for it. (Henry gave only "a trifle," but his father contributed ten dollars.) Few of Brown's supporters knew that he hoped to establish a republic of free men in the Appalachians, and from there wage a war of liberation against the slave states. His raid at Harpers Ferry on October 16–19 was intended to launch this campaign, but in the end Brown was wounded and captured, most of his men were killed, and they had inflicted only one casualty.

Thoreau learned a few of these facts from hasty and imperfect newspaper reports; in the Journal he formed his own opinions, which transformed the peaceful Kalendar into a caldron of boiling rhetoric, 10,000 words written between October 19 and 22. The violent hostility he had felt came surging back, now safely directed away from Concord toward the Church, press, and State. Brown became Thoreau's heroic ideal, the righteous soldier who swept away all contamination.

His absorption of Brown's identity was almost total; on paper Brown became a character who diverted his author's worst impulses: "How many a man who was lately contemplating suicide now has something to live for."

Writing about Brown was cathartic, largely because of Thoreau's anger at the evil, degenerate system Brown had confronted: "A semi-human tiger or ox stalking over the earth, with its heart taken out and the top of its brain shot away." Although Thoreau knew he was using Brown "as a touchstone" to attack larger issues, some entries were almost compulsive: "The very surface of the earth itself has been rapidly imbrowned of late."

Other notes about Brown were unconsciously autobiographical: Thoreau called him "a Transcendentalist above all" and admired him as a surveyor, one of "Spartan habits" who had not attended Harvard. Yet if Brown restored Thoreau's self-regard, he also cleared his mind of politics: "I do not think it is sane to spend one's whole life talking or writing about this matter. . . . A man may have other affairs to attend to."

But for a brief period Thoreau wrote of nothing else. Two-thirds of his entries on Brown appeared under a single date, and he later recalled that during those hours he kept pencil and paper under his pillow; "when I could not sleep, I wrote in the dark" (RP, 118). On October 23 he alluded to a "Supplement" of clippings and notes, where he may have drafted a lecture text. Never before had he worked so rapidly on a public address; Brown's trial began on October 27, and Thoreau wished to speak before a verdict was announced.

He gave the lecture three times in five days, between October 30 and November 3, at Concord, Boston, and Worcester; during that time Brown was found guilty and sentenced to be hanged on December 2. Thoreau impressed his audiences with a rare display of passionate eloquence. Newspapers widely reported his views, and at first he intended to publish the text as a pamphlet, with the profits going to Brown's family. By November 24 an alternate plan had developed; "A Plea for Captain John Brown" appeared in a collection of similar essays, *Echoes of Harpers Ferry* (1860), edited by James Redpath.

This essay on John Brown is an anomaly in Thoreau's career. He wrote and published it quite swiftly, in sharp contrast to his usual working habits, and in the address he used not his familiar style but the pomp and bombast of popular oratory, a forceful mixture of pulpit and platform evangelism: "On the one side, half brutish, half timid questioning; on the other, truth, clear as lightning, crashing into their obscene temples" (RP, 126). The effect is deliberate; Thoreau wraps Brown and his actions in the cloak of liberty and redemption. He is a modern Christ, surrounded by jeering disbelievers who cannot match "for manly directness and force . . . the few casual remarks of crazy John Brown" (RP, 127).

Thoreau also organizes his address quite simply, perhaps taking the cue from his recent court appearances in Concord and Boston. His "Plea" resembles an attorney's summation to a jury, describing the client's history and character, his principal adversaries, his superiority to them, and thus his inherent right to vindication. The argument is *ad hominem*, but not merely through praise: Thoreau seeks to convince his readers that Brown is the incarnation of their unconscious ideals.

On another level Thoreau's "Plea" is an effort to exonerate himself by showing that "insane" actions may express the higher laws of human character. As he tells his townsmen, "I do not wish to force my thoughts upon you, but I feel forced myself" (RP, 111). His portrait of Brown has some features common to a local audience—he was New England born, the scion of Puritan and Revolutionary stock—but others are Thoreau in boldface: "Much of the time for some years he has had to skulk in swamps, suffering from poverty and sickness, which was the consequence of exposure, befriended only by Indians and a few whites" (RP, 116).

Thoreau knew something of Brown's atrocities in Kansas and elsewhere, yet here he is defending not actions but the heroic principles behind them. That he may be wrong about Brown is less important than being right about himself: "Not yielding to a whim or transient impulse, but carrying out the purpose of a life" (RP, 115). Thus the enemies of Brown are not slaveowners but the same forces Thoreau had long opposed; the newspapers, journals, and editors who dare not print words that might reduce their number of subscribers (RP, 122).

Yet identifying with Brown, "the most American of us all" (RP, 125), is an act not of anarchy but of faith in democracy's social contract. Brown represents justice and the Union, values that work for the collective good, and his swift action is more admirable than abolitionist talk. In that respect his character is distinctly American—and Thoreauvian—"proceeding coolly, reverently, humanely to work . . . summering and wintering the thought, without expecting any reward but a good conscience" (RP, 132).

Ultimately Thoreau closes the gap between his audience and Brown by arguing—as in other late writings—that the experience of death unifies all men. Brown's death merely anticipates the fate awaiting his nation; thus his deeds are exemplary: "for in order to die you must first have lived" (RP, 134). Thoreau expresses that paradox in the same terms he had used for fallen leaves: "These men, in teaching us how to die, have at the same time taught us how to live. . . . It is the best news that America has ever heard" (RP, 134–35).

Thoreau never argued for sparing Brown's life, only for understanding his character, and that plea rose from both political and personal motives. Perhaps he spoke out of self-interest more than he realized, yet his concern for Brown did affirm the principle of political liberty. Bronson Alcott admired this address, but years later he said of its author: "Nature, poetry, life—not politics, not strict science, not society as it is—were his preferred themes."

The image of Brown clearly occupied Thoreau's mind during the last weeks of 1859. He joined efforts to raise funds for Brown's family, then helped to plan a memorial service for the day of execution. The selectmen of Concord ruled against allowing a "passing bell" to be tolled at the hour of death, an honor normally accorded only to town residents. In the Journal for November 30 Thoreau wrote that people in Concord were "in the condition of Virginia to-day,—afraid of their own shadows."

On December 2 he played a major role in the service, arranging the order of participants and reading a short address taken from the Journal. In subdued tones he reiterated his sentiments about Harpers Ferry, which had affected him "like an invisible writing held to the fire" (RP, 139). Yet with Brown's death the cipher began to fade from view. On December 3 Thoreau helped transport a fugitive from Harpers Ferry, a man who seemed clearly insane because of "his incessant excited talk." Thoreau's own obsession had ended. Within two weeks he wrote his last entry on Brown and returned to the seasonal motifs of his Kalendar: the winter ice, the pungent style of Gerard's *Herbal* (1633). After a youth's fervor had subsided, an older man remained whose "only resource is to say his prayers."

―――――

Along with studying early naturalists like Aristotle and Gerard, Thoreau read that winter in Charles Darwin's recent treatise, *The Origin of Species* (1859). Over the next year he copied passages into a notebook, defended the "development theory" in conversations, and eventually he used it as the foundation for his own works on plant dispersal and succession.

On the backs of broadside sheets he had printed to announce the memorial service for Brown, Thoreau continued to prepare working drafts of his old Journal entries on wild fruits. These treated well-known species—strawberries, huckleberries, and apples. The large number of entries on wild apples suggested a lecture topic, which he began to draft in January 1860. Since much of the draft came from earlier Journal volumes, he wrote little in his current entries about this work.

The Journal was for other pursuits, like tracking animals in the snow. A long entry for January 4 (1,600 words) reflects his reading in science:

> In Hosmer's pitch pine wood just north of the bridge, I find myself on the track of a fox—as I take it—that has run about a great deal. Next I come to the tracks of rabbits, see where they have travelled back and forth, making a well-trodden path in the snow; and soon after I see where one has been killed and apparently devoured. There are to be seen only the tracks of what I take to be the fox. The snow is much trampled, or rather flattened by the body of the rabbit. It is somewhat bloody and is covered with flocks of slate-

colored and brown fur, but only the rabbit's tail, a little ball of fur, an inch and a half long and about as wide, white beneath, and the contents of its paunch or of its entrails are left,—nothing more. Half a dozen rods further, I see where the rabbit has been dropped on the snow again, and some fur is left, and there are the tracks of the fox to the spot and about it. There, or within a rod or two, I notice a considerable furrow in the snow, three or four inches wide and some two rods long, as if one had drawn a stick along, but there is no other mark or track whatever; so I conclude that a partridge, perhaps scared by the fox, had dashed swiftly along so low as to plow the snow. But two or three rods further on one side I see more sign[s], and lo! there is the remainder of the rabbit,—the whole, indeed, but the tail and the inward or soft parts,—all frozen stiff; but here there is no distinct track of any creature, only a few scratches and marks where some great bird of prey—a hawk or owl —has struck the snow with its primaries on each side, and one or two holes where it has stood. Now I understand how that long furrow was made, the bird with the rabbit in its talons flying low there, and now I remember that at the first bloody spot I saw some of these quill-marks; and therefore it is certain that the bird had it there, and probably he killed it, and he, perhaps disturbed by the fox, carried it to the second place, and it is certain that he (probably disturbed by the fox again) carried it to the last place, making a furrow on the way.

In this entry Thoreau reconstructs the process by which he forms inferences, discards them, and eventually arrives at a proper solution—the predator was a bird, not a fox. But that answer is less important than his procedure, which suggests that close observation is ultimately self-justifying, like the account he has just written: "Every man thus *tracks himself* through life, in all his hearing and reading and observation and travelling. His observations make a chain."

His studies of Concord's natural history were moving toward a grand conclusion, that concord—harmony, integration—is the principal attribute of organic life. Seeds, the stage of life that follows fruits, became a metaphor that expressed this conviction. On January 7 he wrote that seed-eating birds and squirrels do not destroy life, but

". . . some gray or red squirrel or squirrels have been feeding on the pitch pine cones extensively. . . ."

help it to disperse and germinate. Ten days later he described how seeds ripen on an overlapping schedule, which assures animals of a continuous food supply. Seeds express nature's generosity and confidence; of a million offspring only a handful survive to create future crops—and this lesson was not lost on Thoreau, the writer. In a letter for January 19 he told an aspiring author that "the precept 'Write with fury and correct with flegm' required me to print only the hundredth part of what I had written."

In his projects that winter he was trying to germinate old thoughts while collecting new ones. By mid-January he saw how the climate affected seasonal cycles, just as the daily weather affected "a journal of one's walks and thoughts." In February he added to his daily weather report a reading of the midday temperature, along with extra drawings of ice and snow forms to confirm the accuracy of his descriptions. His public work fared less well; some printed extracts from his "Plea" were full of errors, but at least their editor, James Redpath, wrote on February 6 and offered to correct future printings.

"The ice is thus marked under my feet somewhat as the heaven overhead."

Twice in February Thoreau gave his "Wild Apples" lecture
—with success, according to Alcott's diary for February 8. Thoreau
was less content, and a series of Journal entries that month urged him
to use metaphor carefully, in exact keeping with the objects he described. He complained on February 13 that his audiences were too
literal, "more obedient at first to words than ideas," unless the speaker
was a recognized preacher. Two days later he concluded that tropes
must stay close to "the physical fact which in all language is the symbol of the spiritual."

Thoreau planned to bring "Wild Apples" back into a projected
work on wild fruits, but the lecture text changed little beyond this
date. He added a new section after his trip to Minnesota in 1861, then
made only minor revisions in the text he and Sophia prepared for the
Atlantic Monthly in April of 1862.

The lecture he gave in 1860, although modeled on "Autumnal
Tints," was strikingly different in its genesis: "Autumnal Tints" came
mostly from the current Journal of 1858, but two-thirds of "Wild Apples" was from the pre-*Walden* era, one-third from 1850–51 alone. In
those early years Thoreau was far less informed about the organic cycle
of fruition. "Wild Apples" therefore has discrepancies of style and
form uncommon in his later works.

The lecture has subtitled sections and follows an apple's life cycle
of growth, ripening, and decay, but with two digressions—on "The
Crab" and "The Naming of Them"—not strongly attached to the
main discourse. In general Thoreau tries to use the apple as a symbol
of historical progress, the fruit cultivated by successive civilizations on
their westerly course around the world. But that theme forces him into
many pages on domestic apples instead of his title subject.

The wild apple of Concord is his symbol for American culture,
quick to spread in rough, uncultivated lands, "making its way amid
the aboriginal trees" where more delicate fruits cannot (Ex, 279). Like
America's settlers, the apples grow by responding to adverse conditions. Cows that browse the young shrubs from May to October stimu-
late the growth of a tough outer thicket of branches, which protects
the inner shoots that eventually bear fruit: "What a lesson to man!"
(Ex, 287). The fruits of October and November acquire their "racy
and wild American flavor" and a marvelous streaked beauty, even as

they ripen toward decay and death: "apples not of Discord, but of Concord" (Ex, 290, 296).

In the last weeks of November wild apples begin to decay in earnest, falling to the earth where only a solitary gleaner can find their obscure "lurking-places" (Ex, 300). The apples that hold on through December, frozen and then thawed, are miraculously transformed in flavor from bitter acid to "a rich, sweet cider." This fruit of "the frigid North" symbolizes America's destiny: "The era of the Wild Apple will soon be past" (Ex, 303–304). Now domestic fruit is taking over the orchards of New England, bringing an end to part of aboriginal America: "we shall be compelled to look for our apples in a barrel" (Ex, 305).

The historical theme of "Wild Apples," while consistent with Thoreau's works since *Cape Cod*, is nostalgic in mood and tone, a celebration of ideas generated by the sojourn at Walden Pond. And the lecture's formal lapses, its heavy use of authorities, its ponderous moralizing and learned "wit" are characteristic of his earlier style, reflecting its origin in the Journal of 1850–54. These flaws may have intimated to Thoreau that his larger project on wild fruits would face difficulties. He could not celebrate the mystery of organic development with old materials, for they did not accurately measure his own growth.

The work of Conrad Gesner, a Swiss naturalist of the sixteenth century, helped Thoreau to identify his problem in late February. Gesner wrote about purely imaginary beasts with apparent factuality: "The ability to report a thing *as if* [it] *had occurred*, whether it did or not, is surely important to a describer." Thoreau considered the possibility of recasting facts slightly and avoiding scientific jargon in order to make things seem "warm, moist, incarnated."

By early March he was working on a draft called "Wild Fruits," nearly one hundred pages on forty-four species of fruits, arranged in a May-to-August sequence. This text discusses the fruits of plants, shrubs, and trees including some species that are poisonous or not native to Concord. At this early stage in his work Thoreau had no firm definition of a "wild" fruit.

The draft has a calendar arrangement, each species assigned to a single date, and Thoreau wanted this sequence to represent "phenomena in the order in which they are first observed" (WF, 5). But, as his descriptions often note, the fruiting process actually takes several weeks, and this period varies considerably from year to year, depending on the climate. Thoreau's single date is a statistical average of uneven organic processes, and often he has to juggle his criteria in order to make the dates sequential. The early promise to list species *as first observed* does not hold; some appear when they "begin to get ripe" and others when they are "at their height" (WF, 30–32).

The descriptions are of varying quality. Some are fanciful or subtitled, like the sections of "Autumnal Tints" and "Wild Apples"; others are rather plain and literal. Thoreau's persistent theme seems contorted: a sweet table-fruit may fill the belly, but a wild fruit feeds both the palate and the mind. And what of the inedible or poisonous fruits that "actually fur the mouth" when tasted (WF, 60)? For those he suggests that their beauty nourishes the eye, and that vision is a higher faculty than appetite: "Would it not be in *bad taste* to eat these berries which are ready to feed another sense?" (WF, 68). The pun is juvenile, and it obscures a serious point.

Similar problems impair his partial second draft of "Wild Fruits," thirty-six pages dealing with a May-to-July sequence of twenty-two species. This draft follows the previous arrangement but eliminates lesser-known species and expands familiar ones, like wild raspberries (WF, 30). The writing is at times clumsy and prolix, as though Thoreau were uncertain of his theme. In describing his notion of a fruit he uses pedantic terms like *effluence, essence, incidence, excidence* (WF, 2–4); apparently he means that the entity called *fruit* is not fixed but changing, always in transit to a higher state of ripeness. Hence its value lies in higher, nonmaterial uses: "They educate us & fit us to live in New England" (WF, 13).

But the ensuing calendar sequence contradicts that principle; it criticizes farmers who cultivate strawberries for market, without admitting that Thoreau is doing the same with his literary wares. He may have recognized this discrepancy, for eventually he dropped "Wild Fruits" altogether and concentrated on a single species. Late in the second draft he began to write on black huckleberries, a fruit not described earlier (WF, 32). Almost a year later he would return to this suggestion and begin writing an independent lecture, called "Huckleberries."

Early in March Thoreau was also trying to build studies of "General Phenomena" from the Journal, compiling indexes and coding previous entries with footnotes or cross-references to arrange his data systematically. The subject was vast and amorphous, for nature's seasonal phenomena were "full of life," like the great spring flood of March 2; or dense and discordant, like a flock of noisy grackles he saw on March 8: "Yet, as *nature* is a *becoming*, their notes may become melodious at last."

The data soon revealed that nature did not follow the lines of a human calendar. Spring could fluctuate by several weeks, beginning anywhere between early March and late April. For two weeks he tried to summarize characteristics of the February-to-March transition. He made a table of March temperatures and a summary of other events in mid-March, then tried writing an account of "the phenomena of an average March."

But an "average" March was an impossibility. In nature many phenomena unfold simultaneously and on a wide scale, yet his entry for March 22 breaks the data down into a sequence of topics: weather, plants, animals. The result is lifeless, like the printed tables he stuck to the Journal pages with candle wax. On March 25 he tried once more to "speak of the general phemomena of March" with an immense entry (4,000 words) that intimates failure in its early image of a rusty sled: "Examine also its joints, and see if it will cohere when it is started."

By the next day he knew that the story of March would not cohere. Although he could write a narrative that imitated the calendar, one paragraph to a date, his "month" was a botch compared to nature's yearly version. Tested by four criteria alone, the month he called March "receded half-way into February or advanced half-way into April." Although Thoreau kept up these seasonal observations and indexes for another year, he did not try again to write imaginary accounts of the calendar. On April 1 he saw that the Kalendar of his Journal, left to its own ends, more accurately recorded nature's true order: "The fruit a thinker bears is *sentences* . . . my affirmations or utterances come to me ready-made, not forethought."

With that assurance in mind, he intended to write in the Journal only of things and ideas that moved him spontaneously. Consider his

silence about the excitement that stirred Concord on April 3 and 4:
F. B. Sanborn, the town's young schoolmaster and an ardent supporter
of John Brown, was arrested by federal marshals bearing a subpoena
from the U. S. Senate. Sanborn's sister ran screaming into the streets,
fire bells rang, and a sympathetic crowd gathered. After a local justice
issued a writ of habeas corpus the marshals were run out of town in a
hail of sticks and stones. Sanborn obtained a discharge from the state
court in Boston and returned to a hero's welcome in Concord.

The town's antislavery forces had grown since Harpers Ferry. In
December no bell was rung for John Brown's memorial service; now
Thoreau could speak in town hall and be greeted with applause and
laughter, when he thanked the citizens who "didn't ring the fire alarm
bells according to law." That was ironic praise from the man once
branded as a woods-burner, but Thoreau was in no mood to relish his
success. He wrote nothing of this incident in the Journal; Alcott set
down the details and saved clippings in his diary. By April 6 Thoreau
was busy recording the laws and history of nature, the life in Concord
that moved "forward rather by fits and starts than by steady progress."

"The weight of sand suddenly jerked this tremendous weight of mud right back onto the road, bottom up."

Anything unexpected caught his eye and pen in mid-April: the
first sighting of a pair of crossbills, a view of what he thought—mistak-
enly—was a bittern, the sudden collapse of a section of the Bedford
Road. These events were surprising, but in retrospect and with careful
study he could explain them. Anticipation of seasons to come was always inspiring, yet the Journal's real value, he wrote on April 28, lay
in its immediate resonance of the present moment: "You seem to have
a great companion with you . . . as if it were the noise of your own
thinking."

The pleasure of serendipity, and of writing without concern for how the entries might be *used*, made him more like the "old and skillful performer" he described on April 29, playing his music through the birds, his life "ever a prelude or essay with him, as are all good things." And paradoxically, by not seeking to mold his daily entries, he found in them the inner workings of Concord—as on May 6, when he saw that flowers, shrubs, and trees regulated their leafing in order to share the early sun. In projects outside the Journal he could honor that symmetry, but only if he continued to let the Journal leaves grow.

An unusual drought in May confirmed this intuition, for the hot weather accelerated all seasonal events: insects hatched early, threatening the new foliage, but the birds simply ate more insects and so preserved Concord's equilibrium. Plants also adjusted to the drought; their growth slowed down markedly, holding up the dispersal of seed until moist conditions returned.

Thoreau thus held to his own accounts, riding on the flow of time as all of Concord did. The Kalendar of his days had many parables of resurrection. On May 20 he wrote to Blake that "a man never discovers anything, never overtakes anything or leaves anything behind, but himself"; and the next day rain fell at last, restoring the season to normal by early June.

9
WITNESS ON THE STAND

Wherever men have lived there is a story to be told, and it depends chiefly on the story-teller or historian whether that is interesting or not. You are simply a witness on the stand to tell what you know about your neighbors and neighborhood.

—MARCH 18, 1861

By the summer of 1860 Thoreau had decided that works he lifted from the Journal must honor its natural congruity. Concord gave him many examples of disruption, he wrote on June 11, yet a larger order prevailed: "Such is Nature, who gave one creature a taste . . . for another's entrails as its favorite tidbit!!" Nature's metabolism was supreme; it gave and took life with exacting efficiency. Or so he surmised, when examining the life-bearing spores of pines on June 21: "Who knows but the pollen of some plants may be unwholesome to inhale, and produce the diseases of the season?"

Allergies were unknown in his day; Thoreau had sensed that seeds were both the origin and end of life cycles, a paradox worthy of closer study. Scattered in previous entries and his drafts of "Wild Fruits" were many suggestive notes. He had written on tree seeds, on the swift succession of blueberries in cut or burned woods, and on the changing harvest, from soft berries to hard-shelled nuts, between summer and fall. Seeds, succession, and forest management were issues that might form a major study of natural history.

Before he could launch this work Thoreau had to meet a last ob-ligation to John Brown. A memorial service at his graveside in North Elba, New York, was planned for July 4, and Thoreau had been asked to speak. He declined to attend but converted some Journal passages into a brief address and sent it in his place. Printed in *The Liberator* on July 27 as "The Last Days of John Brown," this text measures Tho-reau's withdrawal from partisan affairs. Most of the address came from his Journal for November–December 1859, but he toned down some estimates of Brown's historical importance (RP, 364).

The life-and-death balance of Concord Thoreau now saw in John Brown's last days. His life had reawakened the old revolutionary spirit of America, and the death of his body affirmed that his spirit would survive: "He works in public, and in the clearest light that shines on this land" (RP, 153). Not every abolitionist could agree with this transcendentalist view.

Later that summer a young journalist from Ohio named William Dean Howells paid a visit to Thoreau. Howells had just written a cam-paign biography of Abraham Lincoln; now he wanted to hear about John Brown, that "warm, palpable, loving, fearful old man" of anti-slavery legend. Thoreau disappointed the young man by speaking of "a sort of John Brown type, a John Brown ideal, a John Brown principle, which we were somehow (with long pauses between the vague, orphic phrases) to cherish, and to nourish ourselves upon."

Thoreau's phrasing may have been vague to others, yet privately his ideas and plans were becoming clear. During the summer he had begun to compile materials for the initial chapter of "The Dispersion of Seeds," a botanical treatise that would offer a rational proof of his ideas about life and death. By this date he probably had about 200 pages written on seeds and forest succession, but he could not predict the work's ultimate length or shape.

The demands of this project, far more technical than his previ-ous writings, affected the Journal that summer. As a follow-up to the 1859 survey of rivers, he spent a week in early July measuring the wa-ter temperatures of local springs and brooks. The data gave him a sur-prise: most of the springs had the same temperature, 49° F., close to "the mean annual temperature of the air here." This conclusion,

which limnologists have called a significant discovery, demonstrated
to Thoreau the value of testing hypotheses with copious factual evidence.

Responding to lecture requests in mid-July, he stressed that his
subjects were not scientific but "rather Transcendentalist & aesthetic.
I devote myself to the absorption of nature generally." He also warned
that his talks would be "to the mass of hearers, probably *moonshine*."
Yet this work, "The Dispersion of Seeds," was hardly nonsensical.
From Senator Charles Sumner Thoreau obtained several government
reports on agriculture, which he read throughout July. On August 1 he
wrote in the Journal that a landscape painter needed botany, otherwise "he does not know the species of sedges and grasses which paint
it."

A writer also needed botany. Early in August Thoreau made his
last trip to Mount Monadnock, where he had camped on previous excursions in 1844, 1852, and 1858. The journey of 1858, which included a tour of the White Mountains, had produced long Journal
accounts, dense with facts about plants and rocks, that contrasted
strongly with his romantic effusions about Wachusett, Saddleback,
and Katahdin in the 1840s. The 1860 trip to Monadnock repeated
several aspects of the one in 1858: a similar path of ascent, a camp in
the same location (until he moved to a second site, nearby), a common set of observations on vegetation and scenery. He was trying to
extend his knowledge of the alpine environment, possibly as a topic
for some future project. Monadnock was now as familiar to him as Katahdin had once seemed alien; here he could build a solid hut of spruce
and rocks and poke about for several days, making exact observations.

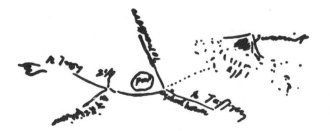

"I should say it
was near two
miles . . . to the
summit,—all the
way up hill to the
meadow."

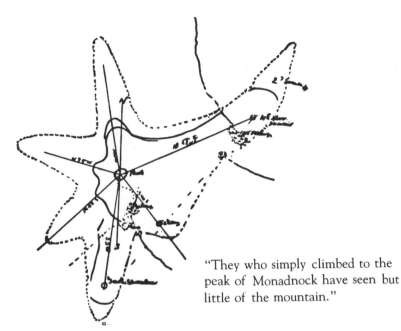

"They who simply climbed to the peak of Monadnock have seen but little of the mountain."

The Journal account of Monadnock, dated August 5–9, reflects an interest in particular facts. Instead of following his usual excursion pattern, Thoreau narrates the trip in topical summaries: general landscape views, foggy mornings, and—in 6,000 words—a complete inventory of the mountain's plant and animal zones. He also draws a survey of Monadnock and enumerates its surface features: "I came not to look *off from* it, but to look *at* it." He clearly planned to write more on mountains, for he made several notes about items to bring or see "next time."

After writing this long account he suspended entries for several days and resumed work on "The Dispersion of Seeds." He had decided to extract from this project a briefer lecture on forest succession, for delivery at the town cattle show in September. Some passages he took from his first-chapter draft, others from old Journal entries. The work was engrossing; when he later resumed the Journal his mind persistently ran to the theme of discovery. He found some Indian pottery and tools on August 22, not solely through logic but also through inspiration: "I have first divined its existence, and planned the discovery of it."

His lecture would illustrate this process by organizing the insights of his Journal, even as he continued in early September to write entries on seeds for possible later use. But fresh divinations were also welcome; when a rare Canadian lynx was killed near town at midmonth, he paused to write several long entries on the animal.

"I judged it to be a Canada lynx. . . . A principal claw was ¾ inch long measured directly, but it was very curving."

Thoreau's growing authority as a naturalist gave him more confidence about delivering lectures. In mid-September he asked the publishers of a New York newspaper to list his services, and he expressed no anxiety about speaking at the local cattle show to an audience of farmers and tradesmen. His lecture, "The Succession of Forest Trees," proved the right mixture of wit and common sense for the audience. After its delivery on September 20 it was printed: in Greeley's *Tribune*, in two official reports, and in a farming journal—making it the most widely distributed work of Thoreau's last years.

He had explained to Greeley on September 29 that the lecture was "part of a chapter on the Dispersion of Seeds," but later Thoreau saw it as a model for three chapters: it differentiates between light and heavy seeds (pine and oak), explains how the trees succeed each other, and makes some comparative remarks on English and American forest management. For several months after its publication he tried to reintegrate the lecture with his working papers, clipping parts of the printed text and waxing them to manuscript leaves. Eventually the project was abandoned, and his posthumous editors could only print the lecture in *Excursions* (1863) as a token of the longer unfinished work.

"The Succession of Forest Trees" combined Thoreau's studies of the Concord woodlots since 1856 with a few earlier notes, but its major inspiration came from reading Darwin in January 1860. *The Origin of Species* described biological development as a process of "natural selection" that explained the succession and distribution of species: it refuted earlier beliefs in a "special creation," which presumed that life forms arose spontaneously, as separate entities. Darwin's ideas confirmed the organic synthesis Thoreau had found in Concord; and Darwin's conclusion urged him to turn from tedious research to interpreting his data more broadly: "A grand and almost untrodden field of inquiry will be opened."

The field for Thoreau was botany, and Concord's woodlots gave him his best opportunity for making an original contribution. In the books of such naturalists as Dwight, Bartram, and Loudon, Thoreau had read about the principle of forest succession, but he was the first to theorize correctly about the adaptational processes of individual species. Ironically, his contribution to succession theory was ignored by scientists for almost a century, and many later readers have assumed that this "purely scientific subject" (Ex, 137) has little value as literature. One early exception was a teacher from Elmira, New York, who asked Thoreau in November for permission to use the essay as a model for classes in "writing and thinking."

In his address Thoreau takes pains to identify himself as "a transcendentalist" (Ex, 135) and to create an expository unit that is instructive rather than technical. He asks a simple question—why do oaks and pines succeed each other?—and answers: because of their differences in seed structure and mode of dispersal. He then suggests some implications for managing woodlots, and closes with a final image of himself, the transcendentalist at work in his garden. The effect is logical but humane; it uses plain facts to explain how men should work the earth.

Thoreau's tone is confident and genial; he mocks himself and—using the language of laymen—stresses his respect for his fellow Concordians. His explanation of their woodlots is equally direct: all trees must come from seeds, and differences in seeds allow them to succeed—to generate and to replace previous species. For convenience he limits himself to two species, the pines and oaks most common to Concord. He demonstrates how their "spontaneous generation" is impossible: the seeds are moved by wind or animals into new territory, and, if conditions are favorable, they germinate. Opposites attract: young pines grow best in a stand of oaks, young oaks under pines; and when the mature species is cut off the new one takes its place. Seeds, trees, and forests: each larger ring of development repeats the archetypal pattern of succession.

"They are small and very neat light-green acorns, with small cups, commonly arranged two by two close together. . . ."

Darwin had said that "the terms used by naturalists . . . will cease to be metaphorical, and will have a plain signification"; but for Thoreau science *is* metaphor. The principle of "succession" says that life is a poem, that history is a long chain of cause and effect. This transcendentalist metaphor he wishes to impart to his countrymen, for they are too credulous in America, where new growth looks "as if it had dropped from the skies" (Ex, 148). But the royal foresters of England, tending the groves of successive monarchs, know that species will alternate, and they adjust their work accordingly, as "the best gardeners" should (Ex, 152).

Dispersal is an equally poetic process, because it works through the simple agency of animals: in seeking food for their own survival, they assure the endless generation of forests. Behind one species' limited designs stands an order of cosmic proportions, all unified by a single, poetic fact: "Convince me that you have a seed there, and I am prepared to expect wonders" (Ex, 158). Thoreau offers a proof from his own experience, six tiny seeds that produce 310 pounds of *poitrine jaune grosse*, large yellow squash. By planting seeds with an Old World name, he had fulfilled a cycle in history: "These talismans had perchance sprung from America at first, and returned to it with unabated force" (Ex, 159).

As a surveyor Thoreau had often feared that he was helping to destroy Concord's forests; but in this address he recognized that the taking of life assures its continuance. Death is the warrant for all creativity; the task of men—and artists—is to minimize waste in their work. Whitman had espoused a similar notion in his latest edition of *Leaves of Grass* (1860). An untitled poem, later called "Out of the Cradle Endlessly Rocking," describes his discovery of song in the sea's lovely "carol" of life and death. For Thoreau the image of forest succession in Concord probably justified his life as an artist: as he cut down one species of thought in the Journal, another had evolved in its place.

––––––––

After the lecture he immediately resumed work on "The Dispersion of Seeds," filing a series of notes and thoughts in Journal entries for September and October. The larger work presented its own problems of form and style. He wanted to be accurate but still metaphorical, and his order should conform to the principle of evolutionary progress—no "spontaneous generation" by manipulating the entries. He studied botanical texts, but they rarely described "living plants," like the blueberries nature used to reclothe her burned-over lands. On October 10 he examined the cemetery pond and saw that turtles and fish had established new patches of kalmiana lily: "Thus in the midst of death we are in life."

Describing these processes in a lively manner was difficult. Having mailed a description of the Canadian lynx to a society of naturalists on October 13, Thoreau complained in the Journal about prolix, Latinate terms that sacrificed delight for the sake of logic. In nature "order or system is not insisted on. . . . It is indispensable for us to square her circles, and we offer our rewards to him who will do it." Those circles appeared in the Journal, but his treatise on seeds had to be linear and hierarchical, its points arranged like an army of soldiers.

The circle was not just a metaphor for nature. He discovered on October 16 that pines literally grew in crescent or balloon patterns, which farmers interrupted with plows and fences: "we square these circles every day in our rude practice." This "forest geometry" reflected a long history of man's blundering and nature's consistency. Thoreau tried to make his entries geometrical by summarizing evidence and arranging the inferences in an ascending order. Two days later he attributed that model to Darwin, whose "development theory" implied that nature was "flexible and accommodating . . . a sort of constant *new* creation."

Each day the entries accommodated new data or insights, their atmosphere charged with the energy of imagination. Never had Thoreau been so captivated by a project, so confident of its purpose. Never had he deposited so much evidence directly in the Journal, breathlessly rushing on each day for more findings. Each new conclusion led to a larger one, yet his treatise would not square that circle. On October 31 he decided not to state facts in the order observed, but to select his most important observations "and describe them in their natural order." He was trying to create a simulacrum of Concord's time, within a three-chapter design that was an expansion—and natural successor—of the September lecture.

In early November his studies turned statistical—dimensions of stumps, counts of growth rings—as he gathered evidence to extend and verify his theories. At the same time, these facts gave him new poetry to justify his work. Nature provided for "countless trees in every stage of growth" because her progress was not rapid or ambitious: "the more slowly trees grow at first, the sounder they are at the core, and I think that the same is true of human beings."

Trees had become the core of his daily life. The Journal said nothing of Lincoln's election; on November 11 Thoreau told Alcott that a free man should not vote for presidents. He thought more important history was written in the Inches Woods near Boxboro, nearly a thousand acres of "primitive oak," rarely cut by man. Thoreau's studies that month revealed that the trees' best period of growth was in their late years, and that gradually they arranged themselves with "the greatest regularity and harmony." The extreme age of trees was impressive; on November 20 he found a cedar, waiting in a pile at the sawmill, that predated the white settlers of New England. As he began volume XXXII, Thoreau anticipated a similar longevity and vitality for his own life: "I would rather that my body should be buried in a soil thus wide-awake than in a mere inert and dead earth."

Death would come soon enough; for the moment he was thinking only of "The Dispersion of Seeds." He kept its soil fresh and vital
by revising these recent entries and copying them for the second and
third chapters. The order of contents affected his studies: because the
chapters moved from germination to growth and maturity, his notes in
the Journal for early December shift from soft-wooded pines to harder
species—oaks, chestnuts, hickories—that grew slowly but attained
greater life spans.

Hickories were especially rugged and enduring because they had
massive underground roots that repeatedly sent up new sprouts:
"Theirs is like the early career of genius." If he was thinking of his own
career, the persistence of hickories must have been encouraging: one
specimen had sent up four sprouts since 1849, and although none had
prospered—like his books—the roots did not "give up the ground."
One day after writing this thought, on December 3, he caught a severe
cold while counting hickory rings, thus beginning the long bout with
pulmonary disease that was to bring him down. That night he anticipated only more days with the Journal, his best correspondent: "by
good deeds or words you encourage yourself, who always have need to
witness or hear them."

". . . a tree has a definite age after which it grows
more languidly or feebly, and then gradually ceases to
grow at all—dies and decays."

His cold became bronchitis, complicated by influenza, and for
several weeks Thoreau was too ill to write Journal entries or work on
his tree project. Until he had recovered sufficiently to conduct more
field research, "The Dispersion of Seeds" would have to wait. He had
not looked at "Wild Fruits" for nearly a year; although the original

plans had collapsed, its last few pages on huckleberries suggested a possible lecture. By late December he was gathering old entries and writing new ones in the current Journal. Long one of his favorite fruits,
the huckleberry might serve as an symbolic nostrum this year: "New
England will bear comparison with the West India Islands."

Thoreau's friends thought he should seek a more favorable climate, for throughout the winter his condition steadily deteriorated.
He coughed and lost weight; his voice was often barely a whisper. But
he worked on his lecture and book in January 1861, setting forth mag-
nanimous themes. In the Journal he framed proposals for public parks
and wilderness areas; then he described the theme of evolution in
philosophic terms: "Nature is slow but sure . . . she knows that seeds
have many other uses than to reproduce their kind."

His visitors were impressed by this activity, but he did not clearly
explain his plans. Early in February Alcott asked Thoreau to contrib-
ute to an "Atlas of Concord, for which he has rich materials and the
genius; but he must work in his own ways and times." Thoreau apparently wanted to give his lecture in March, for he had already drafted
introductions that December and January in an "Indian book" and the
Journal. But his health did not improve. Sometime in February he put
the lecture aside, at a point when it was virtually complete.

"Huckleberries," the title of his draft, is nearly 13,000 words
long; in this form it seems ready for final revising and copying, a process that probably would have reduced and refined the contents. But
even in the unfinished state it is impressive, quite similar to Thoreau's
other late works in natural history. The form is less calendrical than
"Autumnal Tints" and more topical than "Wild Apples"; it argues
that a "small" fruit can symbolize the New World and its wilderness,
in contrast to the large table fruits grown in villages. The implications
grow as he proceeds, swelling and ripening like the process of fruition
itself.

Written in a period of declining health, the lecture has a valedic-
tory air: "I trust I may not outlive the last of the huckleberries" (Hb,
20); but Thoreau is concerned for the nation that will survive him. He
wants to issue a final warning against heartless materialism, a set of
values that deprecates "*little things*" (Hb, 3) or describes objects with

"Thus the roots of huckleberries may survive till the woods are cut again. They certainly will here."

the unfeeling logic of science. The huckleberry is material, but also a symbol of transcendent concerns: often avoided by pickers, the fruit matures into a higher state of beauty and utility, becoming more "fair and memorable" through this postponement (Hb, 7).

For Thoreau the huckleberry expresses America's native potential, for this genus (*Vaccinium*) developed in ancient Greece but now enjoys "a new significance" in the New World (Hb, 10), where a greater number of its species exist than elsewhere. The strength of huckleberries lies in their ubiquity and humility: forming the understory of a woods, they are "the most persevering Native Americans, ready to shoot up into place and power at the next election among the plants . . . and feed all kinds of pensioners" (Hb, 14). These fruits of democracy flourish because they grow wild, "in every soil and locality" (Hb, 14), and their tolerant adaptation to various conditions allows them to survive, to feed animals and men, and also to propagate. Thoreau's implication is clear: a nation that develops rigid and wasteful living requirements will have "a comparatively narrow range" (Hb, 15).

He illustrates this claim by noting that the Algonquin Indians, once masters of North America, have a range "very nearly coterminous" with huckleberries (Hb, 15); and—with a long series of historical extracts—he proves that the Indians saved many white settlers by giving them these edible fruits. But this humane act was the Indians' undoing: the whites prospered, suppressed their dependence on a "savage" diet, and eventually displaced wild berries with fruit grown merely "to gratify an appetite" (Hb, 23). America thus lost contact with its aboriginal past, a simple hardiness that was open and experimental: "Liberation and enlargement—such is the fruit which all culture aims to secure" (Hb, 27).

His message to the living generation is not reactionary. Wild America will never come back, but its remnants should be preserved forever. The Indian notion of communal property can be revived in public parks and forests, held in perpetuity for future Americans. By this means the metaphysic of fruition becomes an ethic, for the land will be held as a spiritual rather than a material resource, "a common possession forever" (Hb, 31–32).

Fruition is the common destiny of all things, berries or men, and in this lecture, the last that he wrote, Thoreau bore witness to the positive creed he had long ago learned from Emerson: "For all nature is doing her best each moment to make us well. She exists for no other end" (Hb, 36). Sadly, in Thoreau's final months the two friends never discussed this work. In his eulogy a year later, Emerson repeated his old charge that Thoreau had no public-spirited ambition: "instead of engineering for all America, he was the captain of a huckleberry party" (Ex, 29).

Thoreau's poor health in the winter and spring of 1861 obviously affected his Journal. During February he wrote of indoor subjects—a playful kitten, a book on hunting—with only slight success, and he was rarely able to take the walks that inspired his best entries. He tried to make some notes on spring, but raised no false hopes for his own recovery. Two neighboring spinsters died, he wrote on February 28, yet bluebirds sang as usual near the deserted cottage. By mid-March Walden Pond had thawed again, earlier than ever, but he could not go to see it for himself.

He was not discouraged. The long years of writing in his Journal had not been wasted, for through its pages he had come to see Concord as a metaphor for the world. On March 18 he compared his town to Shakespeare's Stratford. Though Concord had earned Thoreau far less fame, he was glad to have been its principal historian: "You are simply a witness on the stand to tell what you know about your neighbors and neighborhood."

His testimony to friends was frank and unsentimental. He told Ricketson on March 22 that his work was steady but his fate uncertain: "If I knew how it began, I should know better how it would end." His entry for the same day suggested that nature must take its course;

neither miracles nor human intervention could affect "the principle of growth, of life." Proof was certainly in the daily papers; each day the Union grew weaker; after Lincoln's inauguration many southern states were preparing to secede. In early April Thoreau's letters roundly condemned both sides for the split, while he and Alcott discussed the possibility of creating a "Concord Book," an anthology of essays by local authors that would express their ideal of community.

By mid-April Thoreau had agreed with his doctor to seek a climate that might improve his condition before another winter arrived. The warm West Indies would have been a sound choice, but Thoreau opted for a place more suited to his current interests: Minnesota, where he expected to find Indians living in a savage condition and plants from the grasslands that would extend his Concord research. When he left for the West, in May 1861, Thoreau put aside "The Dispersion of Seeds," expecting to complete it upon his return.

The manuscripts of this last major project were not published by early editors, and eventually some leaves were scattered or lost. Even in 1861 the 400-page text was incomplete, with gaps in its line of argument, notes to revise passages and insert Journal entries, unresolved queries of fact and style everywhere. Yet the outline of Thoreau's ideas was clear; he had reached tentative conclusions that further research would not have altered greatly. Most of his remaining problems were editorial: he had an immense first chapter on seeds, over 200 pages of the total, while the other two chapters gave compact discourses on succession and forest management.

The principles of burning and selective cutting described there had to be applied to his own work, and that task would not have been easy. The first chapter had been gathered from Journal entries from 1850 to 1859, while the last two came almost entirely from September to December 1860. They were a condensed version of the Journal, and their inherent symmetry made a strong contrast to the massive chapter on seeds. Thoreau's problems were of both length and control: in Boxboro he saw that trees arranged themselves in "the greatest regularity and harmony" when men left them alone—yet he needed to arrange this forest to make it tell the story of evolution.

Darwin had spelled out the theory of natural selection before addressing its "difficulties" and "miscellaneous objections," but Thoreau

"a very picturesque large black oak on
the Bee-Tree Ridge"

opens his treatise with an attack on prevailing notions: all species of
trees *do* have seeds, and therefore cannot arise from nothing; the succession of species will not continue unless men find policies of forest
management that accept "the significance of the seed" (DS, 6). * The
seed is his seminal figure; from it arise the themes of his two later
chapters, as this preamble states.

His aim at the outset is to show how seeds are transported from
one place of germination to another. He begins to divide the seeds
according to type (coniferous or deciduous), weight, and agency of
dispersal—light, winged seeds are dispersed by wind and heavy nuts by
animals. But that distinction will not hold: squirrels collect pine cones
before their winged seeds have blown away, then disperse the cones
through burial. Birds and other animals eat deciduous winged seeds,
like those of birches and maples. The mechanics of dispersion are
more complex than his rhetorical plan suggests.

The first chapter is a self-justifying miscellany; one of its persistent themes is that clutter, repetition, and abundance are elements of
the natural order: "In this hap-hazard manner Nature surely creates
you a forest at last, though as if it were the last thing she cared for"
(DS, 32–33). The end result is orderly and productive, even if nature's means are not. Every seed of the pitch pine or white birch has
exactly thirteen lines, yet millions of them are scattered with a profli-
gate hand, some in places where they cannot grow (DS, 139). Larger

*Page numbers as listed in the manuscript: Berg Collection, New York
Public Library.

deciduous seeds, produced in smaller numbers, face even more haz-
ards, for they are more attractive to animals as a food source. (Thoreau
did not quite see this fact as an adaptation: the lower populations of
large trees assure an economical use of soil and water resources.)

In his papers Thoreau also writes on downy herbs, water plants,
and adherent seeds—burrs and ticks—to illustrate other modes of dispersal, but in revising he probably would have dropped them to concentrate on trees. The discussion of heavy, animal-dispersed seeds is
abbreviated by his decision to defer the nut-bearing oaks, chestnuts,
and hickories to later chapters; mostly his argument celebrates the
merits of natural economy: "there is nothing so crabbed but somebody
will be found to eat it somewhere" (DS, 81). He also dwells only briefly on seed morphology, or structure, since nature has not designed
heavy seeds for travel, only made them tempting to eat.

"A pine cone blossoms out now
fully in about three days, in the
house."

His second chapter expands the central argument of "The Succession of Forest Trees," parts of which he had clipped and waxed to
his manuscript pages. He goes beyond pines and oaks to include other
species, mostly deciduous, yet he preserves the lecture's air of informal
science. Thoreau wants not only to explain succession but to evoke a
sense of its beauty. The shrub oaks are an example: thought useless by

most farmers, the trees feed an abundant crop of acorns to squirrels, who in turn plant or leave uneaten the seeds of trees men *do* regard as useful (DS, 320). This food chain is perfectly symmetrical; it stresses the mutual dependency of all forms of life.

In recounting how squirrels, mice, and birds disperse seeds, Thoreau repeatedly attacks the belief in spontaneous generation. The animals collect seeds for food, but always in overabundance, and their caches eventually sprout new seedlings that continue the life cycle (DS, 329). The dispersion of heavy seeds is less accidental than that of windblown varieties; in the relationships of higher life forms a greater degree of interdependency is evident. Chestnut seedlings do not grow near their parent trees, but among the oaks and pines, where their animal collectors live (DS, 292–93). Conversely, oak seedlings grow best in pine woods, surviving as recurrent sprouts until the conifers are cut down (DS, 301–303). Animals are the contractors of species succession; its architects are the innate properties of buried seeds.

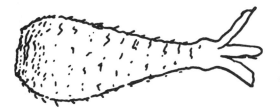

"under a pitch pine, many cores of cones which the squirrels have completely stripped"

Three species—hickories, oaks, and chestnuts—verify this claim, based on Thoreau's research in late 1860. Hickories "succeed" in competition with other species because hickory seeds spend their early years developing thick underground roots (DS, 311–14). Oak seeds are more abundant, and thus a greater number rot or are eaten, but the species also achieves a wider distribution over the countryside (DS, 271–72). Chestnuts, the slowest-growing of seeds, are rewarded with the longest life spans (DS, 274). Each species has its peculiar genius, an adaptation that allows it to survive and propagate. Thoreau,

"Scarlet oak acorn (commonly a broader cup with more shelf)."

Darwin, and Emerson were in agreement: nature is a grand, holistic organism, alive and healthy everywhere: "The very earth is a granary. . . . its surface is regarded as the cuticle of one great living creature" (DS, 338).

The third and final chapter, on "Treatment of Forests," describes the obligations of men, nature's appointed stewards. By Thoreau's account most human activity in the woods has been damaging; practices have to be developed that are more suited to natural selection. The forests grow naturally in circular patterns, which men "squared" with plows and fences, the angular lines of their civilization. Men think trees grow in a random, haphazard fashion, but in fact the "forest geometry" is precise and logical (DS, 383).

Order prevails in Concord, not working as a great static design (the Newtonian universe Thoreau studied at Harvard), but as the dynamic process of struggle that Darwin had outlined. Oaks usually dominate over pines, yet the two species repeatedly succeed each other in Concord. Why?—because of poor forest management. In cutting their woodlots indiscriminately, men retard the course of evolution, forcing nature to repeat weak, short-term cycles instead of proceeding on her instinctively grand scale. Clearing pastures forces new sprouts to return with greater vigor; letting cows browse there destroys a crop more valuable than the animals: "we have thus poor pastures and poor forests" (DS, 397).

The preferred course is to appoint "forest wardens," who manage the land for greater productivity and allow succession to reach its peak in a climax forest, where the noblest trees—maple, hemlock, beech

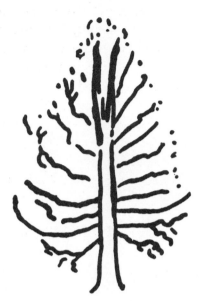

"What singular regularity in the
outlines of a tree!"

—can live in settled, stable conditions. The process of natural selection drives all life in an upward spiral, each succeeding species taller
and stronger than its predecessors. The forest is a profound lesson to
man, its blundering opponent: left to follow an inherent course of development, life will constantly evolve toward the state "of perfect renovation" (DS, 243).

Thoreau had not written a conclusion to "The Dispersion of
Seeds," for his research was incomplete. Modern studies of germination and photosynthesis have confirmed his ideas, if not his belief that
nature progresses toward perfect renovation. The form of his treatise,
even in its unfinished state, is impressive; as a chain of ideas—seeds,
animals, men—it simulates the principle of evolutionary progress he
saw in the forest. Whether or not he could have edited the papers with
the skill of a forest warden will never be known. At best he was a witness to nature's whole and perfect concord, a success that transcends
the blundering efforts of his art.

The trip to Minnesota was Thoreau's last major excursion, planned —as he wrote on May 3—because of the "all absorbing but miserable business [of] my health." This trip pulled him toward that open western country he had long imagined, glimpsed from atop Wachusett in 1842, celebrated in his lecture on "The Wild" throughout the 1850s. And what a grand tour he made in two months, going 3,000 miles by train and boat, seeing the splendors of Niagara Falls, the Mississippi River, and the Great Lakes. Here were the prairies where Channing had once lived, the tribes of Sioux described in many books. Now Thoreau could see the country for himself, gathering notes and plants with the help of his companion, Horace Mann, Jr., a keen young naturalist.

The journey produced a thick packet of field notes, which Thoreau planned to write up as Journal entries back in Concord. But when he returned his health was still miserable; he completed entries only for May 12–14 before abruptly giving up. The loss was considerable, for even those few entries indicate how well he could describe the frontier land and its people.

What Thoreau might ultimately have done with his western notes and entries was uncertain, even to him. A correspondent from Chicago urged him on May 22 to "write a book about the great West," but Thoreau would have needed more years for study and additional trips to write a book to his satisfation. He made some notes on the Indians he saw, others on Minnesota history, but mostly he wrote of his botanical findings—probably for use in the unfinished works on fruits and seeds. His discovery on June 11 of a native wild crab (MJ, 17–18) later went into "Wild Apples" (Ex, 280–81), and a few notes on *Vaccinium* for June 14 (MJ, 18) reached the worksheets of "Huckleberries."

Most of Thoreau's botanical notes are clearly destined for "The Dispersion of Seeds," for they expand his theories beyond Concord and the eastern woodlands. During May and June he observed differences in the distribution of wind-and-animal-borne seeds, summarized the succession of species in various forests, and took measurements to estimate the ages of large specimens. Horace Mann echoed this interest; on June 7 he was informing his mother that small clusters of oaks on the prairies are planted by squirrels, then protected from them by

ensuing thickets of brush (MJ, 52). In late May and early June Thoreau also noted the effects of burning and building on western forests
(MJ, 6, 15, 17). All of this evidence might have found a place in his
chapters on seeds, succession, and management.

But the field notes themselves were of little value; the Journal
entries depended on contributions from his memory and imagination.
The notes are precise and disciplined; entries would have supplied the
softening brushwork of description, thought, and humor. The only
vivid document from his trip is a long letter to F. B. Sanborn, written
on June 25 atop a great loaf-shaped river bluff at Red Wing, Minnesota. From this outpost, a western version of Nawshawtuct or Annursnack, Thoreau describes steamboat travel, councils between Indians
and whites, the political apathy of Minnesotans, all in vivid prose but
with an undercurrent of sad fatalism: "I could tell you more & perhaps
more interesting things, if I had time."

Little time remained. Because his health had not improved in six
weeks of travel, he and Mann returned to Concord a month early, by
July 9. At home he had little strength for writing. After giving up on
his field notes, he wrote no Journal entries for two months. On August
15 he told Ricketson that all his usual pursuits were interrupted by illness, which he saw with a writer's metaphor: "I have almost forgotten
what it is to be well, yet I feel that it all respects only my envelope."

In September he tried writing entries again, making the most of a
playful cat, but he sent the truth to Ricketson on October 14: "It is
easy to talk, but hard to write. From the worst of all correspondents,
Henry D. Thoreau." The changes in his life drastically altered the
Journal. During October he could describe only the birds that he saw
from his windows, or retell others' stories—one traveler said that the
1860 camping shelter was still intact on Monadnock. By month's end
a newly born kitten had become an emblem of his own condition,
"protected by its instinct in its infancy as an old man can be by his
wisdom."

He was wise enough to see that the Journal must end. On November 3 he walked to the railroad causeway. Heavy rain the previous
night had marked the gravel in straight parallel lines. At home he
wrote an exact description, with enough detail for readers to visualize

the phenomenon clearly. Then he took leave of them—and of the long history he had written: "All this is perfectly distinct to an observant eye, and yet could easily pass unnoticed by most. Thus each wind is self-registering."

These closing words of Thoreau's Journal were as deliberate as its opening ones, written twenty-four years ago, on October 22, 1837: " 'What are you doing now?' he asked. 'Do you keep a journal?' So I make my first entry to-day."

As a young man he had stressed his dependency on a mentor's advice; now he gave final witness to the freedom of eye and pen his Journal had fostered. The author of a self-register had the ultimate privilege: he could end the book that someone else once urged him to begin.

Epilogue

10

A DEATH NOT PREMATURE

It appears a rare triumph of Nature to have produced and perfected such a plant, as if this were enough for a summer. What a perfect maturity it arrives at! It is the emblem of a successful life concluded by a death not premature, which is an ornament to Nature.

—"AUTUMNAL TINTS"
OCTOBER 1862

In his last months Thoreau wanted to establish an income for his mother and sister. During November and December of 1861 he made a final survey for Concord officials, cleared up outstanding debts with plumbago customers, and briefly tried to work on "The Dispersion of Seeds." By early January 1862 others knew this task was hopeless. Sophia reported to Ricketson that her brother was still reading and taking notes, though he grew weaker every day. Alcott also heard this news; in his diary he speculated that Thoreau could at best "prepare his manuscripts for others' editing." From Worcester Theo Brown wrote to urge new editions of *A Week* and *Walden*: "Is it discouraging to you to . . . see me sticking at what you have left? *Have* you left it?"

In February Thoreau decided to make use of the works that were nearest to completion. James T. Fields, the publisher of *Walden* and now editor of the *Atlantic Monthly*, asked him to submit his lectures for publication. Fields preferred the natural history papers to moral or po-

litical ones; Emerson later grumbled that the *Atlantic* had not sought
Thoreau's best work. But on February 11 Thoreau said he would com-
ply as long as Fields would send him proofs, not alter or omit words
without his consent, and allow him to retain copyright after publication.

On February 18 Thoreau agreed to submit "Autumnal Tints," a
text that he wanted back because "what I send will be culled out from
a very large imperfect essay, whose integrity I wish to restore." This
cryptic reference was apparently to "The Fall of the Leaf," on which
he had worked intermittently since 1859. He culled the sheets at once
and sent them in on February 20 with little revision. The elegiac
theme of this text had a special pertinence for its author: it opened
with a celebration of the pokeberry, "emblem of a successful life concluded by a death not premature," and climaxed with a moving description of fallen leaves, which lived on in the forests that sprang
from them.

He wanted to assure that his own leaves would survive him.
Fields discussed the possibility of reissuing his two books but made no
firm offer for *A Week*. On February 24 Thoreau agreed to send two
more lectures, "Walking" and what he called "The Higher Law," the
latter first because it was "much shorter & easier to prepare." This was
the old lecture called either "Getting a Living" or "What Shall It Profit," which he had first written in 1854 and delivered often thereafter.
He made few changes on the text, just inserted new sheets of paper
where revisions were necessary. It made a strong contrast to "Autumnal Tints," blasting lyceums and lecture audiences for their indifference to his works.

Fields accepted the paper but requested a change of title; Thoreau suggested "Life Without Principle." He also wrote on March 4
that the title of *Walden* would be improved by dropping the words "Or
Life in the Woods." He could alter the titles, but little time remained
to change his works' contents. In a week he read the proofs of "Autumnal Tints" and submitted the copy of "Walking."

Sophia was now helping him by recopying some pages for clarity,
but "Walking" was not greatly altered from its last major revision of
1857. Fields decided to print it as the first of Thoreau's *Atlantic* essays;

when published in June 1862, one passage was no longer a prophecy:
"If you are ready to leave father and mother, and brother and sister,
and wife and child and friends, and never see them again,—if you
have paid your debts, and made your will, and settled all your affairs,
and are a free man, then you are ready for a walk."

His friends were not ready to see him go. Emerson urged him to
see a Boston doctor, who prescribed daily rations of whiskey, cod liver
oil, and horseback riding. Thoreau allegedly said he would not take
the fluids and could not afford the horse, a reply that made some
neighbors think he was making no effort to survive. He had Emerson
in mind while writing a letter on March 21 to Myron Benton, who
had heard Emerson describe Thoreau's "work . . . on Botany" in 1860.
Thoreau replied, "He is actually more familiar with what I have written than myself. . . . if I were to live, I should have much to report on
Natural History generally."

In 1860 he had first written "Wild Apples," which he was now
preparing for the *Atlantic* with the help of two copyists, Sophia and
her friend Elizabeth Hoar. But he also had *A Week* in mind. During a
visit on March 24 he explained to Emerson that the Concord rivers
formed their bends and banks in a compensatory manner, and when
he sent Fields the text of "Wild Apples" on April 2, Thoreau again
asked for an offer on his old book: "it will be an advantage to advertize
it with Walden." Fields agreed to this arrangement and soon came to
Concord to strike a bargain. The old sheets of *A Week* would be bound
in fresh covers, and after they were sold a new edition would be published.

Thoreau had never been happy with the text of *A Week*. Back in
1849 the printers had ignored many of his corrections, and since then
he had entered over 1,000 additional revisions, including material
from his drafts and commonplace books. Most of the new passages discussed friendship and death, thus clarifying the book's memorial
theme. Just before the invocation to "my Muse, my Brother," he
placed a new motto about himself, the compensatory author who confined the bends of rivers "within their sloping banks." After Thoreau's
death Fields kept the revised text in a company safe until the first edition was out of print, in 1868.

With his *Atlantic* essays completed, Thoreau turned to the only other materials that would readily yield a new book, his three essays on Maine. He drove himself fearfully in these last days, Channing recalled, "as if to live forty years longer; his work was laid out for a long life." Thoreau told one visitor, "You know it's respectable to leave an estate to one's friends"; hence he spent every comfortable hour working on his papers. Daniel Ricketson knew that much of the estate was unpublished; on April 13 he wrote that "your works, and above all, your brave and truthful life, will become a precious treasure."

For his last book Thoreau drew up an outline and gave final titles to the contents, naming the collection *The Maine Woods*. He put the three essays in chronological order but established through cross-references and footnotes several points of connection. In all three Mount Katahdin is a brooding part of the landscape, and the principal Indian figures—Louis Neptune, Joe Aitteon, and Joe Polis—appear in overlapping allusions. An "Appendix" at the end summarizes his notes on the wildlife observed in 1853 and 1857, each list arranged by a different principle: plants by population, habitat, and size; animals by their order of appearance in the essays. Thoreau made only minor revisions in "Ktaadn" and "Chesuncook," but "The Allegash and East Branch" gave him continuing problems. He had never written a proper conclusion to the narrative; it simply ended with his last glimpse of Joe Polis. He told Channing on April 23 that the paper was "in a knot I cannot untie."

Sophia was reading the revised text of *A Week* to him in daily stints; on April 23 he advised Channing of a bird name that was incorrect in the chapter "Thursday." Another late visitor saw Thoreau at work on his papers, trying to strike "the mirthfulness" from his work. The text of *A Week* printed in 1868 does modify some of its jests about religion. He changed none of his beliefs about life or death, but in the last days Thoreau's tone was less combative. His mother and sister surrounded him with flowers, pictures, and books; on his sleepless nights they put a lamp on the floor, and he watched the flickering shadows. The high fever of consumption put him in an exalted mood: he asked to see children, wept when he heard an organ-grinder playing in the street. To his visitors he was courteous, sometimes even playful. His aunt asked if he had made his peace with God: "I did not know we had ever quarrelled." A friend wondered if he could see the opposite shore: "One world at a time."

In this world he was a writer to the very end. He listed the books in his library that would go to close friends: Emerson, Alcott, Channing, Ricketson, Blake, Sanborn. To Edmund Hosmer, whom Thoreau once called "the most intelligent farmer in Concord," went a special gift. Through the years Hosmer had been a good surveying client, always willing to stop his work for a talk about larger matters. He had helped raise the frame and roof of the house at Walden; now Thoreau asked for his company one final night. On the morning of May 6 he gave him an old copy of *A Week*. Inside was a lock of John Thoreau's hair.

After Hosmer left, Henry asked Sophia to continue their proofreading of *A Week*, which had reached "Friday," the final chapter. She soon came to the page where the brothers have entered Massachusetts on their homeward voyage to Concord. Ahead lay a description of traveling fast before the wind, watching the sail's motion, "the play of its pulse so like our own lives" (We, 360). He whispered to Sophia, "Now comes good sailing." Minutes later, still thinking of the book on Maine, he uttered his last distinct words: "Moose—Indian." By nine o'clock he was gone.

Sometime that day a clerk at the town hall entered Concord's latest death: "Henry D. Thoreau. 44 years, 9 months, 24 days. Natural Historian."

On May 7 Bronson Alcott began to plan a funeral, but first he turned for solace to his diary, writing, "It is the departure of many persons from our population, and leaves the town greatly the poorer in virtue and expectation."

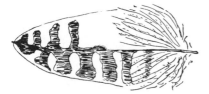

"Few mortals ever look down on the tail-coverts of a young hen-hawk, yet these are not only beautiful, but of a peculiar beauty. . . . Thus she finishes her works above men's sight."

SOURCES

All references in the text to journals, diaries, or letters are by date. Quotations are from the following primary sources:

The Journals of Bronson Alcott, ed. Odell Shepard (Boston: Little, Brown and Co., 1938).

The Letters of A. Bronson Alcott, ed. Richard L. Herrnstadt (Ames, Iowa: Iowa State University Press, 1969).

Manuscript journals of William Ellery Channing at the Pierpont Morgan Library, New York.

The Correspondence of Emerson and Carlyle, ed. Joseph Slater (New York: Columbia University Press, 1964).

The Journals and Miscellaneous Notebooks of Ralph Waldo Emerson, ed. William H. Gilman *et al.* (Cambridge, Mass.: Harvard University Press, 1965–).

Journals of Ralph Waldo Emerson, ed. Edward W. Emerson and Waldo E. Forbes (Boston: Houghton Mifflin Co., 1914).

The Letters of Ralph Waldo Emerson, ed. Ralph L. Rusk (New York: Columbia University Press, 1939).

Nathaniel Hawthorne, *The American Notebooks*, ed. Claude Simpson (Columbus, Ohio: Ohio State University Press, 1972).

The Journal of Henry D. Thoreau, ed. Bradford Torrey and Francis H. Allen (Boston: Houghton Mifflin Co., 1906).

Manuscript Journal of Henry D. Thoreau, transcribed by Thoreau Textual Center, Princeton University, Princeton, N.J.

The Correspondence of Henry David Thoreau, ed. Carl Bode and Walter Harding (New York: New York University Press, 1958).

Manuscript letters to and from Henry D. Thoreau, transcribed by Thoreau Textual Center, Princeton University, Princeton, N.J.

Parenthetical references in the text are to Thoreau's writings, with abbreviations for the following texts:

CC   *Cape Cod* (Boston: Ticknor & Fields, 1865).
CP   *Collected Poems of Henry Thoreau,* ed. Carl Bode (Baltimore: The Johns Hopkins University Press, 1964).
DS   "The Dispersion of Seeds," manuscript transcribed by Thoreau Textual Center, Princeton University, Princeton, N.J.
EE   *Early Essays and Miscellanies,* ed. Joseph J. Moldenhauer, Edwin Moser, and Alexander Kern (Princeton: Princeton University Press, 1975).
Ex   *Excursions* (Boston: Ticknor & Fields, 1863).
Hb   *Huckleberries,* ed. Leo Stoller (New York: New York Public Library, 1970).
MJ   *Thoreau's Minnesota Journey,* ed. Walter Harding (Geneseo, N.Y.: Thoreau Society, 1962).
MW   *The Maine Woods,* ed. Joseph J. Moldenhauer (Princeton: Princeton University Press, 1972).
RP   *Reform Papers,* ed. Wendell Glick (Princeton: Princeton University Press, 1973).
Wa   *Walden,* ed. J. Lyndon Shanley (Princeton: Princeton University Press, 1971).
We   *A Week on the Concord and Merrimack Rivers,* ed. Carl Hovde, William Howarth, and Elizabeth Witherell (Princeton: Princeton University Press, 1980).
WF   "Wild Fruits," manuscript transcribed by Thoreau Textual Center, Princeton University, Princeton, N.J.
YC   *A Yankee in Canada, with Anti-Slavery and Reform Papers* (Boston: Ticknor & Fields, 1866).

The following is a selective list of secondary sources that influenced my ideas or provided basic facts.

BIBLIOGRAPHY

Allen, Francis H. *A Bibliography of Henry David Thoreau* (Boston, 1908).
Burnham, Philip E., and Carvel Collins. "Contribution to a Bibliography of Thoreau, 1938–1945," *Bulletin of Bibliography* (September–December 1946), 16–18ff.
Harding, Walter. "Additions to the Thoreau Bibliography," *TSB* 1–155 (1941–81); cumulated as *A Bibliography of the Thoreau Society Bulletin Bibliographies, 1941–1969* (Troy, N.Y., 1971).
———, and Michael Meyer. *The New Thoreau Handbook* (New York, 1980).
Leary, Lewis. "Henry David Thoreau," *Eight American Authors: Revised Edition*, ed. James Woodress (New York, 1971), pp. 128–71.
White, William. *A Henry David Thoreau Bibliography, 1908–1937* (Boston, 1939).
Woodress, James, *et al. American Literary Scholarship: An Annual* (Durham, N.C., 1965–).

REFERENCE

Harding, Walter. "A Check-List of Thoreau's Lectures," *BNYPL* 52 (February 1948), 78–87.
———. *Thoreau's Library* (Charlottesville, Va., 1957).
Howarth, William. *The Literary Manuscripts of Henry David Thoreau* (Columbus, Ohio, 1974).
Stowell, Robert. *A Thoreau Gazetteer*, ed. William Howarth (Princeton, 1970).

BIOGRAPHY

Canby, Henry S. *Thoreau* (Boston, 1939).
Channing, William Ellery. *Thoreau, the Poet-Naturalist*, ed. F. B. Sanborn (Boston, 1902).
Harding, Walter. *The Days of Henry Thoreau* (New York, 1965).
Krutch, Joseph Wood. *Henry David Thoreau* (New York, 1948).
McGill, Frederick T., Jr. *Channing of Concord: A Life of William Ellery Channing II* (New Brunswick, N.J., 1967).

Porte, Joel. *Representative Man: Ralph Waldo Emerson in His Time* (New York, 1979).

Salt, Henry S. *The Life of Henry D. Thoreau* (London, 1896).

Sanborn, Franklin B. *The Life of Henry David Thoreau* (Boston, 1917).

————. *The Personality of Thoreau* (Boston, 1901).

Turner, Arlin. *Nathaniel Hawthorne: A Biography* (New York, 1980).

THOREAU STUDIES

Cavell, Stanley. *The Senses of Walden* (New York, 1972).

Christie, John Aldrich. *Thoreau as World Traveler* (New York, 1965).

Cook, Reginald L. *Passage to Walden* (Boston, 1949).

Garber, Frederick. *Thoreau's Redemptive Imagination* (New York, 1977).

Glick, Wendell. *The Recognition of Henry David Thoreau* (Ann Arbor, Mich., 1970).

Harding, Walter. *Thoreau: A Century of Criticism* (Dallas, Tex., 1954).

Hicks, John H. *Thoreau in Our Season* (Amherst, Mass., 1966).

Lebeaux, Richard. *Young Man Thoreau* (Amherst, Mass., 1977).

McIntosh, James. *Thoreau as Romantic Naturalist* (Ithaca, N.Y., 1974).

Meyer, Michael. *Several More Lives to Live: Thoreau's Political Reputation in America* (Westport, Conn., 1977).

Miller, Perry. *Consciousness in Concord* (Boston, 1958).

Paul, Sherman. *The Shores of America: Thoreau's Inward Exploration* (Urbana, Ill., 1958).

————. *Thoreau: A Collection of Critical Essays* (Englewood Cliffs, N.J., 1962).

Porte, Joel. *Emerson and Thoreau: Transcendentalists in Conflict* (Middletown, Conn., 1966).

Sayre, Robert. *Thoreau and the American Indians* (Princeton, 1977).

Seybold, Ethel. *Thoreau: The Quest and the Classics* (New Haven, 1951).

Shanley, J. Lyndon. *The Making of Walden* (Chicago, 1957).

Stoller, Leo. *After Walden: Thoreau's Changing Views of Economic Man* (Stanford, 1957).

Wagenknecht, Edward. *Henry David Thoreau: What Manner of Man?* (Amherst, Mass., 1980).

————

GENERAL STUDIES

Anderson, Quentin. *The Imperial Self* (New York, 1971).

Bates, Marston. *The Nature of Natural History* (New York, 1950).

Bercovitch, Sacvan. *The Puritan Origins of the American Self* (New Haven, 1975).

Brooks, Van Wyck. *The Flowering of New England* (New York, 1936).

Buell, Lawrence. *Literary Transcendentalism* (Ithaca, N.Y., 1973).

Clough, Wilson O. *The Necessary Earth: Nature and Solitude in American Literature* (Austin, Tex., 1964).

Ekirch, Arthur. *Man and Nature in America* (New York, 1963), pp. 58–69.

Farb, Peter. *Face of North America* (New York, 1963).

Fussell, Edwin. *Frontier: American Literature and the American West* (Princeton, 1965).

Gura, Philip F. *The Wisdom of Words: Language, Theology, and Literature in the New England Renaissance* (Middletown, Conn., 1981).

Harris, Neil. *The Artist in American Society, 1790–1860* (New York, 1966).

Hoffman, Daniel G. *Form and Fable in American Fiction* (New York, 1961).

Huth, Hans. *Nature and the American* (Berkeley, 1957).

Lewis, R. W. B. *The American Adam* (Chicago, 1955).

Marx, Leo. *The Machine in the Garden* (New York, 1964).

Matthiessen, F. O. *American Renaissance* (New York, 1941).

Mitchell, Lee Clark. *Witnesses to a Vanishing America* (Princeton, 1981).

Nash, Roderick. *Wilderness and the American Mind* (New Haven, 1967), pp. 84–95.

Poirier, Richard. *A World Elsewhere: The Place of Style in American Literature* (New York, 1966).

Richardson, Robert D., Jr. *Myth and Literature in the American Renaissance* (Bloomington, Ind., 1978).

Smith, Henry Nash. *Virgin Land: The American West as Myth and Symbol* (Cambridge, Mass., 1950).

Tanner, Tony. *The Reign of Wonder: Naivety and Reality in American Literature* (New York, 1967).

NOTES

An abbreviated citation here refers to the previous list of sources. Biographical facts lacking a specific note are from Walter Harding, *The Days of Henry Thoreau*. Abbreviations for periodical titles are:

AL	*American Literature*
AQ	*American Quarterly*
ATQ	*American Transcendental Quarterly*
BNYPL	*Bulletin of the New York Public Library*
CS	*Concord Saunterer*
ESQ	*Emerson Society Quarterly*
JHI	*Journal of the History of Ideas*
NEQ	*New England Quarterly*
PMLA	*Publications of the Modern Language Association*
SAR	*Studies in the American Renaissance*
TJQ	*Thoreau Journal Quarterly*
TSB	*Thoreau Society Bulletin*

1. HIS BROKEN TASK

pages

3. "a clerk enters": Concord town records for 1862, Concord Free Public Library (Special Collections).

3. "obituary tribute": Joel Myerson, "Emerson's 'Thoreau': A New Edition from Manuscript," SAR (1979), 17–92.

4. "Louisa May Alcott": *Ibid.*

5. "Journal volumes": Howarth, *The Literary Manuscripts of Henry David Thoreau*, pp. 247–79.

6.   "summer of 1862": Gabrielle Fitzgerald, " 'In Time of War': The Context of Emerson's 'Thoreau,' " *ATQ* 41 (Winter, 1979), 5–12.

6.   "Emerson portrays": Leonard Neufeldt, "The Severity of the Ideal: Emerson's 'Thoreau,' " *ESQ* 58 (1970), 77–83. William M. Moss, "So Many Promising Youth," *NEQ* 49 (March 1976), 46–64.

7.   "the legend of Thoreau": Ellen R. Ballou, *The Building of the House: Houghton Mifflin's Formative Years* (Boston, 1970), pp. 597–98. George Cooke, "The Two Thoreaus," *The Independent* 48 (December 10, 1896), 1671–72.

7.   "published excerpts": A. Bronson Alcott, *Concord Days* (Boston, 1872), p. 264.

7.   "this plan agreed": William Ellery Channing, *Thoreau, the Poet-Naturalist*, pp. ix–xvi, 14, 67–68, 341–44; Channing, *Poems of Sixty-five Years*, ed. F. B. Sanborn (Philadelphia, 1902), p. xxxviii. *See also* McGill, *Channing of Concord*, p. 157–59.

8.   "calendar excerpts": Henry D. Thoreau, "April Days," "May Days," "Days in June," ed. H. G. O. Blake, *Atlantic Monthly* 41 (April–June 1878), 445ff., 567ff., 711ff.

8.   "apparently complete": "General Introduction" in Henry D. Thoreau, *Journal* Vol. I, 1837–1844, ed. John C. Broderick *et al.* (Princeton, 1981), pp. 578–91.

8.   "provoked controversy": Mark Van Doren, *Henry David Thoreau: A Critical Study* (Boston, 1916), pp. 109–28. Norman Foerster, "Thoreau as Artist," *Sewanee Review* 29 (January 1921), 2–13.

8.   "readers have speculated": Leon Balzagette, *Henry Thoreau, Bachelor of Nature*, trans. Van Wyck Brooks (New York, 1924), p. 119. Henry Seidel Canby, "The Man Who Did What He Wanted," *Saturday Review of Literature* 15 (December 26, 1936), 3–4, 15. Canby, *Thoreau*, p. 336. Canby, "Foreword," *The Journal of Henry David Thoreau* (Boston, 1949). Paul, *The Shores of America*, pp. 399–400; Laurence Stapleton, *Thoreau: A Writer's Journal* (New York, 1960), pp. 178-79. Fussell, *Frontier*, p. 329.

8.   "an opposite view": Miller, *Consciousness in Concord*, p. 4.

9.   "book on Indians": Sayre, *Thoreau and the American Indians*, pp. 101–22.

9.   "born to be a writer": E. B. White, "The Talk of the Town," *The New Yorker* (May 7, 1949), 23. White, *The Points of My Compass* (New York, 1962), pp. 15–26.

2. GLEANINGS FROM THE FIELD

16.   "Emerson . . . a journal": William H. Gilman *et al.*, "Introduction," *The Journals and Miscellaneous Notebooks of Emerson* (Cambridge, Mass., 1960), I, pp. xxiv–xliii.

16.   "The earliest volumes": "Historical Introduction," in Henry D. Thoreau, *Journal*, Vol. I, 1837–1844, pp. 592–612.

16.   "to live in Concord": Townsend Scudder, *Concord: American Town* (Boston, 1947). Ruth Robinson Wheeler, *Concord: Climate for Freedom* (Concord, Mass., 1967). Wheeler, "Thoreau's Village Background," *TSB* 134 (Winter 1975), 1–2. Lebeaux, *Young Man Thoreau*, pp. 1–27.

18.   "Harvard gave him": Kenneth W. Cameron, *The Transcendentalists and Minerva* (Hartford, Conn., 1958), pp. 223–25; Cameron, *Thoreau and His Harvard Classmates* (Hartford, Conn., 1965); Cameron, *Thoreau's Harvard Years* (Hartford, Conn., 1966); Cameron, "A Tabular View of Thoreau's Harvard Curriculum," *ESQ* 51 (1968), 10–24.

19.   "boat and hiking journey": Christopher McKee, "Thoreau's First Visit to the White Mountains," *Appalachia* 31 (December 1956), 199–209. Raymond P. Holden, "New Men for a New World," *The Merrimack* (New York, 1958), pp. 243–59.

20.   "series of early notebooks": Cameron, *The Transcendentalists and Minerva*, pp. 130–358, 374–80, 871–82.

20.   "career had bloomed": Joel Myerson, "Convers Francis and Emerson," *AL* 50 (March 1978), 17–36. Lebeaux, *Young Man Thoreau*, pp. 79–90.

20.   "Lowell met Thoreau": Joel Myerson, "Eight Lowell Letters from Concord in 1838," *Illinois Quarterly* 38 (Winter 1975), 20–42. Raymond Adams, "Thoreau and his Neighbors," *TSB* 44 (Summer 1953), 2.

23.   "formally 'signed off' ": Transcript at Thoreau Textual Center, Princeton University.

24.   "moved into Emerson's": Porte, *Emerson and Thoreau*, pp. 98–99; Lebeaux, *Young Man Thoreau*, pp. 151–66.

26.   "anthology of English verse": Robert Sattlemeyer, "Thoreau's Projected Work on the English Poets," *SAR* (1980), 239–58.

27.   "a verse translation": Leo M. Kaiser, "Remarks on Thoreau's Translation of Prometheus," *Classical Weekly* 46 (January 5, 1953),

69–70. Text in *The Writings of Henry David Thoreau* (Boston, 1906), V, 337–75. *See also* Kevin Van Anglen, "The Sources for Thoreau's Greek Translations," *SAR* (1980), 291–300.

28.   "this problem was common": Buell, *Literary Transcendentalism*, pp. 55–74. Harris, *The Artist in American Society*, pp. 170–86. *See also* Joel Myerson, *The New England Transcendentalists and The Dial* (Rutherford, N.J., 1980).

29.   "old nature album": Howarth, *The Literary Manuscripts of Henry David Thoreau*, pp. 306–307. Transcript at Thoreau Textual Center, Princeton University.

29.   " 'A Walk to Wachusett' ": Richard Fuller, "Visit to the Wachusett, July 1842," ed. Walter Harding, *TSB* 121 (Fall 1972), 1–4. Raymond Adams, "Thoreau's Mock-Heroics and the American Natural History Writers," *Studies in Philology* 52 (January 1955), 86–97.

30.   "unity of form": Leo Marx, "Thoreau's Excursions," *Yale Review* 51 (Spring 1962), 363–69. Donald R. Swanson, "Far and Fair Within: 'A Walk to Wachusett,' " *ESQ* 56 (1969), 52–53.

30.   " 'long book' ": Transcript at Thoreau Textual Center, Princeton University.

31.   "To Emerson": Transcript at Thoreau Textual Center, Princeton University.

32.   "months in New York": Paul, *The Shores of America*, pp. 139–72. Max Cosman, "Thoreau and Staten Island," *Staten Island History* 6 (January–March 1943), 1–2, 7–8.

32.   " 'A Winter Walk' ": Gordon E. Bigelow, "Summer under Snow: Thoreau's 'A Winter Walk,' " *ESQ* 56 (1969), 13–16. James Morse Marshall, "The Heroic Adventure in 'A Winter Walk,' " *ESQ* 56 (1969), 16–23.

33.   "translation of Aeschylus": Henry D. Thoreau, "The Seven Against Thebes," ed. Leo Max Kaiser, *ESQ* 17 (1959), 1–30.

33.   "future in journalism": Joseph M. DeFalco, " 'The Landlord': Thoreau's Emblematic Technique," *ESQ* 56 (1969), 23–32. Frederick Carpenter, "The American Myth: 'Paradise (to be) Regained,' " *PMLA* 74 (December 1959), 599–606.

33.   "Pindaric odes": Texts in *The Writings of Henry David Thoreau* (Boston, 1906), V, 375–92.

33.   " 'Herald of Freedom' ": Wendell Glick, "Thoreau and the 'Herald of Freedom,' " *NEQ* 22 (June 1949), 193–204.

34. "repressed guilt": Harding, *The Days of Henry Thoreau*, pp. 158–59. Lebeaux, *Young Man Thoreau*, pp. 209–13. Miller, *Consciousness in Concord*, p. 119.

34. "a summer hike": Thomas Woodson, "Thoreau's Excursion to the Berkshires and Catskills," *ESQ* 21 (1975), 82–92.

35. "to build a house": Roland W. Robbins, *Discovery at Walden* (Concord, Mass., 1947).

3. THE CUBES OF PYTHAGORAS

36. "At Walden Pond": "Reminiscences of Augustus Bowers French," *TSB* 130 (Winter 1975), 5–6.

36. " 'wooden inkstand' ": Harding, *The Days of Henry Thoreau*, p. 182.

37. "outline of A *Week*": Linck C. Johnson, "Historical Introduction," *A Week on the Concord and Merrimack Rivers*, ed. Carl Hovde et al. (Princeton, 1980), pp. 433–500.

37. "untitled notebooks": Transcripts at Thoreau Textual Center, Princeton University.

37. "gleaned the volumes": Walter Harding, "The Influence of Thoreau's Lecturing upon His Writing," *BNYPL* 60 (February 1956), 74–80. Carl Hovde, "Nature into Art: Thoreau's Use of His Journals in A *Week*," *AL* 30 (May 1958), 165–84.

39. "he was arrested": John C. Broderick, "Thoreau, Alcott, and the Poll Tax," *Studies in Philology* 53 (October 1956), 612–26. Walter Harding, "Thoreau in Jail," *American Heritage* 26 (August 1975), 36–37.

39. "Horace Greeley": Helen B. Morrison, "Thoreau and the New York Tribune: A Checklist," *TSB* 77 (Fall 1961), 1–2.

40. " 'Thomas Carlyle' ": R. P. Adams, "Romanticism and the American Renaissance," *AL* 23 (January 1952), 419–32. Perry Miller, "Thoreau in the Context of International Romanticism," *Nature's Nation* (Cambridge, Mass., 1967), pp. 175–83.

41. " 'n book' ": Transcripts at Thoreau Textual Center, Princeton University.

41. "writings about Walden": Shanley, *The Making of Walden*, pp. 18–27.

43. "Thoreau wrote him": Transcript at Thoreau Textual Center, Princeton University.

44. "essay on Maine": Robert C. Cosbey, "Thoreau at Work: The Writing of 'Ktaadn,' " *BNYPL* 65 (January 1961), 21–30.

45.   "source is not nature": For other readings, *see* Paul, *The Shores of America*, pp. 358–362. John G. Blair and Augustus Trowbridge, "Thoreau on Katahdin," *AQ* 12 (Winter 1960), 508–17. Nathaniel Nitkin, "Wild, the Mountain of Thoreau," *NEQ* 9 (Fall 1967), 35–43.

46.   "The excursion to Maine": *See also* Loren Eisley, *The Man Who Saw Through Time* (New York, 1973), pp. 110–15; Garber, *Thoreau's Redemptive Imagination*, pp. 75–101.

47.   " 'Civil Disobedience' ": Wendell Glick, "Civil Disobedience: Thoreau's Attacks upon Relativism," *Western Humanities Review* 7 (Winter 1952–53), 35–42. Richard Drinnon, "Thoreau's Politics of the Upright Man," in Hicks, *Thoreau in Our Season*, pp. 154–168. Edward H. Madden, *Civil Disobedience and Moral Law in Nineteenth-Century American Philosophy* (Seattle, 1968), pp. 96–98.

48.   "prophet of its redemption": *See also* Hannah Arendt, "Reflections: Civil Disobedience," *The New Yorker* (September 12, 1970), 70–105. Meyer, *Several More Lives to Live*, pp, 157–92.

49.   "their reactions": Walter Harding, "Thoreau on the Lecture Platform," *TSB* 125 (Fall 1973), 6. Canby, *Thoreau*, pp. 248–49.

49.   " 'I have thought of you' ": Transcript at Thoreau Textual Center, Princeton University.

51.   "flawed in design": For other readings, *see* Paul, *The Shores of America*, pp. 191–233. J. J. Boies, "Circular Imagery in Thoreau's *Week*," *College English* 26 (February 1965), 350–55. Jonathan Bishop, "The Experience of the Sacred in Thoreau's *Week*," *English Literary History* 33 (March 1966), 66–91. John Conron, "Bright American Rivers: The Luminist Landscapes of Thoreau's *A Week on the Concord and Merrimack Rivers*," *AQ* 32 (Summer 1980), 144–66.

52.   "poems and quotations": Ernest E. Leisy, "Sources of Thoreau's Borrowings in *A Week*," *AL* 18 (March 1946), 37–44. William Brennan, "An Index to Quotations in Thoreau's *A Week*," *SAR* (1980), 259–90.

52.   "contradictory ideas": *See also* Leslie A. Fiedler, *The Return of the Vanishing American* (New York, 1968), pp. 104–19. David B. Hock, "Theory of History in *A Week*: Annals and Perennials," *ESQ* 56 (1969), 32–35. Buell, *Literary Transcendentalism*, pp. 208–38.

53.   "widely reviewed": Harding, *Thoreau: A Century of Criticism*, p. 3. Glick, *The Recognition of Henry David Thoreau*, p. 4. Walter Har-

ding, "An Early Review of Thoreau's *A Week*," *TSB* 130 (Winter 1975).

53. "in a letter": Dated February 2, 1849; transcript at Thoreau Textual Center, Princeton University.

4. SAYS I TO MYSELF

60. "an English translation": Henry D. Thoreau, *The Transmigration of the Seven Brahmans*, ed. Arthur Christy (New York, 1931).

61. " 'Places to Walk To' ": Transcript at Thoreau Textual Center, Princeton University.

62. "slant-top desk": Anne McGrath, "Henry Thoreau's Desk," *CS* 9 (March 1974), 6–9.

62. "friendship with Ellery Channing": McGill, *Channing of Concord*, pp. 47–62, 83–85, 99–104. Francis B. Dedmond, "William Ellery Channing on Thoreau: An Unpublished Satire," *Modern Language Notes* 67 (January 1952), 50–52.

63. "a surveyor's practice": Channing, *Thoreau, the Poet-Naturalist*, pp. 65–66; Canby, *Thoreau*, pp. 220–22; Albert F. McLean, Jr., "Thoreau's True Meridian: Natural Fact and Metaphor," *AQ* 20 (Fall 1968), 567–79.

66. "set of 'Fact books' ": Howarth, *The Literary Manuscripts of Henry David Thoreau*, pp. 304–305. Analysis of contents supplied by Robert Sattelmeyer.

68. " 'the motto of my journal' ": Malcolm W. Ferguson, "Thinks-I-to-Myself," *CS* 7 (December 1972), 8–9.

69. "trip to Canada": Kenneth W. Cameron, *Thoreau's Canadian Notebook and Record of Surveys* (Hartford, Conn., 1968). Lawrence Willson, "Thoreau's Canadian Notebook," *Huntington Library Quarterly* 22 (May 1959), 179–200.

73. "mean-spirited elements": Willson, "Thoreau and Roman Catholicism," *Catholic History Review* 42 (July 1956), 157–72. Willson, "Thoreau and the French in Canada," *Revue de l'Université d'Ottawa* 29 (July–September 1959), 281–97. Barrie Davies, "Sam Quixote in Lower Canada: A Reading of Thoreau's *A Yankee in Canada* Revisited," *CS* 13 (Spring 1978), 7–11.

73. "Grindell Reynolds": Edward W. Emerson, *Henry Thoreau as Remembered by a Young Friend* (Boston, 1917), p. 148.

75. "fiasco in Boston": Thomas W. Higginson, "Glimpses of Authors," *Brains* 1 (1891), 105.

77.   "hope and despair": Miller, *Consciousness in Concord*, Paul, *The Shores of America*, Porte, *Emerson and Thoreau*, *passim*. Lewis P. Simpson, "The Short Desperate Life of Henry Thoreau," *ESQ* 42 (1966), 45–56. J. Lyndon Shanley, "Thoreau: His Lover's Quarrel with the World," *Four Makers of the American Mind*, ed. T. E. Cawley (Durham, N.C., 1976), 25–42.

78.   "philosophers of Worcester": Salt, *The Life of Henry D. Thoreau*, p. 118. Ruth H. Frost, "Thoreau's Worcester Friends: II, III," *Nature Outlook* (May 1945; May 1947), 116–18; 4–7.

79.   "Thoreau's sexuality": For other views, *see* Frank Preston Stearns, *Sketches from Concord and Appledore* (New York, 1895), pp. 24–25. Krutch, *Henry David Thoreau*, p. 207. Henry Miller, *Stand Still Like a Hummingbird* (New York, 1962), pp. 111–18. James Armstrong, "Thoreau as a Philosopher of Love," *Henry D. Thoreau: A Profile*, ed. Walter Harding (New York, 1971), pp. 222–43. Mary Elkins Moller, "Thoreau, Womankind and Sexuality," *ESQ* 22 (1976), 122–48. Jonathan Katz, *Gay American History* (New York, 1976), pp. 481–94.

5. A FAITHFUL RECORD

80.   "on birds and plants": McGill, *Channing of Concord*, pp. 112–16.

80.   " 'Fact book' ": Analysis of contents supplied by Robert Sattelmeyer.

81.   "gunpowder mill": Stoller, *After Walden*, pp. 126–27.

83.   "Underground frost crystals": Information supplied by Henry Horn, Department of Biology, Princeton University.

83.   " 'Country Walking' ": Channing, *Thoreau, the Poet-Naturalist*, pp. 132–33. McGill, *Channing of Concord*, p. 129. Letter from F. B. Sanborn to F. H. Allen (July 7, 1917) in Concord Free Public Library (Special Collections).

86.   "a miniature of the world": William Howarth, "Travelling in Concord: The World of Thoreau's Journal," *Puritan Influences in American Literature*, ed. Emory B. Elliott (Urbana, Ill., 1979), pp. 143–66. John A. Christie, *Thoreau as World Traveler* (New York, 1965), pp. 201–11.

86.   "Moncure Conway": Moncure Conway, *Autobiography: Memoirs and Experiences* (Boston, 1902), pp. 141–42, 148.

88.   "The Journal entries": Transcript at Thoreau Textual Center, Princeton University. *See also* Joseph J. Moldenhauer, "Textual Introduction," *The Maine Woods* (Princeton, 1972), pp. 359–63.

89. "Melville's new story": Egbert S. Oliver, "A Second Look at Bartleby," *College English* 6 (May 1945), 431–49. Frederick Busch, "Thoreau and Melville as Cellmates," *Modern Fiction Studies* 23 (Summer 1977), 238–42.

89. "the Channings separated": McGill, *Channing of Concord*, pp. 131–35, 141–44.

90. "versions of *Walden*": Shanley, *The Making of Walden*, pp. 34–94, Shanley, "Historical Introduction," *Walden* (Princeton, 1971), pp. 361–68.

92. "Thoreau's only great book": Robert Frost and Reginald Cook, "Thoreau's *Walden*," *Listener* 52 (August 26, 1954), 319–20. Wright Morris, *The Territory Ahead* (New York, 1958), pp. 39–50.

92. "style and structure": Stephen J. Sherwin and Richard C. Reynolds, *A Word-Index to Walden* (Hartford, Conn., 1969). Phillip Gura, "Henry Thoreau and the Wisdom of Words," *NEQ* 52 (1979), 38–54. Michael West, "Scatology and Eschatology: the Heroic Dimensions of Thoreau's Wordplay," *PMLA* 89 (October 1974), 1043–64. Cavell, *The Senses of Walden*, pp. 35–67. Charles Anderson, *The Magic Circle of Walden* (New York, 1968). Poirier, *A World Elsewhere*, pp. 84–89. Northrop Frye, "Varieties of Literary Utopias," *Daedalus* 94 (Spring 1965), 323–47. Marx, *The Machine in the Garden*, pp. 242–65. Lewis, *The American Adam*, pp. 20–27. Charles Fiedelson, Jr., *Symbolism and American Literature* (Chicago, 1953), pp. 135–42. Matthiessen, *American Renaissance*, pp. 166–75.

92. "notable disputant": B. F. Skinner, "*Walden* (One) and *Walden Two*," *TSB* 122 (Winter 1973), 1.

92. "cycles of time": Aldous Huxley, *Beyond the Mexique Bay* (New York, 1934), pp. 176–84. Georges Poulet, *Studies in Human Time*, trans. Elliot Coleman (Baltimore, 1955), pp. 334–37.

93. "the story of *Walden*": Barry A. Marks, "Retrospective Narrative in Nineteenth-Century American Literature," *College English* 31 (January 1970), 366–75. James M. Cox, "Autobiography and America," *Aspects of Narrative*, ed. J. Hillis Miller (New York, 1971), pp. 143–72. G. Thomas Couser, *American Autobiography: The Prophetic Mode* (Amherst, Mass., 1979). William Howarth, "Some Principles of Autobiography," *Autobiography: Essays Theoretical and Critical*, ed. James Olney (Princeton, 1980), pp. 84–114.

97. "his survey map": Edward S. Deevey, Jr. "A Re-examination of Tho-

reau's *Walden,*" *The Quarterly Review of Biology* 17 (March 1942), 1–11. Melvin E. Lyon, "Walden Pond as Symbol," *PMLA* 82 (May 1967), 289–300. Eugene H. Walker, "Walden's Way Revealed," *Man and Nature* (Lincoln, Mass., 1971), pp. 11–20. Edward C. Jacob, "Thoreau and Modern Psychology," *TSB* 127 (Spring 1974), 4-5. Walter Harding, "Walden's Man of Science," *Virginia Quarterly Review* 57 (Winter 1981), 45–61.

99. "Melville's later stories": Frank Davidson, "Melville, Thoreau, and 'The Apple-Tree Table,' " *AL* 35 (January 1954), 379–88.

99. "widely reviewed": J. Lyndon Shanley, "Historical Introduction," *Walden* (Princeton, 1971), pp. 368–77. Harding, *Thoreau: A Century of Criticism,* pp. 8–11. Glick, *The Recognition of Henry David Thoreau,* pp. 5–13. James H. Matlack, "Early Reviews of *Walden* by the *Alta California* and its 'Lady Correspondent,' " *TSB* 131 (Spring 1975), 1–2.

99. "sales of *Walden*": Walter Harding, "The First Year's Sales of Thoreau's *Walden,*" *TSB* 117 (Fall 1971), 1–3.

100. " 'Slavery in Massachusetts' ": Wendell Glick, "Historical Introduction," *Reform Papers* (Princeton, 1974), pp. 331–35. Stoller, *After Walden,* pp. 140–149. Howard R. Floan, *The South in Northern Eyes: 1831–1861* (Austin, Tex., 1958), pp. 63–71. Lauriat Lane, Jr., "The Structure of Protest: Thoreau's Polemical Essays," *Humanities Association Bulletin 20* (Fall 1969), 34–40.

100. "Daniel Webster": Leonard Neufeldt, "Emerson, Thoreau, and Daniel Webster," *ESQ* 26 (1980), 26–37.

101. "his 'moonlight walks' ": William Howarth, "Successor to *Walden?* Thoreau's 'Moonlight: A Course of Intended Lectures,' " *Proof 2* (1972), 89–115.

101. "monthly transcripts": Copies and transcripts at Thoreau Textual Center, Princeton University.

6. A CERTAIN GREENNESS

108. "*liber naturae*": Rensselaer Lee, *Names on Trees: Ariosto into Art* (Princeton, 1977), pp. 3–9.

109. " 'in a far country' ": Charles J. Woodbury, *Talks with Ralph Waldo Emerson* (New York, 1890), pp. 78–79. *See also* Albert Gilman and Roger Brown, "Personality and Style in Concord," *Transcendentalism and its Legacy,* ed. M. Simon and T. H. Parsons (Ann Ar-

bor, Mich., 1966), pp. 87–122. Joel Porte, "Emerson, Thoreau, and the Double Consciousness," *NEQ* 41 (March 1968), 40–50.

110. "April 13 and 20": Transcript of letter at Thoreau Textual Center, Princeton University.

111. "dispute had arisen": Gordon Milne, *George William Curtis and the Genteel Tradition* (Bloomington, Ind., 1956), pp. 66–67.

111. "*Cape Cod* is a solemn trek": For other readings, *see* Krutch, *Henry David Thoreau*, p. 250. Harding and Meyer, *The New Thoreau Handbook*, pp. 66–69.

113. "the Pilgrim dream": *See also* Lawrence Willson, "Another View of the Pilgrims," *NEQ* 34 (June 1961), 160–77. Martin L. Popps, "An Analysis of Thoreau's *Cape Cod*," *BNYPL* 67 (September 1963), 419–28. John McAleer, "Thoreau's Epic, 'Cape Cod,' " *Thought* 43 (Summer 1968), 227–46.

115. "the discovery of America": *See also* Joel Porte, "Henry Thoreau and the Reverend Plouphloisbois Thalassa," *The Chief Glory of Every People*, ed. M. Bruccoli (Carbondale, Ill., 1973), pp. 191–210. Donald Federman, "Toward an Ecology of Place: Three Views of Cape Cod," *Colby Library Quarterly* 13 (1977), 209–22.

116. "Thoreau himself wrote": Transcript of letter at Thoreau Textual Center, Princeton University.

117. "young Emily Dickinson": Richard B. Sewell, "Kindred Spirits," *Harvard Magazine* (March 1978), 71–72.

118. "no longer the poet": Canby, *Thoreau*; Krutch, *Henry David Thoreau*; Paul, *The Shores of America*; Porte, *Emerson and Thoreau*—all *passim*. For contrary views, *see* William Drake, "Spiritual and Scientific Fact: Thoreau's Search for Reality," *The Western Thoreau Centenary*, ed. J. G. Taylor (Logan, Utah, 1963). Horace Taylor, "Thoreau's Scientific Interests as Seen in His *Journal*," *McNeese Review* 14 (1963), 45–59. Nina Baym, "Thoreau's View of Science," *JHI* 26 (April–June, 1965), 221–34.

122. "Thoreau's fieldwork": Channing, *Thoreau, the Poet-Naturalist*, pp. 220–21. Sanborn, *The Life of Henry David Thoreau*, pp. xi, 55, 198. For informed views, *see* Henry S. Salt, "A Botanophilist's Journal" in *The Call of the Wildflower* (London, 1922), pp. 133–38. Alex Lucas, "Thoreau, Field Naturalist," *University of Toronto Quarterly* 23 (April 1954), 227–32. Robert Henry Welker, *Birds and Men: American Birds in Science, Art, Literature, and Conservation* (Cambridge, Mass., 1955), pp. 91–115.

124. "father's prize boar": Another version is in *Thoreau: Man of Concord*, ed. Walter Harding (New York, 1960), p. 65.
127. "Alcott had promised": Transcript at Thoreau Textual Center, Princeton University.
128. "deep sexual neuroses": Raymond Gozzi, "Tropes and Figures: A Psychological Study of David Henry Thoreau" (New York University Ph.D., 1957). Carl Bode, "The Hidden Thoreau," *The Half-World of American Culture* (Carbondale, Ill., 1965), pp. 3–15.
128. "a lapsed commune": "Eagleswood, a Local Social Experiment," *Perth Amboy Evening News* (November 12, 1949). Maud H. Green, "Raritan Bay Union, Eagleswood, New Jersey," *Proceedings of the New Jersey Historical Society* 68 (January 1950), 1–20.
129. "Whitman later recalled": Horace Traubel, *With Walt Whitman in Camden* (Boston, 1906), I, pp. 212–13; III, pp. 318–19, 403. *See also* Andrew Schiller, "Thoreau and Whitman: the Record of a Pilgrimage," *NEQ* 28 (June 1955), 186–97. Charles R. Metzger, *Thoreau and Whitman: A Study of their Aesthetics* (Seattle, Wash., 1961).
132. "curvature in 'Walking' ": For other readings, *see* Stoller, *After Walden*, pp. 115–20. John C. Broderick, "The Movement of Thoreau's Prose," *AL* 33 (May 1961), 133–42. Frederick Garber, "Unity and Diversity in 'Walking,' " *ESQ* 56 (1969), 35–40.
133. "myth of western settlement": *See also* Arthur Ekirch, *The Idea of Progress in America, 1815–1860* (New York, 1951), pp. 162–64. Fussell, *Frontier*, pp. 181–87. Clough, *The Necessary Earth*, pp. 97–115. Tanner, *The Reign of Wonder*, pp. 46–63. Gay Wilson Allen, "How Emerson, Thoreau, and Whitman Viewed the Frontier," in *Toward a New American Literary History*, ed. Louis Budd (Durham, N.C., 1980), pp. 111–28.
133. "the Wild": *See also* Robert P. Cobb, "Thoreau and 'the Wild,' " *ESQ* 18 (1960), 5–7. Jonathan Fairbanks, "Thoreau: Speaker for Wildness," *South Atlantic Quarterly* 70 (Autumn 1971), 487–506.

7. THE ACCUMULATING GRISTS

136. "local antiquities": Ruth Robinson Wheeler, "Thoreau's Concord," *Thoreau: Studies and Commentaries*, ed. Walter Harding (Ruther-

ford, N.J., 1972), pp. 25–33. *See also* Robert A. Gross, " 'The Most Estimable Place in All the World': A Debate on Progress in Nineteenth-Century Concord," *SAR* (1978), 1–15.

136. "his place in society": Mary Elkins Moller, *Thoreau in the Human Community* (Amherst, Mass., 1980).

137. "Daniel Ricketson": Anna and Walton Ricketson, *Daniel Ricketson and his Friends* (Boston, 1902). Earl J. Dias, "Daniel Ricketson and Henry Thoreau," *NEQ* 26 (September 1953), 388–96.

138. "Kate Brady": Walter Harding, "Thoreau and Kate Brady," *AL* 36 (November 1964), 347–49; Harding, *The Days of Henry Thoreau*, p. 379.

138. "Surveying had also helped": Benton L. Hatch, "Thoreau's Plan of a Farm," *Papers in Honor of Andrew Keogh* (New Haven, 1938). Thorkild Hoy, "Thoreau as a Surveyor," *Surveying and Mapping* (March 1976), 59–65. A *Catalog of Thoreau's Surveys in the Concord Free Public Library*, ed. Marcia Moss (Geneseo, N.Y., 1976). Rich Howard, "Thoreau as a Surveyor," *TSB* 139 (Spring 1977), 3.

139. "Melville's bitter travesty": Egbert S. Oliver, "Melville's Picture of Emerson and Thoreau in 'The Confidence-Man,' " *College English* 8 (November 1946), 61–72. Herschel Parker, "Melville's Satire of Emerson and Thoreau: An Evaluation," *ATQ* 7 (1970), 66–74. Herman Melville, *The Confidence-Man*, ed. Herschel Parker (New York, 1975).

139. "Edward Hoar": Edward S. Burgess, "Notes on Concord People," Concord Free Public Library (Special Collections).

140. " 'Tom Bowling' ": Caroline Moseley, "Henry D. Thoreau and His Favorite Popular Song," *Journal of Popular Culture* 12 (1979), 624–29.

140. "notes in a 'Fact book' ": Analysis of contents supplied by Robert Sattelmeyer.

140. "he told one host": Harding, *The Days of Henry Thoreau*, p. 383.

143. "collecting rare plants": Virginia S. Eifert, *Tall Trees and Far Horizons* (New York, 1965), pp. 239–56.

143. "entries on Maine": Transcripts at Thoreau Textual Center, Princeton University.

145. "Ruskin's *Modern Painters*": Roy Gridley, " '*Walden* and Ruskin's 'The White-Thorn Blossom,' " *ESQ* 26 (1962), 31–34. Roger Stein, *John Ruskin and Aesthetic Thought in America, 1840–1900* (Cambridge, Mass., 1967), pp. 90–93.

147. "Thoreau and Lowell": Martin Duberman, *James Russell Lowell* (Boston, 1966), pp. 169–72, 429–30. Austin Warren, "Lowell on Thoreau," *Studies in Philology* 27 (July 1930), 442–61. Wesley Mott, "Thoreau and Lowell on 'Vacation': The Maine Woods and 'A Moosehead Journal,' " *TJQ* 10 (July 1978), 14–24.

151. " 'the Indian' and himself": Sayre, *Thoreau and the American Indians*, pp. 155–87.

153. "the story's wilderness setting": Fannie Hardy Eckstorm, "Thoreau's Maine Woods," *Atlantic Monthly* 102 (July 1908), 242–50. Mary P. Sherwood, "Fannie Eckstorm's Bias," in Hicks, *Thoreau in Our Season*, pp. 58–66. Lew Dietz, *The Allegash* (New York, 1968), pp. 151–63.

154. " 'Chesuncook' is briefer": *See also* Joseph J. Moldenhauer, "Introduction," *The Illustrated Maine Woods* (Princeton, 1974), pp. xi–xxiii.

8. MY KALENDAR

161. "his mountain trips": Christopher McKee, "Thoreau: A Week on Mt. Washington and in Tuckerman Ravine," *Appalachia* 30 (December 1954), 169–83. Christopher Collins, "Thoreau, the Mountain Climber," *The Uses of Observation* (The Hague, 1971), pp. 58–81. *See also* William Howarth, *Thoreau in the Mountains* (New York, 1982).

163. "vegetative zones": Henry I. Baldwin, "The Vegetation of Mt. Monadnock," *Forest Notes* 99 (Fall 1968), 12–13.

168. "auditors at Worcester": Joseph Slater, "Caroline Dall in Concord," *TSB* 62 (Winter 1958), 1.

169. " 'The Fall of the Leaf' ": Howarth, *The Literary Manuscripts of Henry David Thoreau*, pp. 172, 313–16. Partial transcript at Thoreau Textual Center, Princeton University.

169. " 'Autumnal Tints' ": Krutch, *Henry David Thoreau*, p. 278. Bernard B. Cohen, "The Perspective of an Old Master," *ESQ* 56 (1969), 53–56. Bernard Rosenthal, "Thoreau's Book of Leaves," *ESQ* 56 (1969), 7–11.

170. "reprise of American history": Lauriat Lane, Jr., "Thoreau's Autumnal Indian," *Canadian Review of American Studies* 6 (Fall 1975), 228–36. Willard H. Bonner, "The Harvest of Thought in Thoreau's 'Autumnal Tints,' " *ESQ* 22 (1976), 78–84.

170. "death is the destiny": G. Thomas Couser, "The Shape of Death in American Autobiography," *Hudson Review* 31 (Spring 1978), 53–66.

173. " 'General Phenomena' ": Howarth, *The Literary Manuscripts of Henry David Thoreau*, pp. 306–31. Aldo Leopold and Sara E. Jones, "A Phenological Record for Sauk and Dane Counties, Wisconsin," *Ecological Records* (January 1947), 83–112. Leo Stoller, "A Note on Thoreau's Place in the History of Phenology," *Isis* 47 (June 1956), 443–61.

173. "studied the rivers": Marcia Moss, *A Catalog of Thoreau's Surveys in the Concord Free Public Library* (Geneseo, N.Y., 1976). Laurence Eaton Richardson, *Concord River* (Barre, Mass., 1964).

174. "river entries": Transcripts at Thoreau Textual Center, Princeton University. *See also* R. S. McDowell and C. W. McCutcheon, "The Thoreau-Reynolds Ridge, a Lost and Found Phenomenon," *Science* 172 (May 28, 1971), 975. A. G. Volkman, "Henry Thoreau, Physicist," *TSB* 123 (Spring 1973), 4.

175. " 'Life Misspent' ": Partial transcript at Thoreau Textual Center, Princeton University.

176. " 'Getting a Living' ": Walter Harding, "Thoreau at the Boston Music Hall," *TSB* 105 (Fall 1968), 7.

176. "new work on fruits": Howarth, *The Literary Manuscripts of Henry David Thoreau*, pp. 306–31.

177. "Thoreau had met Brown": Bronson Alcott, *Concord Days* (Boston, 1872), pp. 11–17. G. M. Ostrander, "Emerson and Thoreau and John Brown," *Mississippi Valley Historical Review* 39 (March 1953), 713–26.

178. "Writing about Brown": For other views, *see* Krutch, *Henry David Thoreau*, p. 162. Paul, *The Shores of America*, pp. 237–39.

179. "platform evangelism": *See also* Robert Albrecht, "Thoreau and his Audience: 'A Plea for Captain John Brown,' " *AL* 32 (January 1961), 393–402. Truman Nelson, *The Old Man: John Brown at Harpers Ferry* (New York, 1973). Lauriat Lane, Jr., "Thoreau's Autumnal, Archetypal Hero: Captain John Brown," *Ariel* 6 (January 1975), 41–49.

179. "Brown's atrocities": Michael Meyer, "Thoreau's Rescue of John Brown from History," *SAR* (1980), 301–16.

184. " 'Wild Apples' lecture": Frank Preston Stearns, *Sketches from Concord and Appledore* (New York, 1895), pp. 27–28.

184. "style and form": Leo Stoller, *After Walden*, p. 121.

184. "apple as a symbol": Robert Sattelmeyer, "Introduction" to Henry D. Thoreau, *The Natural History Essays* (Salt Lake City, Utah, 1980), pp. xxx–xxxiv. Kevin Van Anglen, "A Paradise Regained: Thoreau's 'Wild Apples' and the Myth of the American Adam," *ESQ* 27 (1981), 28–37.

185. " 'Wild Fruits' ": Transcripts at Thoreau Textual Center, Princeton University.

187. " 'General Phenomena' ": Howarth, *The Literary Manuscripts of Henry David Thoreau*, pp. 309–18.

188. "F. B. Sanborn": John W. Clarkson, Jr., "Wanted in Concord," *Yankee* (April 1969), 129–32. Clarkson, "F. B. Sanborn, 1831–1917," *CS* 12 (Summer 1977), 7–8.

9. WITNESS ON THE STAND

191. "journalist from Ohio": William Dean Howells, *Literary Friends and Acquaintances* (New York, 1911), pp. 58–60.

191. "springs and brooks": Donald G. Quick, "Thoreau as Limnologist," *TJQ* 4 (April 1972), 13–20.

192. "trip to Mount Monadnock": Elliott S. Allison, "Thoreau of Monadnock," *TJQ* 5 (October 1973), 15–21. Allison, "Alone on the Mountain," *Yankee* 37 (June, 1973) 158–165.

194. " 'The Succession of Forest Trees' ": *Transaction of the Middlesex Agricultural Society . . .* (Concord, Mass., 1860), pp. 8–9. Walter Hesford, "The 1860 Concord Cattle-Show: An Official Account," *TSB* 132 (Summer 1975), 6–7.

195. "Darwin's ideas": Charles Darwin, *The Origin of Species* (New York, 1938), pp. 371–74. John Byron Wilson, "Darwin and the Transcendentalists," *JHI* 26 (April–June 1965), 268–90. Loren Eiseley, "Nature's Golden Alphabet," *The Unexpected Universe* (New York, 1969), pp. 120–46.

195. "an original contribution": Raymond Adams, "Thoreau's Science," *Scientific Monthly* 60 (May 1945), 379–82. Kathryn Whitford, "Thoreau and the Woodlots of Concord," *NEQ* 23 (September 1950), 291–306. Stoller, *After Walden*, pp. 70–78. Walter Harding, "Thoreau and Timothy Dwight," *Boston Public Library Quarterly* 10 (April 1958), 109–15.

195. "teacher from Elmira": Transcript of letter at Thoreau Textual Center, Princeton University.

196. "principle of 'succession' ": W. H. Drury and I. C. T. Nisbet, "Succession," *Journal of the Arnold Arboretum* LIV (1973), 331–68. Henry S. Horn, "Succession," *Theoretical Ecology*, ed. R. May (Oxford, 1976), p. 187. Robert Edward Cook, "Long-Lived Seeds," *Natural History* 88 (February 1979), 55–60.

200. " 'Atlas of Concord' ": A. Bronson Alcott, *Essays on Education*, ed. Walter Harding (Gainesville, Fla., 1960). Anton Huffert, "Alcott on Thoreau's *Atlas of Concord*," TSB 56 (Summer 1956), 1–2.

200. " 'Huckleberries' ": Transcript at Thoreau Textual Center, Princeton University. A new version of the Stoller text (Hb) is in Henry David Thoreau, *The Natural History Essays* ed. Robert Sattelmeyer (Salt Lake City, 1980), pp. 211–62.

202. "public parks and forests": Paul Oehser, "Pioneers in Conservation," *Nature Magazine* 38 (April 1945), 188–90. Phillip and Kathryn Whitford, "Thoreau: Pioneer Ecologist and Conservationist," *Scientific Monthly* 73 (November 1951), 291–96. Stoller, *After Walden*, pp. 95–108. Millard C. Davis, "The Influence of Emerson, Thoreau, and Whitman on the Early American Naturalists John Muir and John Burroughs," *Living Wilderness* 30 (1967), 18–23.

203. " 'Concord Book' ": John C. Broderick, "Bronson Alcott's 'Concord Book,' " *NEQ* 29 (September 1956), 365–80.

203. " 'The Dispersion of Seeds' ": Transcript at Thoreau Textual Center, Princeton University.

203. "the story of evolution": Dirk J. Struik, *The Origins of American Science: New England* (New York, 1957), pp. 217–19. Stoller, *After Walden*, p. 84. Charles R. Metzger, "Thoreau on Science," *Annals of Science* 12 (September 1956), 206–11.

208. "Modern studies": Information supplied by Gordon G. Whitney, School of Forestry and Environmental Studies, Yale University.

208. "evolutionary progress": *See also* Donald W. Cox, *Pioneers of Ecology* (Hammond, Ind., 1971), pp. 25–29. Donald Worster, "The Subversive Science: Thoreau's Romantic Ecology," *Nature's Economy* (San Francisco, 1977), pp. 57–112. John Fowles, *The Tree* (Boston, 1980).

209. "Channing had once lived": McGill, *Channing of Concord*, pp. 156–57.

209. "western notes and entries": Lawrence Willson, "The Transcendentalist View of the West," *Western Humanities Review* 14 (Spring

1960), 183–91. Sayre, *Thoreau and the American Indians*, pp. 194–215.

210. "letter to F. B. Sanborn": F. B. Sanborn, *The First and Last Journeys of Thoreau* (New York, 1905).

10. A DEATH NOT PREMATURE

215. "James T. Fields": Walter Harding, "Notes and Queries," *TSB* 109 (Fall 1969), 7. Annie Fields, *James T. Fields* (Boston, 1881), p. 102. James C. Austin, *Fields of the Atlantic Monthly* (San Marino, Cal., 1953).

216. "Emerson later grumbled": Charles J. Woodbury, *Talks with Ralph Waldo Emerson* (Boston, 1895), p. 89.

217. "Thoreau allegedly said": Thomas Blanding, "Beans, Baked and Half-Baked," *CS* 12 (Winter 1976), 18.

217. "A *Week* in mind": Carl Hovde, "Textual Introduction," *A Week on the Concord and Merrimack Rivers* (Princeton, 1980), pp. 501–44.

218. "these last days": F. B. Sanborn, *The Personality of Thoreau*, pp. 66–69. Edward Emerson, *Henry Thoreau as Remembered by a Young Friend* (Boston, 1917), p. 117.

219. "homeward voyage to Concord": Thomas Blanding, "A Last Word from Thoreau," *CS* 11 (Winter 1976), 16–17. Thomas Woodson, "Another Word on Thoreau's Last 'Good Sailing,' " *CS* 12 (Spring 1977), 17.

INDEX